OREGON PLANS

 *Culture and Environment in the Pacific West*

◉ *Culture and Environment in the Pacific West*
Series Editor: William L. Lang

OTHER TITLES IN THE SERIES

Oregon Plans

THE MAKING OF AN UNQUIET LAND-USE REVOLUTION

Sy Adler

Oregon State University Press
Corvallis

The paper in this book meets the guidelines for permanence and durability of the Committee on Production Guidelines for Book Longevity of the Council on Library Resources and the minimum requirements of the American National Standard for Permanence of Paper for Printed Library Materials Z39.48-1984.

Library of Congress Cataloging-in-Publication Data

Adler, Sy, 1950-
   Oregon plans : the making of an unquiet land use revolution / Sy Adler.
     p. cm.
   Includes bibliographical references and index.
   ISBN 978-0-87071-651-5 (pbk. : alk. paper) — ISBN 978-0-87071-652-2 (e-book)
   1. Land use—Law and legislation—Oregon. 2. Land subdivision—Law and legislation—Oregon. 3. City planning and redevelopment law—Oregon.
4. Zoning law—Oregon. I. Title.
   KFO2858.A93 2012
   333.7309795--dc23
                         2011052235

Contents

Acknowledgments

It's a great pleasure for me to acknowledge the many people who were actively involved in the events discussed in this book who spoke with me, made materials available, and read and gave me invaluable comments on chapter drafts. Arnold Cogan, Edward Sullivan, Ron Eber, and Jim Knight each talked with me on several occasions, and commented on drafts of many of the chapters. Robert Stacey made available archival material at 1000 Friends of Oregon's Portland office and talked with me several times. Richard Benner spoke with me, commented on drafts and made available materials from his personal files, as did Larry Frazier. Fred VanNatta and Gordon Fultz gave me interviews, and read and commented on draft chapters. My Portland State University colleagues Carl Abbott and Ethan Seltzer discussed the overall project me with on numerous occasions, read and commented on several draft chapters, and gave me many valuable suggestions.

Other active participants and knowledgeable individuals who granted me interviews include: David Aamodt, Vic Affolter, John Anderson, Ward Armstrong, Dave Barrows, Adrianne Brockman, Ginny Burdick, Wallace Carson, Kathleen Carter, Neal Coenen, Joyce Cohen, Margaret Collins, Steve Corey, Keith Cubic, Carolyn Gassoway, Mark Greenfield, Craig Greenleaf, Eldon Hout, Stephen Kafoury, Paul Ketchum, Doug McClain, Janet McLennan, Brent Lake, Dave Leland, Robert Liberty, Steven McCarthy, Lee Miller, John Platt, John Porter, Lidwein Rahmin, Henry Richmond, Dick Roy, Steve Schell, Anne Squier, Rod Stubbs, and Greg Winterowd.

John Gray very generously gave me financial support that expedited the completion of the research, and also granted me an interview.

Librarians at University of Oregon's Special Collections Department and the Oregon Historical Society's Research Library were very helpful, as were staff members at the Oregon State Archives and Cristine Paschild,

University Archivist and Head of Special Collections at the Portland State University Library.

The Oregon Department of Land Conservation and Development made available to me material about the early years of the program at its Salem Office.

Thanks to Meg Merrick for producing the maps.

Thanks to Mary Braun, Oregon State University Press acquisitions editor, for her support of this project, and to the other members of the Press for their valuable contributions.

Thanks to Bill Lang, editor of the series within which this book appears, for shepherding drafts of the manuscript through the process, and to Marianne Keddington-Lang for her expert editing, which greatly improved the readability of the manuscript.

Ellen Shoshkes read draft chapters, made many valuable comments, and sustained me throughout the research and writing process with her love and support.

Series Editor's Preface

In January 1971, on the eve of his second term as governor of Oregon, Tom McCall responded to an interviewer's question with an iconic quotation that proclaimed Oregon's distinctive take on population growth and defending the state's livability. Almost rhetorically, the national television interviewer asked: "What could be done about population growth?"

McCall forcefully answered: "Come visit us again and again. This is a state of excitement. But for heaven's sake, don't come here to live."

McCall seemed to post a sign at the stateline, declaring that growth had become an endangered species in Oregon. What he wanted was not an end to growth, but a smarter growth that preserved Oregon's quality of life. Still, many commentators chastised him, questioning whether he believed in the "visit but don't stay" motto. McCall assured them that he did, telling all who would listen that everyone who comes to Oregon must "play the game by our environmental rules, and be members of the Oregon family."

That was Oregon's marker on the future. In a series of laws enacted in the early 1970s, the state embraced regulations that prized livability as the ultimate goal and maintaining "the sanctity of the environment" as a constant guide. Burgeoning public opinion supported the idea, especially the protection of farm and forest lands from the "grasping wastrels of the land," as McCall characterized the developers of residential sprawl and recreational properties. Passage of Senate Bill 100 in 1973 and the consistent refinement and defense of the state's progressive land-use planning system ever since has impressed the nation. Oregon's success has prompted many to ask how it accomplished what so many states had quailed to even contemplate. Were Oregonians so much different than everyone else who worried about growth? Did they know something unique? Was there something in the rain that fell on a greening Oregon? Oregon's system appeared to work, and more, its creation seemed almost unbelievable, if not a bit mysterious.

In *Oregon Plans*, Sy Adler demystifies the story. It is a complex story, with sufficient twists and turns, surprising bedfellows, and strong personalities to produce a gripping melodrama. Adler offers the first thorough investigative account of how environmentalists, including professional planners, lawyers, and legislators, teamed up with farmers and business people to hammer out the system. Reading Adler's account, it is clear that there was little foregone about the process and even less in the results. There was no mysterious and deterministic key to the pattern of events and their outcomes. In fact, readers will be struck by a fragility that pervades the episodes Adler explains in intimate detail. If there is an exceptionalism buried in the story, it is likely inherent in the people who built the system, fine-tuned its workings, and defended it against determined foes.

At its heart, the drama Adler lays out in *Oregon Plans* is about a community wrestling with two inherently democratic challenges: how can the public's interest in land use temper the prerogatives of private property owners, and how can people insure that their use of the environment ensures a viable future for themselves and the nature they need for survival? These questions are at the center of what books in the *Culture & Environment in the Pacific West* series are meant to address. In *Oregon Plans*, the focus is on public policy and political decisions about highly contested issues. It is a story about political culture and environmental goals, and it is also about specific people who chose not to avoid the contests.

The story has heroes, but many are unlikely allies, such as Hector S. Macpherson, Republican farmer-legislator from Albany, and Democrat Ted Hallock, a liberal legislator from Portland. The two men agreed on a strategy that matched local participation with state-based planning to find a workable mix of land-use restrictions and controlled development that Oregonians could willingly adopt. It meant establishing potentially cumbersome regulatory structures, such as the Land Conservation and Development Commission (LCDC), and it also stimulated opposition that reared its head in every legislative session since 1973. In Adler's storyline, though, other people come forward to defend the plan, such as Henry Richmond, creator of the 1000 Friends of Oregon. Add other players, such as L. B. Day, the strong-willed director of LCDC, and Fred VanNatta of the Oregon Home Builders Association, and it quickly becomes clear that the state land-use planning drama could have ended in a much different place.

Adler's story is about unusual conditions, purposeful action, dynamic personalities, and the messiness of democratic and bureaucratic processes. His conclusions reveal much about how Oregonians defined livability in the late twentieth century. He also makes clear that many issues in contest during the creation of the historic land-use system are still unresolved. The most recent evidence came in November 2007, when voters over-whelmingly reaffirmed the system in a referendum. They kept the faith in a complex and potentially fractious method to assure the Oregon ideal of a livable future. Sy Adler's *Oregon Plans* tells readers how people created the system and perhaps why it should continue to be defended.

William L. Lang

Introduction
Oregon Plans

Oregon's Senate Bill 100—commonly called simply SB 100—and the state-wide land-use planning program it initiated were controversial from the start. Passed by the legislature in 1973, the program would affect in various ways the daily lives of everyone in the state, and would earn Oregon a reputation as a leader among states in the field. Those who led the effort to pass the revolutionary legislation included environmental activists—some of them attorneys, professional planners, legislators, and state officials—business people, and farmers. Their goal was to insert what they saw as statewide interests into land-use decision-making processes that had been up to that point resolutely local. They were motivated by pragmatic concerns about the future of critical sectors of the state's economy and increasing costs to taxpayers, as well as by desires to protect the state's natural beauty and livability. This is the story of the path to SB 100, what it took to get it passed, and how it was implemented during the critical early period of the mid-1970s.

Context
Advocates for statewide land-use planning expected opposition to SB 100, and they got it—from local governments that were competing with each other to attract population and economic growth, state agencies that pursued projects shaped by local growth-promoting interests, and property owners and developers hoping to reap speculative gains associated with growth. Advocates wanted to address the resulting environmental, economic, and social problems that transcended local government boundaries, and the transformation of land-use planning institutions and practices became the vehicle to accomplish that.

Modernizing those institutions and practices involved elaborating a complex set of legal mandates and establishing a new agency to administer them. It also meant enlarging the role of professionals in making and implementing plans and requiring them—and the officials they worked for—to base their work on objective information about current and likely future conditions. Enacting and implementing SB 100 involved many thousands of Oregonians who sought to shape land-use-related actions at state and local levels in a variety of forums and provided intense scrutiny of what planners and elected officials at all levels were doing every controversial step along the way.

Oregon began to chart a path toward SB 100 in the early 1960s. The legislature, traditionally attentive to agricultural interests, attempted to preserve farmland on the fringes of growing urban areas by borrowing and tinkering with methods that had been used in states such as Hawaii and California. The effects of urbanization were most clearly evident in the Willamette River Valley, where about two-thirds of the state's population lived and where the most productive agricultural land was located. Oregon's population grew by 18 percent during the 1960s. The Willamette Valley accounted for 86 percent of that growth, 54 percent of it in the Portland metropolitan area. During the 1970s, the state population grew by another 26 percent, this time with a larger proportion occurring outside the Willamette Valley. Land-use issues were becoming increasingly important throughout the state as a result.

State lawmakers were also revising land-use planning laws that had been adopted in the 1940s and 1950s to facilitate farmland preservation. Those laws enabled county governments to zone land for a variety of uses, but a county's zoning code had to be consistent with a land-use plan. Most counties showed little interest in taking advantage of the opportunity to plan. In the early 1960s, the legislature authorized counties to create exclusive farm-use zones, a different approach to farmland preservation than was emerging in other states. Farmers in those zones would automatically be entitled to property-tax breaks that were intended to give them an incentive to keep their land in agricultural production. The path to farmland preservation in Oregon, though, still required comprehensive plans that designated land for farm use. With continuing resistance to planning in most counties, relatively little land in rural Oregon was planned or zoned into the early 1970s.

Interest in farmland preservation increased dramatically in the United States during the 1960s and 1970s, especially from 1972 through 1974.

Map of Oregon counties (the Willamette Valley counties are unshaded)

Map of Willamette Valley counties and some key cities

National and global developments affected the agricultural sector world-wide, producing rising prices for agricultural products. There was also a concern that productivity-enhancing technical innovations had reached their limits, and, starting in 1973, a growing national interest in using income earned by agricultural exports to offset higher prices for imported oil (Lehman, 1995; Peterson and Yampolsky, 1975). Those developments were especially significant for Oregon, where agriculture was the second largest economic sector in the state.

While the threat to the agricultural economy was the prime motivation for state involvement during the early years, the concurrent rise of new social and political movements shaped the state's intervention in local land-use decisions. Environmentalists, proponents of citizen empowerment, feminists, public interest lawyers, and advocacy planners pursued overlapping agendas. Many public interest attorneys, for example, worked on environmental protection issues, and women were prominent among those advocating for citizen empowerment. Many planners were both involved in the environmental movement and supported efforts to give citizens more power. Activists saw land-use planning processes as arenas within which to articulate social, economic, and environmental concerns and to challenge the capture of local government decision making about land use by property owners and developers, which often led to projects and policies that activists saw as being environmentally destructive and socially inequitable.

Laws

The key structural feature of Oregon's land-use program was the preeminent role SB 100 assigned to comprehensive plans produced by local governments. A law passed in 1969—Senate Bill 10 (SB 10)—had mandated that every city and county government adopt a comprehensive land-use plan and zone its jurisdiction "border-to-border" by the end of 1971. The Governor's Office was authorized to take over planning and zoning if a local government failed to meet that deadline, and ten goals were included in the law to guide the Governor's Office in the event it did. Oregon was the second state in the country, after California, to require local governments to produce plans and the first to require them to adopt zoning ordinances. It was a dramatic move, elevating the status of local comprehensive plans to a level well above what they occupied elsewhere in the nation. The shift from enabling to requiring local governments to plan and zone proved to be highly contentious, and SB 100 was crafted to overcome the obstacles that the implementation of SB 10 revealed.

SB 100 maintained the SB 10 mandates and stipulated clearly that zoning ordinances had to be consistent with plans. The plans and projects of special districts—such as those providing water, sewer, school, and port facilities—and of state agencies—such as those dealing with transportation, economic development, and environmental quality—also had to be coordinated with local comprehensive plans. SB 100 assigned to counties the critical role of coordinating the planning efforts of all cities in their jurisdictions, especially regarding growth outside city boundaries, as well as the plans and projects of special districts and state agencies.

The mandated plans and zoning ordinances and all state and special district programs affecting land use had to conform to a set of legally binding goals adopted by a new state agency, the Land Conservation and Development Commission (LCDC). The new agency would review the plans, ordinances, and programs that cities and counties created for conformance with statewide goals, and was authorized to assume responsibility for planning and zoning if a local government failed to comply before the end of 1975. LCDC also had to ensure that citizens were involved at all stages of the process, from developing goals and making plans through implementation. At the time, this ensemble of mandates was unique in the United States. Norman Williams, Jr., a law professor who worked closely with national planning organizations, wrote: "The new Oregon Planning Act [SB 100] . . . represents the most advanced step yet taken in American planning legislation" (Williams, N., 1975).

The Quiet Revolution in Land Use Control, a landmark book published in 1972, significantly influenced the development of SB 100. Underlying an enhanced role for state governments, the authors argued, was a transition underway in the status of land, from an individually owned commodity bought and sold in the marketplace to a common property resource in which the larger community had an interest. Because local officials often resented the notion that there were statewide interests in the resources in their jurisdictions that they were failing to protect, one piece of advice offered by the authors was that state governments begin with modest efforts to regulate land uses to achieve a few select goals. That approach would be more successful, they predicted, than imposing a planning mandate that might generate resistance and undermine the state's ability to achieve its larger land-use objectives (Bosselman and Callies, 1972). By that time, though, the Oregon legislature was already headed down the mandate path.

Another influential source for those working on SB 100 was the American Law Institute's *Model Land Development Code* project (American Law Institute, 1974). The original version of SB 100 included several Model Code proposals, including state-designated areas of critical concern and activities of statewide significance. A state agency would be centrally involved in planning and regulating those areas and coordinating those activities.

Hawaii in the early 1960s and the Canadian province of British Columbia in the early 1970s pursued versions of the critical-area approach to preserve farmland on the fringes of rapidly growing metropolitan areas. They created state/provincial agencies that directly zoned land for farm use after consulting with local and regional governments and taking their planning considerations into account. Oregon interposed local planning and state acknowledgment of local plans between the state goal of preserving farmland and zoning land to achieve that objective. Local planners, especially in rural areas, often faced resistance from property owners and officials that prolonged those processes and threatened the achievement of the state's goal.

Plans

Many city planners in Oregon had concerns about implementing the local comprehensive planning mandate. They were often more interested in doing short- and intermediate-range plans and more specific plans that targeted particular districts than doing the long-range comprehensive plans SB 100 and LCDC required. While population in the Portland metropolitan area grew substantially between 1960 and 1980, the City of Portland's population increased just 2 percent between 1960 and 1970, and declined by 4 percent between 1970 and 1980. Acutely concerned about the competitive position of its central business district, the city adopted an ambitious downtown plan just before SB 100 was enacted, and city officials were looking forward to creating additional such plans and projects to implement them. The legislature defined comprehensive as "all-inclusive, both in terms of the geographic area covered and functional and natural activities and systems occurring in the area covered by the plan." Producing such a plan would clearly be a very complex, time-consuming, and resource-intensive process. Portland planners, as well as their city and county counterparts elsewhere, were reluctant to allocate the time and resources to the state-mandated effort.

Oregon enacted its local planning mandates at a time when the U.S. government sometimes required and often encouraged state and local governments to plan before spending federal money. In the 1960s, for example, comprehensive metropolitan-area transportation plans had to be created before federally financed highway projects would be approved for construction. State and local governments also had to create associations of local governments to review and approve applications for a wide range of federal program grants, including law enforcement, social services, and physical infrastructure projects. Those new regional entities were required to prepare and adopt plans to guide their reviews. The federal government also mandated planning for water-quality-related facilities, air-quality-related projects and programs, and health care facilities.

The planning mandates were intended to rationalize federal expenditures during a time when rapid metropolitan population and economic growth were creating turmoil. The actions of federal agencies that affected the location of growth were often in conflict with each other; and federal agencies, each pursuing its own mission and cultivating its own relationships, were drawn into the competition for investments that raged among state and local governments. In the absence of explicit national goals for the location of population and economic activity—Congress was particularly reluctant to adopt such goals—executive branch officials hoped that regional planning processes would produce the coordinated allocation of resources they were unable to implement themselves and mitigate the troubling social, economic, and environmental impacts generated by competitive pressures operating at state and local levels.

The lack of coordination of the projects and programs initiated by state and local agencies and private developers motivated Governor Tom McCall to support SB 100, and coordination objectives figured prominently in the preamble to the bill. McCall strongly supported authoritative planning roles for regional agencies in metropolitan areas, in the Oregon coastal zone, and in nonmetropolitan regions to address coordination issues. During his first term, McCall was officially the state's chief planner, a role that he relished.

McCall was also an outspoken advocate of the National Land Use Policy Act, a much-amended bill that Congress debated between 1970 and 1975.

The act proposed to give money to states to develop plans and regulations, just as McCall strongly supported giving local governments money to plan and zone. In fact, the governor fervently hoped that federal money would be available to finance state and local land-use planning in Oregon. Lobbyists for homebuilders, realtors, farmers, and large business organizations were centrally involved at both federal and state levels. Although the national land-use law did not pass, in part due to the opposition of those groups, the federal government enacted several laws that had profound effects on land use during that period (Lehman, 1995; Lyday, 1976; Plotkin, 1987; Weir, 2000). It clearly made a difference to its success that SB 100 had the strong support of a popular Republican governor, key legislators, many of who were also Republicans, and leading members of the business community, including farmers.

Zones

At the same time that some reformers and practitioners were questioning the value of long-range comprehensive plans and state planning mandates, zoning was getting its share of criticism. Many land-use planning advocates and some homebuilders were troubled by the use of zoning to exclude lower-cost housing in the suburbs, and exclusionary zoning was a major concern for the reformers working on the Model Code project. The creation and changing of zoning designations were critiqued more generally by planners and environmental activists because those decisions focused primarily on enhancing the value of private property without regard for social consequences, and sometimes involved corrupt practices by appointed members of planning commissions and elected officials, many of whom were involved in property development. In rural areas, decisions to establish zones and to change them often reflected personal relationships among elected and appointed officials and their constituents (Rudel, 1989). Given those relationships, advocates of resource land preservation were skeptical that local government officials would or could apply zoning to preserve farmland or sensitive natural areas when landowners wanted zoning designations that would permit more intensive uses of their land. The 1969 mandate to zone all privately owned land had generated substantial controversy in rural Oregon, including an unsuccessful 1970 ballot measure to repeal the requirement. Protecting resource lands required changing county decision-making practices, but many county officials and their constituents were ideologically opposed to SB 100 on the grounds that its mandates violated private property rights.

Local Coordination and Citizen Participation

Assigning county governments the responsibility of coordinating the plans, regulations, and projects of local and state government agencies in their jurisdictions was both controversial and problematic. The legislature said in SB 100 that a plan would be coordinated "when the needs of all levels of governments, semi-public and private agencies and the citizens of Oregon have been considered and accommodated as much as possible." The definition included a pragmatic element, but it was still a daunting prospect. Many of Oregon's thirty-six counties, especially those outside the state's four metropolitan areas—Portland, Salem, Eugene, and Medford—had little, if any, planning experience and limited technical and financial capacities. In addition, the requirement to open plan-making and implementation processes to participation by all of a jurisdiction's residents, and to include opportunities for citizens to appeal government actions, challenged the practice—widespread in city residential neighborhoods, suburban municipalities, and rural areas—of planning land uses according to the desires of property owners, realtors, and developers. Participation requirements also appeared to challenge representative government; there were worries that the authority of elected and appointed officials would be undermined. Citizen involvement through legal proceedings before LCDC and in the state courts emerged early on and became increasingly central to the evolution of the statewide program, which increased the level of contention.

Goals

SB 100's requirement that zoning ordinances had to be consistent with comprehensive land-use plans, and that both plans and ordinances had to conform to statewide planning goals, was another Oregon first. The consistency requirement, the deadlines, the review process, and the threat of the state's big stick all heightened the tensions associated with developing statewide goals and producing local plans.

Formulating those goals and processes was a massive, complex, and controversial undertaking for the Land Conservation Development Commission. The lightning rod issue of whether statewide goals should be detailed and specific in order to create a more certain environment or more general to provide flexibility at the local level to adjust to changing circumstances was heatedly debated. Stakeholders clashed regarding how much discretion state and local governments should have in establishing priorities, resolving conflicts, and reaching judgments about the balance between state interests and local aspirations during plan making and implementation.

Watchdog

All of the legal requirements, though, enhanced the status of local plans and their significance for Oregonians. Lobbyists representing local governments, industry, and property rights groups, as well as environmental, citizen empowerment, and planning activists, participated, often passionately, during goal development and local plan making. There were some differences between planners and environmental activists. The activists, especially the attorneys among them, were skeptical about the ability of local planners to effectively protect environmental resources. They believed that detailed, specific laws and goals and a state agency that was committed to enforcing compliance were necessary to counterbalance the power of local development interests. The lawyers carved out a critically important watchdog role in relation to state and local planners to increase public capacity to monitor and enforce. They were especially worried that the Herculean tasks looming for LCDC, a new agency with seriously limited resources, would lead to a loss of focus, especially on the preservation of farmland. After statewide land-use goals were adopted, LCDC had to allocate public funds to thirty-six counties and 241 cities to produce plans and ordinances and evaluate their products. State and local land-use actions were subject to a great deal of scrutiny—an unprecedented situation.

Several national organizations were doing public interest legal work at the time, but 1000 Friends of Oregon was unique in its concentration on land-use issues in one state. As a land-use rather than an environmental organization, 1000 Friends communicated clearly its support for both conservation and appropriate development, an approach that was consistent with a strategic re-orientation nationally among environmental activists (Popper, 1981). The new organization advocated strongly on behalf of farmland preservation as a key part of a state economic policy, as well as for compact urban development as a way to reduce the cost of infrastructure investments. It sought allies among both farmers and homebuilders to implement its growth-management agenda. 1000 Friends also emphasized the importance of basing plans on objective, fact-filled analyses of current and likely future conditions and doing so in the context of detailed laws and goals. The specifics were intended to reduce what Friends' attorneys saw as the tendency of local planners and elected officials to inappropriately "politicize" land-use decision-making processes and to enhance the chances that regulations would survive legal challenges.

An Unquiet Revolution

Oregon's land-use revolution was noisy and lengthy. Ballot measures—all unsuccessful—challenged SB 100 in 1976, 1978, and 1982. The legislature considered dozens of bills every session that sought to change the program in ways large and small. The last local comprehensive plans were not acknowledged by LCDC until 1986, thirteen years after the passage of SB 100. The broad outlines that shaped conflict about the program's evolution as well as the sources of its accomplishments were visible during the mid-1970s. Frank Popper captured a key aspect of the Oregon experience:

> There may never have been a time when it was as good to be an American city planner or land use lawyer as the late 1960s and early 1970s. Planning was coming alive; huge segments of the public were interested in it and its possible contributions, probably for the first time in American history. The post-World War II building boom, culminating in the record-high development rates of the late 1960s, had produced a professionally exhilarating set of environmental problems . . . planners, lawyers, and environmentalists were animated by a truly public-spirited desire to show how well they would perform if given the opportunity. (Popper, 1988, 292-93)

Professional and civic activists played major roles in the unfolding drama of Oregon's land-use planning revolution. Many were young, had time on their hands, and were passionately concerned about those environmental problems. Elected and appointed state officials, business leaders, and representatives of industry groups and local governments joined them in constructing the statewide program. Everyone wanted good planning, but differences among the stakeholders about what that meant guaranteed that conflict and compromise would shape the specific outcomes that emerged over time.

Chapter 1
The Laws, 1961-1969:
The Path to Farmland Preservation

". . . the scatteration of unimaginative, mislocated urban develop-
ment introducing little cancerous cells of unmentionable ugliness
into our rural landscape . . ."—Governor Tom McCall

The Oregon legislature first identified the loss of farmland on the fringes
of growing urban areas as a problem in 1959. Two years later, legislators
began to address the issue with the Greenbelt Law, a novel approach that
linked a county's creation of exclusive farm-use zones to property tax
breaks for owners of farmland (Roberts, 1967; Sullivan, E., 1973b).

A 1947 statute already enabled Oregon counties to plan and zone (Oregon, 1947). Under the law, those counties choosing to do so first had to
prepare and adopt a land-use plan and then ensure that any proposed zoning regulations followed the pattern of development set forth in that plan
(Sullivan and Kressel, 1975). By 1961, only three of Oregon's thirty-six
counties had been zoned pursuant to the 1947 act. In six other counties,
voters had decided to reject zoning altogether. Elected officials in about
half the state's counties had zoned parts of their jurisdictions in response to
petitions by local landowners, the approach to land-use planning that was
the most frequently used in rural Oregon at the time. The Greenbelt Law
didn't have much of an impact. Just two counties created exclusive farm-
use zones in 1961-1962—Polk, on the edge of Salem, and Washington,
outside Portland.

In 1963, House Bill 1230 entitled landowners whose farms were located outside exclusive farm-use zones to apply to county assessors for tax
breaks. The law also stipulated that "farm-use zones shall be established
only when such zoning is consistent with the over-all plan of development

of the county" (Oregon, 1963). County governments were authorized to enforce interim zoning ordinances for up to three years while they pre-pared new plans. The legislature also designated five nonfarm uses that were permitted in farm-use zones: schools; churches; golf courses; parks, playgrounds, or community centers owned and operated by governments and nonprofit organizations; and public service utility facilities.

The property-tax break approach to farmland preservation was a widely adopted strategy in the United States during the 1960s. The 1961 and 1963 laws used a more unusual approach, one that reinforced the Oregon leg-islature's understanding of the appropriate relationship between land-use planning and zoning: zoning had to be consistent with adopted plans. If farm-use zones were going to be created, then counties would have to adopt comprehensive plans that contained the long-term objectives those zones were designed to achieve. The legislature also demonstrated that it was willing to engage the details of zoning when it declared that certain activities would not conflict with farm uses. Still, planning and zoning remained voluntary choices at the local level.

In 1967, L. B. Day, a state representative from Marion County, intro-duced a bill to preserve prime agricultural land in Oregon. Day was an of-ficial with a Teamsters Union local based in the Willamette Valley's Marion County, one of the leading food-processing counties in the United States, and he was concerned about the negative impact on his union's members of farmland losses caused by urban development. Day reported to the House Agriculture Committee that Oregon had lost about 20 percent of its prime farmland during the previous ten years and that population and economic growth, especially in the Portland area, threatened to urbanize a great deal more. Modeled on a California law passed a few years earlier, his bill aimed to bring about voluntary agricultural zoning to conserve prime resource lands and to pay landowners who were willing to sign contracts to keep their land in exclusive farm use. County governments, using state funds, would purchase the right to develop from willing owners of prime farmland—that is, soils classified by the U.S. Soil Conservation Service as I and II of eight classifications—for a minimum of ten years. Because the agricultural sector was so important to the state's economy, he argued that growth had to be accommodated in ways that did not undermine the capacity of the agricultural sector to sustain production (Day, 1967).

Day's bill did not pass, but the House did adopt Joint Resolution 53, which asked a legislative Interim Committee on Agriculture to study problems associated with the urbanization of prime agricultural lands and the role of zoning in addressing those problems. A land-use subcommittee was established to take testimony on the issues and to develop possible legislative proposals for the interim committee to present to the 1969 legislature.

In late 1967, Day led off the subcommittee hearings by reiterating the facts that had motivated him to sponsor legislation earlier that year. Wesley Kvarsten—planning director for the City of Salem and Marion and Polk counties and the director of the Mid-Willamette Valley Council of Governments, one of the first such entities established in the United States—strongly urged the subcommittee to adopt statewide zoning as a way to preserve farmland. World population was growing faster than world food production, he testified, and Willamette Valley farmland was disappearing. Kvarsten believed that zoning would have to be mandatory, and he supported "rigid laws that designate . . . land as agricultural" and that prohibited farmland from being subdivided (1967-69 Interim Committee on Agriculture, 1967a).

Soil scientists at Oregon State University (OSU) stressed the critical role that soil surveys should play in classifying land and reported that new soil maps were almost complete for all areas of the state with potential for agricultural development. They strongly suggested that the legislators talk with Ted Sidor, an OSU Agricultural Extension agent (1967-69 Interim Committee, 1967b). Sidor had been talking with farmers about the losses of farmland to urbanization. He was especially troubled by the conversions taking place in the Willamette Valley, the location of much of Oregon's most productive agricultural lands, where he estimated that 4 acres of land were lost to farming for every acre that contained a house. In Washington County, a rapidly growing part of the Portland metropolitan area, he calculated a loss of $35 million per year in farm income as a result of suburban sprawl. Scattered houses took thirty-five years of tax revenue before they began to pay their own way, he reported, while compact housing located near already built-up areas paid its way in seven years (Interim Committee on Agriculture, 1968a). Sidor's presentation made an impression: "Following Ted Sidor's remarks . . . the subcommittee agreed that there should be bills drawn . . . because we are losing too much valuable farm land that is going to be necessary to our state, and because we are losing too much income" (1967-69 Interim Committee on Agriculture, 1968b).

The subcommittee developed a package of four bills that aimed to address the issues that had been identified. Senate Bill 13 allocated money for OSU to complete work on soil classification and finish mapping the state. Senate Bill 11 reflected Oregon's experience with two conditions that were becoming increasingly widespread in suburban and rural America: failing septic tanks and unrecorded, sometimes fraudulent, land sales to unsuspecting home-site buyers who ended up with lots that had no access to water (Rome, 2001). The bill required that people building homes on fewer than 10 acres get a permit from the county health officer stipulating that there was adequate water and sewage disposal capacity within the boundaries of the plot.

Senate Bill 12 sought to prevent land classified as agricultural from being taken by eminent domain for the construction of new roads or telephone or power lines, except when the governor declared there was no feasible alternative. The bill was a response to Kvarsten's report to the subcommittee that the construction of Interstate 5 had paved over 1,500 acres of prime agricultural land in the Willamette Valley. He had also expressed concern about land being taken in eastern Oregon for power lines.

The most far-reaching and consequential bill proposed by the subcommittee was Senate Bill 10, which stipulated that counties must plan and zone all of their land by January 1, 1972. If counties missed that deadline, then the State Land Board would plan and zone whatever land remained unzoned. Kvarsten was asked to submit two versions of Senate Bill 10 to the interim committee. The first was to lay out a set of planning standards that would apply to a state agency producing plans and zoning ordinances in place of a local government; the second was to incorporate additional zoning guidelines that applied, for example, to industrial and recreational development (1967-69 Interim Committee on Agriculture, 1968c; 1968d). Kvarsten worked with three other planners to draft goals and guidelines: Arnold Cogan, the planning coordinator in Governor McCall's office and a former City of Portland planner; Robert Baldwin, the planning director for Multnomah County and a leader in the Oregon chapter of the American Institute of Planners; and Lloyd Anderson, the founding director of the Multnomah County planning department and a City of Portland council member. Their work was reviewed and endorsed by Willamette Valley planners, and Kvarsten presented the two versions of the bill to the full interim committee in September 1968.

Kvarsten anticipated that few people would disagree with the generally stated goals that he and his colleagues recommended. It was a comprehensive list: preserving air and water quality; conserving prime farmlands and open space; protecting natural and scenic resources and life and property in hazardous areas; providing recreational opportunities and transportation facilities; improving and diversifying the economy; and managing an orderly and efficient transition from rural to urban land uses, including supplying public facilities and services to serve as a framework for urban and rural development. The planners also proposed a goal that reflected increasing environmental awareness—the idea of carrying capacity, to "ensure that the development of properties within the state is commensurate with the character and the physical limitations of the land."

The other proposal also contained a set of more specific standards that would be applicable to zoning ordinances. Those standards aimed at preventing or mitigating conflicts between different kinds of land uses—for example, between farm and nonfarm uses and between industry and surrounding uses. The proposed standards also attended to the effects of land uses on air and water quality, calling for environmental impact analyses as part of development plans. There was also a requirement to coordinate the supply of infrastructure with demand for services.

The Interim Agriculture Committee decided to sponsor a bill that contained only the general goals that would apply directly to a state agency and leave it up to individual members of the committee either to introduce amendments or to prepare a new bill that contained specific standards and would apply to all local governments. The committee-sponsored version of Senate Bill 10 was referred to the Agriculture Committee. During the 1969 session, most of the members of the land-use subcommittee co-sponsored another bill that embodied all elements of Kvarsten's other proposal, including zoning standards and environmental impact and coordination requirements. That bill became Senate Bill 195; it was referred to the State, County, and City Affairs Committee.

The 1969 Legislative Session

Oregon Governor Tom McCall strongly supported Senate Bills 10 through 13 and the zoning standards embodied in Senate Bill 195. A leader among governors nationwide on growth management, McCall defended the need for the bills and the approach they embodied. In a special message to the legislature (McCall, 1969), he forecast "an urban explosion of environmental pollution . . . threatening the livability of Oregon." Dramatically, he warned of a "scatteration of unimaginative, mislocated urban development introducing little cancerous cells of unmentionable ugliness into our rural landscape whose cumulative effect threaten to turn this state of scenic excitement into a land of aesthetic boredom."

McCall was referring to recent flooding in the Willamette Valley, which had disrupted the lives of hundreds of people, including nursing home occupants. "If adequate zoning restricted flood plain use to nonresidential needs," he said, ". . . the discomfort . . . would not have occurred." He cited the added costs that uncontrolled urban sprawl imposed on local governments, the premature urbanization of prime farmlands, the negative environmental effects of highways and industries, and the insufficient attention given to the possibilities of new towns and the revitalization of older towns to take pressure off metropolitan areas. He also noted problems associated with the lack of coordination on land-use issues between state and local governments.

Land-use planning and zoning—including an important, explicit role for state government—was necessary to address those issues, McCall argued. He reminded the legislators:

> As Oregon's first governor whose staff includes state planners, I can hardly be accused of having an antiplanning bias when I say that our planning has been proceeding on a false premise: We have assumed that our historic concept of a separation of powers demands that state program planning should be the exclusive concern of state agencies and that land-use planning should be the exclusive responsibility of local government. The results have been disappointing.

The legislature should support a new state role in land-use planning and zoning, McCall urged, because of pragmatic statewide interests as well as philosophical ideas about human nature and human communities. A sprawling pattern of development, he pointed out, increased the cost of supplying infrastructure and services that unnecessarily burdened all Oregonians. The urbanization of prime farmlands could no longer be justified by the growth of a local government's tax base: "It is a direct personal threat to the economic livelihood of every Oregon farmer and employee of our growing food-processing industry at a time when Oregon is bidding to become a vital grocery basket for the Far East and American Southwest."

The governor sought to focus the legislators' attention on these kinds of problems because "our society's reflexes are remedial, causing decisions to be made away from ills rather than toward goals." He wanted Oregon to transcend a crisis-response mode and orient its citizens and government agencies toward the future. While he shared with the legislature a belief in subsidiarity—that "problem solving should take place as close as possible to the governed themselves"—he also thought that the Interim Agriculture Committee had chosen wisely when it authorized the state to plan and zone when necessary. "We recognize that all of us are guilty of a sometimes fatal narrowness of viewpoint," he said. "It is to anticipate this perfectly human deficiency that the Ag Interim committee recommends that the State Land Board step in and act when a county refuses to zone or zones in a manner inimical to the best interests of its residents or the general citizenry of the state."

SB 10 and its companion bills were intended to address the all-too-human frailties of individual property owners and developers, the local governance agencies whose decisions were too often influenced by them, and the bureaucratic structures that hindered cooperative approaches to solving Oregon's land-use problems. On behalf of the state, McCall wanted to save owners and developers from their speculative selves and to save government agencies from their territorial instincts.

The governor had suggestions for amending the land-use bills that had been submitted to the legislature. He had created fourteen new administrative districts that covered the state to increase cooperation between state agencies and local governments, and to require local governments to address issues that crossed jurisdictional lines. McCall wanted to allocate state financial resources to those districts to ensure that land-use planning was done on a regional basis and coordinated across levels of government. He would ask technical assistance units at the University of Oregon and Oregon State University to provide on-call help to district planning groups engaged in long-range physical planning. Once area-wide plans were produced, McCall thought, local governments could prepare their own zoning ordinances.

Arnold Cogan, the governor's planning coordinator who had worked on the SB 10 goals with Wes Kvarsten, elaborated forthcoming amendments to SB 10: zoning ordinances should be based on area-wide land-use plans done on the basis of administrative districts, so that regional concerns about transportation, air and water quality, and other cross-jurisdictional issues would be addressed; the language used in local government zoning ordinances should be standardized; and a standardized land-use classification system should be used during planning. Finally, Cogan told the legislature, "land-use planning and zoning should be undertaken on a cooperative basis between state and local government—rather than the adversary role assumed in the present bill which depends on county inaction prior to state involvement." The governor did not want the state to be the planner and zoner of last resort (Cogan, 1969a).

OREGON ENVIRONMENTAL COUNCIL

The Oregon Environmental Council (OEC) clearly established itself as an influential participant in legislative debates during the early 1970s. OEC had been created in late 1968 as an umbrella organization for conservation, planning, and sportsmen's groups to engage in political action. The Oregon chapter of the American Institute of Planners was a member. The 1969 legislative session was the OEC's first foray into legislative politics. The council's executive director, Larry Williams, established a close relationship with Governor McCall and his staff and was eager to make recommendations about the governor's appointments to state commissions and boards, including those for fish, game, environmental quality, transportation, water, forestry, and the Oregon Coastal Conservation and Development Commission. Williams told a reporter for the *Los Angeles Times*, who wrote a lengthy story about Oregon's environmental record and land-use politics: "In a way we are spoiled in this state. Environmentalists have had it easy. The state has picked up on our causes and we just supply support" (Fradkin, 1973).

In addition to mobilizing environmental activists to engage with elected officials at state and local levels, OEC also enjoyed the support of key members of the business community, among them Wade Newbegin, Jr., and John Gray. Newbegin's family owned and operated R. M. Wade and Company, a very large distributor of farm equipment. The company was founded in Oregon in 1865, and was one of the oldest—possibly the oldest—continuously operated family-owned businesses in the state. Taking a long-run view of its industry, the company had supported soil and water conservation for years (Newbegin, 1991).

Maxine Banks, a representative of the recently created Oregon Environmental Council and a planning commission member in Polk County in the Willamette Valley, expressed the council's support for SB 10 and statewide zoning. Leaning heavily on the soil conservation maps prepared by the OSU Extension Service and the U.S. Soil Conservation Service, Polk County had recently established an exclusive farm-use zone and was discussing adding more. The chair of the county planning commission, she reported, had said that "statewide zoning would be definite help because then we wouldn't have to argue whether to zone—only how" (Banks, 1969). The chair also supported incorporating the specific zoning

In response to a contribution that Wade Newbegin, Jr., gave in early 1971, OEC executive director Larry Williams wrote, "We hardly know what to say! The contribution from you and your family is the largest one that we've ever received" (Williams, 1971). As mentioned in connection with the 1970 campaign against Ballot Measure 11, John Gray owned Omark, one of the largest manufacturers of saw chains in the world, and also was an environmentally sensitive land developer. Requesting another donation from his firm, Williams, who had worked at Omark, pointed out to Gray, "Over the last three years, Omark Industries has been kind enough to provide a donation to the OEC. Omark is still the only business in the state which has given any financial support to the OEC on a regular basis" (Williams, 1972b, 2007).

In a speech to the National Association of Home Builders in 1973, Gray pointed out:

One of the first steps in the early planning stage [for John's Landing, a mixed-use land development project just south of downtown Portland] was to call in the Oregon Environmental Council, a non-profit citizens group that is a militant, but not obstinate, guardian of the state's environmental integrity. We described what we wanted to do and we asked these environmentalists if they could see any objections from an ecological point of view. As you might expect, they did have some objections . . . My associates and I pondered their reservations and decided the criticisms had merit . . . It shouldn't surprise you when I say that John's Landing has the OEC as a staunch ally. (Gray, 1973a) standards set out in SB 195 into SB 10 in order to strengthen both planning and zoning.

SB 10 was amended as it moved successfully through the legislative process. One amendment gave the authority to take over local planning and zoning, if necessary, to the Governor's Office rather than the State Land Board. An amendment requiring a public hearing on zoning plans in each county was adopted, as was authorization to permit the governor to grant a reasonable time extension to complete planning and zoning when a local government demonstrated that satisfactory progress was being made. Senate Bills 11, 12, and 13 failed to pass; SB 195 never made it out of committee. The governor's suggested amendments to SB 10 weren't incorporated.

Mandatory planning and zoning were getting off to a less auspicious start than planners and environmental activists had hoped. Clearly, the legislature was reluctant to go much further into the details of how local governments should zone land or to empower newly created regional entities to plan on an area-wide basis. The legislature was not yet willing to regulate in more detail the actions of state and private infrastructure agencies. It was also significant that there was no money associated with SB 10 to help local governments implement the new mandate.

Led by the politically powerful Senate Agriculture Committee, legislative majorities in both chambers were nevertheless willing to mandate planning and zoning statewide and to position the Governor's Office to intervene. The path to a zoning-based approach to farmland preservation, initiated by the legislature in 1961, continued to run through comprehensive plans. The goals embedded in SB 10 had been intended to apply directly only to the governor, but they were in the enacted legislation for all local governments and state agencies to see. It was a high point for the organized professional planning community.

Implementing SB 10

As of November 1969, an estimated 12 percent of unincorporated territory in county jurisdictions was zoned, and cities in which about 55 percent of urban Oregonians lived had adopted zoning ordinances. A lack of qualified planners was clearly evident at the county level (Logan, 1969). To that point, it had been primarily cities and suburbs that had undertaken land-use planning—both in Oregon and throughout the country—and there were relatively few land-use professionals with rural planning experience. But, within a year after the law was enacted, six of the state's thirty-six counties had permanently zoned border-to-border, five had adopted interim countywide zoning ordinances, and another twenty had planning directors working fulltime to produce comprehensive plans and regulations. Some counties thought this would take longer to complete than was contemplated in SB 10, but not too much longer (Sidor, 1970).

As local governments engaged with SB 10, a movement to challenge the law developed among rural property owners and elected officials, primarily on the coast and in eastern and southern Oregon. Ballot Measure 11, "Restricts Governmental Power over Rural Property," appeared on the November 1970 ballot, an election that also featured a gubernatorial contest. That summer, John Gray, the developer of two of Oregon's most important destination resorts and chair of Omark Industries, a major manufacturing concern linked to the forest products sector, wrote Governor McCall and his opponent, Robert Straub, about his strong support for statewide planning and zoning. He was opposed to Ballot Measure 11 and offered to help campaign against it (Gray, 1970; McCall, 1970a). Gray was joined in his opposition by Associated Oregon Industries, the chief lobbying group for the state's larger firms, an indication that key business leaders and their organizations agreed on the importance of state-mandated planning and zoning as part of an overall approach to economic growth and land development issues.

Lee Miller, director of the Lane County Planning Department and chair of the Oregon Planning Directors' Association, also told Governor McCall that his association was on record in opposition to the ballot measure. They were concerned that "the measure has a chance of passage if voters react only to the emotional appeal of the ballot title . . . without being further informed." Miller offered the services of his organization to call attention to the damage the ballot measure would do to "the future growth, environment, and livability of Oregon." For his part, McCall told Oregon citizens that if they planned to vote for Ballot Measure 11 then they should also vote to replace him as governor, since he did not want to preside over the degradation of the state's livability. He forwarded Miller's letter to the district manager of Pacific Power and Light (PP&L), who, McCall said, was organizing the opposition (Miller, 1970; McCall, 1970b). The willingness of Glenn Jackson, chair of both PP&L and the Oregon Transportation

Commission, to allocate his firm's resources to the opposition campaign is another indication of support for a stronger state role in planning and zoning among larger businesses.

Not surprisingly, the environmental community also opposed Ballot Measure 11. Oregon Environmental Council activist Martin Davis, a Portland landscape architect who played an important role in the development of land-use legislation, chaired a No on 11 committee that conducted intensive word-of-mouth and direct-mail campaigns in the state's urban areas and among land-use professionals (Leland, 1970). Oregon Sierra Club groups also actively opposed the measure.

Ballot Measure 11 was defeated in November 1970 by a vote of 56 to 44 percent, and Tom McCall was re-elected governor. A more interventionist state role in local land-use planning and implementation had survived its first political test. Professional planners, environmental activists, business and labor leaders, good-government advocates, and editorial writers—all led by Governor Tom McCall—had persuaded a majority of voters, especially those in urban areas, that mandatory land-use planning and zoning were necessary.

As of the end of March 1972, though, a few months past the deadline SB 10 had mandated for land-use plans and border-to-border zoning, a state survey found that just eleven counties had adopted both permanent plans and zoning ordinances for the unincorporated areas within their jurisdictions. The rest of the counties had received extensions from McCall, and almost all said they were still at work. As expected, the completion rate

Senate Bill 10 (1969) compliance

Jurisdictions in compliance	Jun 1969*	Jul 1970	Feb 1971	Jan 1972**	Mar 1972	Jan 1973	June 1973	1974***
Cities	17% 38/228			34% 79/230	40% 93/230	55% 129/234		65% 154/238
Counties	14% 5/36	17% 6/36	42% 15/36	28% 10/36	31% 11/36	50% 18/36	53% 19/36	64% 23/36

*At the end of the 1969 Legislative session
** Effective date to comply with Senate Bill 10
*** Two years after effective Senate Bill 10 compliance date
(Sources: Sidor, Ted, 1970; Local Government Relations Division, 1971c; Local Government Relations Division, 1972b; Local Government Relations Division, 1973b; Local Government Relations Division, 1974b.)

among cities was higher (Local Government Relations Division, 1972b); planning and zoning were more familiar to those in the cities, and they had been at it longer. Given the farmland-protection emphasis of SB 10, most of the controversial issues flared in county territory. In some cases, proposed county zoning ordinances were voted down and some officials faced recall elections. Growing dissatisfaction with the ways in which many local governments were implementing SB 10 and awareness of the limits inherent in the law triggered efforts to go beyond it.

Chapter 2
The Laws: The Path from SB 10

"Counties were doing their own thing. Some of them were doing a fairly good job; others were doing a lousy job. It was time to get some statewide standards set up to make a more credible job of the planning process."—Hector Macpherson

While local governments struggled to produce and adopt comprehensive plans and zoning ordinances to implement them, development pressures continued to build on resource lands in the Willamette Valley and on the Oregon coast. The Governor's Office initiated a wide-ranging process to address the land-use conflicts that were increasingly evident in the valley, and the legislature created a new agency to propose strategies to manage the conflicts on the coast. Those efforts, as well as programs emerging in other states and at the national level, informed a project spearheaded by Hector Macpherson, a freshman Republican state senator, Willamette Valley dairy farmer, and county planning commissioner, who pulled together a group of people to formulate Senate Bill 100.

The Willamette Valley
In February 1970, Governor McCall and Robert Logan, the former city manager of Tigard (south of Portland) and head of the Local Government Relations Division (LGRD) in the Governor's Office, called together about forty local government officials and several state agency leaders to discuss a development plan for the Willamette Valley. Intergovernmental coordination was a key concern for the two men. As Logan frequently pointed out, hundreds of local government units and state and federal agencies were involved in one way or another in development issues in the valley. A steering committee was formed consisting of two members of the Governor's Office

and two representatives from each of the four Councils of Governments (COGs) operating in the Portland, Salem, Corvallis, and Eugene areas.

The committee identified the conditions that necessitated a planning program: deteriorating air, water, and land resource quality; a lack of common policies with respect to growth; a lack of coordination among local planning efforts and state and federal agency plans; and conflicts between those interested in urban expansion and those interested in rural protection. It proposed a program with three components: a scenario that outlined the future of the valley if current trends continued unchecked; goals that expressed an alternative, environmentally sensitive future development pattern; and a plan to manage development consistent with those goals. It was an extremely ambitious undertaking.

Data would be assembled about the likely future levels of employment and population and the consumption of natural resources associated with growth in both areas. Public opinion would be surveyed and incorporated into goals, which would then be used to frame a plan that would set a twenty-year course to the desired future state of the valley. The Environmental Protection and Development Plan, as it was called, would address transportation, power, water, sewage, health, education, and land use, with recommendations for new policies and legislation to implement it.

In November 1970, forty-eight thousand questionnaires were mailed to Willamette Valley residents and several thousand more were distributed via valley newspapers. A Medford, Oregon, planning and urban design firm was hired to prepare a work program to develop the plan. "This kind of regional planning has never been done before," one of the consultants said. "It's going to be done here though because the valley doesn't want to become another California, where unchecked sprawl and spew has ruined many areas" (Hider, 1971; Local Government Relations Division, 1971a; McCall, 1971).

By the next spring, the consultants had outlined basic policy recommendations that took into account the roughly fourteen thousand responses to the survey. They recommended that the plan and the planning process focus on those regional activities that would or could have significant environmental impacts on the valley—regional functions that, "without positive regional management, will have a debilitating effect on the Valley's environment and will diminish the livability factors which the people have expressed their desire to preserve and protect." The recommendations continued: "The Plan and the process should set forth, in a balanced and equitable program, the means and methods of protecting the environment while still recognizing that growth and development will continue." Either a valley-wide Council of Governments, comprising representatives of the four existing COGs, should be established to exercise regulatory authority, or a state agency should be empowered to regulate regionally significant environmental issues. An advisory approach, they believed, would not be an effective method of implementation. They also suggested producing a professional film on the current state of the valley and its possible futures (Langford and Stewart, 1971). The firm's recommendations were rejected when the Governor's Office balked at the staffing costs.

In August 1971, Governor McCall announced the creation of the Willamette Valley Environmental Protection and Development Planning Council, an intergovernmental task force composed of personnel from state agencies responsible for natural resources, transportation, and economic development and representatives from local and federal governments. Coordination of the projects and programs of those entities would be a key objective. With Secretary of State Clay Myers as chair, the council's members were state legislators, citizens, local officials, and state agency representatives, many of whom were "progressive . . . forward-looking Republicans" (Myers, 1997). The council would oversee the work of the four Willamette Valley COG directors, staff from the relevant state agencies, and LGRD. One way in which the staff geared up was to watch *Multiply and Subdue the Earth* (Logan, 1971), a film by landscape architect/planner Ian McHarg, who had recently published *Design with Nature*, a book that was inspiring many planners and environmental activists (McHarg, 1969). In September 1971, the council announced Project Foresight, a new direction for planning in the Willamette Valley.

The key aspects of Project Foresight were two scenarios that expressed alternative development patterns and citizen participation in resolving conflicts over key values. One scenario projected that current urban and rural growth policies would continue between 1972 and 2000, as would economic and environmental policies, transportation trends, and the rate of consumption of natural resources. The scenario assumed that policy conflicts would be resolved in favor of economic growth. The other scenario assumed growth policies that limited the outward expansion of urban centers in the Willamette Valley. State and local policies would encourage the concentration of urban growth and the preservation of agricultural and other open-space lands. Industry and housing would be limited to areas within urban growth boundaries established by the four Councils of Governments, and surface travel would be limited to mass transit and the existing and presently committed system of highways. Resource conflicts would be resolved in favor of environmental protection (Local Government Relations Division, 1972a).

A case study of Charbonneau informed the current-trends scenario. Charbonneau was a proposed subdivision of 477 acres that would consist of a village center, churches, stores, professional offices, an elementary school, a restaurant, a golf course, a swimming pool, tennis courts, and two thousand upscale residential units. The total investment was projected to be $100 million. The subdivision was located on prime agricultural land (soil classes I and II) just south of the expanding Portland metropolitan area. LGRD staff chose to analyze Charbonneau because of its size and because the developers had followed all the rules then in place. It was acknowledged to be a high-quality proposal.

LGRD worried that the effect on property values of such a development would exacerbate already existing upward pressure on the price of surrounding farmland. Similar developments, mostly smaller, had been proposed for locations throughout the Willamette Valley. "At stake is the economic vitality of Portland, of Salem and Eugene, and the vitality of farms and ranches intervening," the LGRD report warned. "At stake is the consumption of our natural resources, our land, air and water. At stake is intelligent use of all our resources be they fiscal, natural or human." No agency had the authority to deal with the "big picture" issues presented by such a development (Local Government Relations Division, 1971b).

The Charbonneau proposal plunged the Columbia Region Association of Governments (CRAG), which was the Council of Governments for the Portland metropolitan area, into crisis. Don Clark, a member of the Multnomah County Commission, was a member of the CRAG executive committee. He recalled that the Oregon Highway Division had come to CRAG because it had been asked to include water and sewer lines to serve Charbonneau in its plans to reconstruct a freeway bridge across the Willamette River. In addition, the state-created Metropolitan Area Local Government Boundary Commission, which had to approve an annexation to the City of Wilsonville to accommodate the subdivision, wanted to know if Charbonneau was in line with CRAG land-use plans.

Although CRAG had an interim plan showing that Charbonneau would be built five miles beyond its proposed urban boundary, members of the CRAG executive committee, with one exception, refused to oppose the development. Clark, the lone opponent, remembered telling his fellow committee members: "What we do is pass a resolution here and now, and we say, 'Don't do it,' and then the State won't do it and you will not get that sprawl into the agricultural land." Another committee member, Lloyd Anderson from the City of Portland, responded: "Do you realize what a political firestorm you'd create by doing that?" Clark recalled saying: "I don't care; we ought to do it . . . This is our one shot. They're before us right now, they've asked us, we ought to tell them, and we ought to stop it. The thing was, everybody agreed with that position, but nobody would do it" (Clark, 2002). The CRAG majority was concerned that, since it had not yet formally adopted its own plan, it lacked the political and legal capacity to impose restrictions on cities that wanted to grow.

Lawrence Halprin and Associates, a San Francisco-based consulting firm, was hired to develop the Project Foresight scenarios. After extensive revision by LGRD, the project staff held 275 meetings in the valley, involving twenty thousand residents, to discuss them (Logan, 1997; Allen, 1972; LGRD, 1974a). In November 1972, an editorial on a Portland television station framed the issues this way: "Project Foresight . . . offers valley residents two clear-cut choices: wall-to-wall suburbs cloaked in a blanket of air pollution; or a melding of open space and farm land with suburban development, and mass transit facilities from Eugene to Portland." Looking ahead to the 1973 legislative session, the station said that even though the choice was obvious, state legislators might not agree.

> Time and again housing developments and shopping centers have won out over open space and environmental considerations when the alternatives were presented to local officials. Local governments simply have not exhibited the backbone necessary to reject a proposal that may have short-run economic advantages but also entail long-range ecological destruction. The future of the Willamette Valley must not be left in the hands of capricious local officials, else the tragedy of Project Foresight's first alternative might soon be upon us; a nightmare alley between Portland and Eugene. But that decision can only be made by the legislature, whose individual

members are responsible to local constituencies and may find support of statewide zoning politically suicidal. (KATU, 1972)

Project Foresight also triggered a letter to Governor McCall from two members of the Winegrowers Council of Oregon, which had its own land-use committee. Richard Ponzi and William Blosser wrote: "Vineyardists and vintners of the Willamette Valley are concerned that present and proposed land use plans, including 'Project Foresight,' will destroy hillside areas of prime grape land and prevent the development of Oregon's new and flourishing wine grape industry" (Ponzi and Blosser, 1973). They outlined the land-related requirements of the new industry in the valley and projected its potential dollar contribution to the economy:

> Our plea in this statement is for *time* and sensible land use planning *now* for a wine industry in Oregon. Wine grapes in the Willamette Valley must be grown on hillsides, but the comprehensive plans and zoning ordinances [being prepared under the auspices of SB 10] are fostering development on the hillsides, presumably because they are less valuable for agriculture than valley floor lands. Even Scenario II of "Project Foresight" shows the hills as residential and the valley floor as agricultural.

Ironically, classifying hillsides in this way was inspired by the McHargian approach, which had informed the valley project.

Bob Logan attempted to maintain citizen interest in and support for land-use planning by creating Feedback, a nonprofit organization that distributed information about land-use issues. Supported by funds from the U.S. Department of Housing and Urban Development, Feedback staff passed out cards at the end of every Project Foresight meeting, asking people if they wanted to get involved. Logan later recalled that as many as fifteen thousand people gave their names and addresses, and every several weeks they received a Feedback newsletter (Logan, 1997).

That November, LGRD continued to build on Project Foresight and Feedback at the governor's Land Use Conference in Portland. McCall and LGRD persuaded Glenn Jackson to chair the conference, which was attended by more than six hundred people from around the state. The gathering was intended to galvanize leaders and activists to support land-use planning legislation that would be introduced in January. The plan was to begin the

conference with a slickly produced slide show on the effects of development, with a Cat Stevens song ("Where Will the Children Play?") providing the background music. Jackson joined Logan for a preview. "This was
the early seventies," Logan said, "and we got Cat Stevens, a long-haired
hippie, singing to a bunch of straights . . . Jackson came up to me after the
preview and I said, 'What'd you think?' He replied, 'I don't understand
that stuff too well, but my wife liked it.'" Logan thought the show and the
conference were great successes. Jackson's willingness to chair the meeting
and to publicly support strengthened land-use planning legislation did a
great deal to alleviate potential concerns among the business leaders who
attended (Logan, 1997; LGRD, 1974a).

The Coast

In 1971, the legislature created the Oregon Coastal Conservation and
Development Commission (OCCDC), which was charged with preparing a coastal resources management plan by 1975. Logan and his staff,
who put together the original proposal (Logan, 1997), were motivated
by several concerns. There were sewage-disposal issues associated with
development projects running ahead of adequate infrastructure to accommodate them. A county planning commission had asked Governor McCall
to intervene to prevent the construction of a high-rise apartment building
on the beach, but he was reluctant to do so. There was a troubling proposal to fill an estuary that had been approved locally but then rejected
by the U.S. Department of the Interior on resource-conservation grounds.
There was also an ongoing controversy about the environmental impacts
of the location of U.S. 101, the coast highway. Because of these and other
concerns, the governor issued an executive order in March 1970 that
placed a hold on state construction projects on the coast that might have
damaging environmental impacts, an action that angered many local officials (McCall, 1970c).

    At the same time, Congress was considering coastal zone management
legislation. McCall wanted to prepare for a possible national coastal zone
program, which would involve intergovernmental coordination. It was an
issue about which he cared deeply. Moreover, the California and Washington legislatures were debating a coastal management program, and McCall
was concerned about Oregon maintaining its standing as an innovator in
the field of environmental policy.

OCCDC was modeled, to a limited extent, on the San Francisco Bay Conservation and Development Commission. The major difference between the two commissions was that OCCDC could not regulate development, a deep disappointment to Oregon environmental activists who had supported giving the agency such authority. Moreover, Oregon Environmental Council and another new organization, Oregon Shores Conservation Coalition, had been troubled by the proposed composition of OCCDC: twenty-four representatives appointed by local city and county elected officials. Representatives of coastal port districts, traditionally the point agencies for local economic development aspirations, would be able to serve as commissioners, something that was not permitted in San Francisco. Environmentalists had worried that a commission that included people with such interests would skew the OCCDC's planning agenda, and they had persuaded legislators to add six positions filled by gubernatorial appointment so statewide interests would be represented. McCall's first appointees included OEC founding president Maradel Gale and two founding members of Oregon Shores (Davis, M., 1971a; Fitzgerald and Watkins, 1992).

Environmentalists soon clashed with OCCDC chair Wilbur Ternyik, who was the Siuslaw port district representative. Steve Schell, a Portland attorney who was active in Oregon Shores, urged Ternyik to make recommendations about proposed landfill and development projects even though OCCDC did not have permitting authority (Schell, 1971). OCCDC balked, and environmentalists sought McCall's help. On behalf of OEC, Martin Davis wrote the governor in June 1972 telling him that motel and condominium projects were threatening fragile sand dune areas. Because the new commission was refusing to act—in fact, it had not yet inventoried those critical areas—OEC urged the governor to freeze development in that zone (Davis, M., 1972b). McCall wrote to Ternyik, asking OCCDC to begin immediately to survey all proposed development plans that might endanger sensitive areas such as sand dunes and to inventory other areas that might require special protection (McCall, 1972).

The Oregon Student Public Interest Research Group (OSPIRG) also had begun to scrutinize the agency. Inspired by consumer and environmental protection advocate Ralph Nader, OSPIRG was financed by a fee paid by students attending Oregon colleges and universities. In May 1973, OSPIRG staff attorney Henry Richmond supervised a published study that was harshly critical of OCCDC. Richard Benner, a University of Oregon law student, charged that

> OCCDC's present planning approach fails to concentrate limited development funds in the coastal ports offering the greatest benefit to Oregon. Instead, OCCDC is developing general policies which apply uniformly up and down the coast, without setting regional priorities in basically different areas . . . Unless some regional priorities are set which reflect these differences, fifteen coastal ports will continue a wasteful competition for limited development funds, each trying to be Oregon's gateway to the Orient, and Oregon's most pristine estuaries will continue to be slowly destroyed.

Benner's critique incorporated an analysis of the relationship between science and politics. He argued that competition among local governments to attract development was trumping science-based arguments for the preservation of coastal resources (Benner, 1973a). In addition to sounding the alarm about the decline of critical estuarine resources and the need for shorelands protection, Benner asked the Army Corps of Engineers to deny two permits for dredging and filling on coastal rivers ("Benner Asks . . .,"1973). He wrote directly to Ternyik:

> OCCDC was established because, among other reasons, it was recognized that inappropriate development is taking place on the Oregon coast. Planning is one way to deal with such development, but planning on a city and county basis is clearly not enough. If it were, the OCCDC would not exist. Planning with a regional and state perspective is the essence of a coastal comprehensive plan. (Benner, 1973b)

OSPIRG followed with a press release that called on OCCDC to classify estuaries along the lines that Benner proposed (OSPIRG, 1973).

Ternyik anticipated that Benner would be pleased with OCCDC's draft of estuary policies, but Benner worried that OCCDC still "refuse[d] to wrestle" with the kind of regional planning that he believed was both necessary and required (Ternyik, 1973; Benner, 1973c). Oregon Shores board member Anne Squier, who was also on an OCCDC advisory board, wrote Benner to thank him for his efforts: "Your . . . letter [to Ternyik] is great. Expresses well and documents the state of affairs in which OCCDC has not faced the fact that they must make some hard decisions despite a lack of unanimous approval of those decisions. I trust your careful work will help push us closer to some real planning" (Squier, n.d.).

For Richmond and Benner, and for their environmentalist colleagues in Oregon Shores and OEC, the OCCDC experience reinforced one of their major concerns: the capture of the commission by local interests who wanted to promote short-term economic development projects, some with the potential for environmental harm. Richmond also charged that the inventory work the commission had been mandated to do was coming along too slowly and would not be completed in time to provide a solid basis for the policy choices the commission was supposed to incorporate in its 1975 plan (Richmond, 1973b).

OSPIRG

Henry Richmond was impressed by Ralph Nader's 1970 speech at the University of Oregon, where Richmond was a third-year law student. "Nader came to speak to us at a time when there was a lot of violence and unrest going on," he later remembered, "and he presented to us a model that would influence society by working within the system." Campus-based public interest research groups, Nader said, could revitalize American democracy (Richmond and OSPIRG, 1991). Inspired, Richmond helped create OSPIRG—the Oregon State Public Interest Research Group—in 1971. It was the first organization of its kind in the United States to be based in a university system, and it began with a budget of about $150,000 and a staff of nine (Buckhorn, 1972).

A set of philosophical ideas rooted in the concerns of the 1960s New Left informed the approach: a critique of corporate capitalism and big government and a demand for widespread citizen participation in governance (Handler et al., 1978; Harris and Milkis, 1989; McFarland, 1976; Vogel, 1980-81). OSPIRG's role was to create civic balance and to prevent the capture of administrative agencies by those entities the agencies were supposed to regulate. OSPIRG would testify at legislative and administrative hearings and meet with and develop alliances with representatives of interest groups. As an information and referral source for like-minded Oregon groups, OSPIRG should both criticize others' policies and plans and present its own. After graduation and

The inventory work was taking so long largely because of a reality the Oregon coastal commission shared with local government planning agencies: the legislature had not allocated money to fund them. The coastal counties kicked in an amount sufficient to hire a part-time staff person, a part-time secretary, and a couple of firms that were asked to produce a study design for the plan OCCDC was mandated to deliver. The joint venture disintegrated, however, and the separate products did not provide what the thirty-member commission had hoped to receive. During its first year, OCCDC struggled to define an approach for itself. Some state and federal funding became available in July 1972, which allowed the agency to hire James Ross as executive director, its first full-time position, but tension among commission members surfaced early on. The six gubernatorial appointees were often characterized

a year of clerking for Federal District Judge Gus Solomon, Richmond became staff attorney at OSPIRG in September 1972.

Steve McCarthy, a board member of Oregon Environmental Council, was the OSPIRG executive director who hired Richmond. A recent law school graduate, McCarthy had a long-standing connection to Governor McCall; the McCall and McCarthy families were neighbors, and when McCarthy was a college student he had worked for McCall. McCarthy was grateful for the governor's support of OSPIRG: "Your attitude has helped to set the tone of government's response to us and to our work. I think it is a good comment on the state and its leadership that we have become the strongest PIRG in the country" (McCarthy, 1974).

Richmond also brought family-related assets to OSPIRG. His father, Henry "Russ" Richmond II, had worked at Bonneville Power Administration (BPA) during the 1940s and was proud of his contribution to the power-line extensions into eastern Oregon. Russ Richmond had returned to the agency in 1963 at the invitation of Charles Luce, BPA administrator, and he had been appointed deputy administrator in 1966. When Luce left to become undersecretary of the Department of the Interior in 1967, Richmond succeeded him and held the position through 1972. Russ Richmond's connections with government officials and private industry leaders (Luce, n.d.; Tollefson, 1987) were important to his son and McCarthy as they positioned OSPIRG to play a substantial role in Oregon's consumer and environmental protection affairs, especially on land-use matters.

as "unyielding conservationists who wanted to make the coast a playground for the rest of the state and country" (Thompson, J., 1975).

In a related case, another OSPIRG law student intern, together with OEC and Oregon Shores members, argued that appointees involved in real-estate development controlled a coastal county planning commission and that the commission had been captured by the same sorts of actors that Richmond believed had captured OCCDC. They advocated on behalf of requiring changes in the occupational composition of such commissions ("Land Use Planners Hit," 1972; "Tillamook County Planning Commission Makes Waves," 1971).

These kinds of experiences in the Willamette Valley and on the coast shaped the developing critique of SB 10. Whether it was the urbanization of farmland or development on fragile sand dunes and in estuaries, local governments were seen as lacking the political will or technical ability to protect critical natural resources. Aside from the remote possibility that the Governor's Office would displace a local government if it failed to act, SB 10 did not insert statewide interests any more authoritatively into local land-use planning and zoning than before. The gubernatorial appointees to the Oregon coastal commission, who were trying to change the dynamic in that particular area, represented a partial exception. The television station editorial about the future of the Willamette Valley expressed the concern unambiguously and without any sense that anyone would or should be surprised.

In December 1972, Governor McCall received an urgent—and highly unusual—request from Jefferson County elected officials who wanted him to declare a moratorium on all subdivisions and partitions in the county until their plan and zoning ordinance were adopted. The county had no planner on staff, and they felt vulnerable. Because some counties already had met their SB 10 responsibilities, Jefferson County worried that "subdividers are congregating on the counties that do not have adequate ordinances." Even when the county planning commission and the county commissioners refused permission, they told the governor, "the subdividers are by-passing the County by partitioning through the State Realtors Board therefore the property is being sold without the county having any record of these transactions as all contracts are not recorded" (Read, et al., 1972). The episode supplied an exclamation point to the growing awareness of the limits of SB 10 and strengthened the support to address them during the 1973 legislative session.

Hector Macpherson and the Evolution of SB 100

At the end of the 1971 session, OEC president Maradel Gale wrote to several legislators to tell them how pleased the council was with new legislation. She specifically mentioned two precedent-setting bills that reinforced Oregon's position as a national leader in the environmental field. The Bike Bill opened the state's highway trust fund to bicycle-related investments, and the Bottle Bill placed a mandatory deposit on beer and soda containers to encourage recycling and reuse. Both were firsts in the nation. The legislature also had created OCCDC and passed laws regulating billboards and authorizing special tax assessments for open-space lands. "We hope that you have found this a stimulating session," Gale concluded, "and that the OEC has been of help to you on matters of environmental policy. We are honored to have been able to work with you in this session, and look forward to a similarly productive 1973 legislative session" (Gale, 1971).

Freshman Republican legislator Hector Macpherson was not as sanguine. He was deeply disappointed that the Senate leadership had not granted his request for an interim committee to develop stronger land-use legislation for the next session. Determined to forge ahead even without legislative support, he sought assistance from OEC and wrote Maradel Gale to ask for help. He agreed that the session had been a productive one, environmentally speaking, and that the relationship he had established with OEC had been critically important to its success.

> It would not have been possible without the widespread public support mobilized by your organization. Your personal contributions to the shaping of public policy were great. I want to personally thank you for taking the moderate view in the field burning issues so important to the farm economy of my area.

As he told Gale, however, "our real tragedy is that we did nothing in the land use planning field, not even the study I desired." He asked: "Have you members of your group who would work with me in the next two years to develop a plan of action? I would like to put together an unofficial task force to develop legislation" (Macpherson, 1971a).

Gale forwarded Macpherson's letter to Martin Davis, chair of OEC's Environmental Planning Committee. Davis also was disappointed:

> [T]he State . . . must move to protect Oregon's critical environ-
> mental areas as well as the prime agricultural lands on which we
> eventually depend for survival. I do not think cities and counties
> can do this on their own or that the established councils of govern-
> ments are in any way effective. Legislation to give planning and
> development power to the State is needed. Perhaps we should be
> thinking of state zoning.

He was very interested in working with Macpherson on new legislation (Davis, M., 1971b).

Macpherson also connected with Robert Logan in LGRD, who agreed to coordinate the work of the unofficial task force that Macpherson wanted to convene. The work of the task force would be assigned to two groups. The Land Use Policy Committee would "concentrate on the broad issues of how to guide and monitor city and county planning to achieve state and regional goals," while the Rural Planning and Conservation Committee would "concentrate on slowing urban sprawl and conserving our farm and timber land base" (Macpherson, 1971b).

The list of committee members included Martin Davis, whom Macpherson considered his "right-hand person" on the policy committee; and he assigned Steve Schell, who was active in the Oregon Shores Conservation Coalition, to the rural planning group (Macpherson, 1997). Lane County Planning Director Lee Miller served as a staff member to the policy committee, along with Logan. Macpherson chose additional group members who he believed would be responsive to the concerns he wanted to address from OSPIRG, Oregon Shores, Associated Oregon Industries, academia, state and local government, and farm-related and other business groups (Macpherson, 1971b).

Macpherson was troubled by the ways some counties were implementing SB 10. He observed:

> Senate Bill 10 said, counties, you've got to go out and zone from
> border to border . . . some counties simply went in and asked every
> landowner, Well, what do you want your land to be zoned? What-
> ever you want it to be zoned, we'll try and block it up, and this
> will be your zone, and that's it. To my way of thinking, that was
> not planning, and we had to get some statewide standards in this

thing . . . Counties were doing their own thing. Some of them were doing a fairly good job, others were doing a lousy job. It was time to get some statewide standards set up to make a more credible job of the planning process. (Macpherson, 1997)

Some farmers, he thought, especially those in the Willamette Valley who were increasingly confronting urbanization, would be willing to support zoning to preserve farmland in the short and medium term. He was less certain about their support for the longer term. "Scratch a farmer and you'll find a subdivider," he said in 1974, a belief that was widespread among his legislative colleagues (Little, 1974; Wingard, 1993). Macpherson's assessment of landowners' participation in rural county planning disposed him to believe that regional agencies and the state had to play a direct role to preserve farmland. For him, land was more than a privately owned commodity exchanged in the marketplace; it was "precious," and the public must be involved in deciding what happened to it (Macpherson, 1997).

The American Law Institute's evolving *Model Land Development Code* project and the Council on Environmental Quality's *The Quiet Revolution in Land Use Controls* influenced Macpherson's thinking and the approach taken by his groups (Macpherson and Paulus, 1974). Both discussed the shift in the status of land from a commodity to a resource in which the public had a deep and abiding interest, and sought to analyze and shape the state-level government interventions emerging across the country that reflected it. The Macpherson group members educated themselves about the theories and practices outlined in those sources and debated their implications for a new Oregon statewide land-use planning program.

Environmental activists were reading those documents and also studying recent developments in Hawaii, Vermont, and Florida. OEC Executive Director Larry Williams, alerted to promising land-development policies in England, was also seeking information about the British planning system. He wrote to the Council for the Preservation of Rural England asking for information about restricting the conversion of agricultural land to nonfarm uses and about the betterment tax, "an 80% tax on the sale of certain types of land so as to discourage speculation in rural and urban areas." OEC was contemplating proposing its own legislation if Macpherson's effort didn't turn out as the organization hoped it would (Williams, 1972a).

Three ideas set out in the *Model Code* and in the studies of what was happening in other states were especially important to environmentalists: areas of critical state concern, activities of statewide significance, and developments of regional impact. They believed that state governments, acting either through a new agency or through a reconfigured existing agency, should play much more directive roles regarding those.

In the OEC newsletter, Martin Davis outlined a proposal he had advocated at a Macpherson group meeting: a state plan, prepared by a state land-planning agency, that would include areas of critical state concern such as farmland; critical environmental areas; significant historical, cultural, recreational, and social areas; and open space. He argued that the state plan should include the location of key facilities such as airports, freeways, ports, transmission corridors, new communities, and major industries. A state growth policy would also be prepared.

Existing Councils of Governments would prepare regional plans consistent with a set of standards that a new state agency would enforce on sewage treatment facilities, roads and mass transit routes, parks and open space, low-cost housing, solid-waste disposal sites, and sand and gravel extraction sites. The state would develop rules and regulations to govern land use in areas of critical concern and would issue permits regarding significant activities and developments that had regional impact. The state also would approve regional plans, and local plans would have to be consistent with them. For good measure, Davis wanted to require an Oregon State University planning course for all local government planning commissioners (Davis, M., 1972a).

In no uncertain terms, Davis told the Macpherson group that "the critical areas provision is the most important feature of the proposal. It is imperative for the state to act quickly to discourage 'misdevelopment,' especially in areas of great environmental concern" (Zachary, 1978). Richard Cohan, a law school student who was an OEC-OSPIRG intern with the Macpherson group, also was active in discussions about critical areas, activities, and developments. Davis and Cohan advocated strongly for including some specific areas, activities, and developments in the proposed legislation rather than leaving all designations to a state agency.

Macpherson met with Davis and Cohan and representatives of Associated Oregon Industries to draw up a list. Cohan later reported that the industry people wanted to leave "as much as possible in local control, while Martin and I pushed for inclusion of . . . specific areas" (Cohan, 1973). AOI was persuaded, though, that land-use legislation would pass in the 1973 session, Cohan thought, and its representatives figured they had a better chance of limiting the impact of state influence if specific areas were included in a law rather than left to a state planning agency. Thinking strategically, Cohan predicted: "We will have a hard time keeping the good stuff in the bill, and may well have to push for inclusion of more areas . . . to give the wolves something to snap at" (Cohan, 1972a). Macpherson acknowledged the political conflict likely looming ahead: "Probably the most controversial concept in the bill is that of critical areas of state-wide concern. It gives to the state the power to overrule local decisions in critical areas of state-wide concern" (Macpherson, 1972).

The original version of SB 100 included a compromise list of critical areas, incorporating much of what Martin Davis (Davis, M., 1972c) had proposed to the Macpherson policy group: Oregon-designated scenic waterways and related adjacent land; wild and scenic rivers designated by the federal government and related adjacent land; state parks and recreation areas, including land within a quarter-mile of their boundaries; environmentally sensitive lands managed by state and federal agencies; parks in unincorporated areas managed by local governments; lands within a half-mile of the intersection of an interstate highway with any other public highway when it is in an unincorporated area and within a quarter-mile in an incorporated area; most land west of the Oregon Coast Highway; all estuaries, including all land up to 1,000 feet east of the mean high-tide mark on the coast; the Columbia River Gorge; and all lands within 1,000 feet of the edge of Oregon-designated scenic highways in unincorporated areas and within 200 feet in incorporated areas. Farmland was not on the list, though. A new state agency would write rules and regulations governing uses within the critical areas, and local governments would have to plan and implement in ways consistent with those mandates.

The activities of statewide concern included the planning, siting, and construction of airports; state and federal highways; mass transit systems; high-voltage power, gas, and oil transmission lines; sewerage and water supply systems; and thermal power plants and nuclear installations. All would require permits from the state agency. Cohan advocated strongly for an industrial siting provision, based on a Maine Site Location law, which would authorize the state to regulate the location of heavy industry; Macpherson refused to agree to its inclusion (Cohan, 1972b). Regarding critical state-wide activities, the original version of SB 100 held that "a state agency may neither implement any such activity nor adopt any plan relating to such an activity without the prior approval" of a new state land-use agency.

Appeal procedures were extremely important to environmentalists, and Cohan was pleased that the Macpherson group was willing to support easy access to challenge decisions (Cohan, 1972a). The original version of SB 100 stipulated that any person or group of persons could petition the new state agency to review a provision of an adopted comprehensive plan. In addition, the agency would use a hearings officer to review petitions, a procedural requirement that appealed to environmentalists. Such an ap-proach, they believed, would increase the likelihood that decisions would be based on factual evidence and would reduce the chances that the state agency would be captured. The commission and the hearings officer were authorized to approve participation in state agency review proceedings by any person or group of persons, and any party to a proceeding who was aggrieved by a commission order could appeal.

While the environmentalists focused on critical areas, activities, and le-gal processes, Bob Logan and his colleagues in LGRD sought an enhanced regional level of coordination as well as a strong coordinating role for a new state land-use agency. In 1969, Governor McCall had wanted region-al entities incorporated into SB 10 to coordinate planning by cities and counties. Logan and his staff persuaded Macpherson to designate Councils of Governments to play that role. The original version of SB 100 created fourteen planning districts based on Councils of Governments, eleven of which were already operating. Planning committees within each district would coordinate the efforts of local governments within their jurisdic-tions. They would review comprehensive plans and implementing ordi-nances to make sure they complied with statewide planning guidelines and with the rules and regulations that would be adopted by a new state agency. An action taken by one of the regional planning councils could be appealed.

The Land Conservation and Development Commission (LCDC), the name suggested for the new state agency by Logan, would be composed of five citizens appointed by the governor (Logan, 1997). The agency would be authorized to establish statewide planning goals; issue permits for criti-cal statewide activities; prepare statewide objectives and regulations for critical areas and activities; recommend to the legislature the designation of additional critical areas and activities; prepare statewide guidelines for all local governments to follow when preparing mandated comprehensive plans and implementing ordinances; review plans for conformance with statewide planning goals and statewide objectives and regulations; and prepare inventories of land uses.

In the proposed bill, the Macpherson group carried forward the SB 10 mandate that all local governments would be required to prepare comprehensive plans and ordinances to implement them. An important point for Macpherson was "to give . . . city and county plans 'some teeth' . . . The net effect of state activity is to give those plans a certain uniformity through state-wide planning policies" (Zachary, 1978). As local government representatives told the Macpherson group, however, they had been preparing and adopting plans and ordinances pursuant to SB 10 since 1969. A Deschutes County commissioner, for example, told the group that "he was unable to support the proposed bill until something was done which assured cities and counties that their planning work of the past several years was not to be entirely scrapped" (Zachary, 1978).

The group agreed to place more emphasis on past planning efforts during a transition period, with LCDC directed to take into account local plans and ordinances when it formulated statewide objectives and regulations for critical areas and activities. Once the objectives and regulations were promulgated, though, existing plans and ordinances would have to be revised to come into compliance. Until LCDC adopted statewide planning goals—it would get one year to do so—the list of statewide planning goals set out in SB 10 was to be used by local governments to prepare their own plans.

The link between SB 10 and SB 100 was evident in other ways, too. Local governments were given a deadline to bring plans and ordinances into conformance with statewide goals and guidelines that LCDC was mandated to adopt. If they failed to meet the deadline, then the governor and the new state agency either would take over planning and zoning or approve an extension, just as under SB 10. The original version of SB 100 stipulated that local governments had just one year after LCDC's adoption of statewide goals and guidelines to ensure that their plans and ordinances were in compliance. The one-year deadline likely reflected both a sense of urgency in light of the Charbonneau experience and similar pressures on resource lands elsewhere, and a sense that it would not take much time

to whip local plans and ordinances into shape since most local governments had already been actively developing plans and zoning ordinances
for several years.

The more specific set of zoning-related standards that planners had
proposed for incorporation into SB 10, and which had ended up in SB 195
in 1969, were also included. All governments adopting zoning and subdivision ordinances following the effective date of the act were directed to
state explicitly that their ordinances would ensure that the specified zoning standards would be met. There was an interesting addition to the SB
195 standards: a required finding that zoning regulations did not prevent
"adequate housing for persons of low income within the area." Eliminating
zoning ordinances that excluded low-cost housing was a major objective
of the *Model Land Development Code*, and SB 100 aimed to accomplish that.

As formulated by Macpherson and his associates, the original version of
SB 100 was a very complex, far-reaching piece of legislation that embodied much of what environmental activists, planners, and officials in the
Governor's Office wanted to see. Based on the philosophical shift in the
understanding of land that Macpherson had articulated, the proposed new
state and regional agencies and the powers given them, the substantive
planning and zoning objectives incorporated into the bill, and the acces-
sibility to citizens of appeal procedures aimed to bring about a profound
transformation of relationships among state, regional, and local governments, and of relationships between governments and private investors
in land development. Although it originated in the context of discussions
about revolutionary changes in the land-use field that were "quietly" taking place around the country, SB 100 proposed to go well beyond what
had happened elsewhere, and its trajectory in the legislature and afterward
wasn't at all quiet.

Chapter 3
SB 100 in the 1973 Legislative Session

"Regarding the protection of our land . . . the lateness of the hour
for remedial and preventive moves is almost cause for despair . . .
Why the hell don't you just give me $500,000, and I'll zone the
goddamn state?"—Governor McCall

Democrat Ted Hallock, a flamboyant legislator who was highly regarded for his intelligence and his oratorical skills, had represented his Portland district in the state Senate since 1963. Hallock had been a broadcast journalist, as had Tom McCall, and he owned a public relations firm. He chaired the Senate Environment and Land Use Committee (SELUC) during the 1973 session. Hector Macpherson had alerted Hallock that he and his land-use policy group were preparing legislation. Hallock was interested and asked a Portland engineer who was a member of Macpherson's group to keep him informed.

SELUC had seven members, four Democrats and three Republicans. Democrats Hallock and John Burns represented Portland metropolitan area counties, as did Republican Vic Atiyeh. Democrats Jack Ripper and Michael Thorne represented two southern coastal counties and three counties in the northeastern corner of the state, respectively. Republican George Wingard came from the Eugene area, and Hector Macpherson was a Republican from the Willamette Valley's Linn County. Macpherson, Hallock, and Wingard solidly supported SB 100; the others were troubled by various aspects of the bill.

In a stirring speech to the opening session of the 1973 legislature, Governor McCall tried to persuade legislators and the public that passing SB 100 was an urgent necessity. A few days later, in a special message to the legislature, he discussed a report documenting "an unbelievable devastation of land and pollution of resources, both inviting a serious public health problem" on the coast in Lincoln County. He also reported on the results of a 1972 study done at his request by the state Health Division about the subsurface sewage capability of 356 residential subdivisions involving 16,850 parcels of land totaling about 85,000 acres. "Nearly 25 per cent of the acres," McCall said, "have been found inadequate for any sewage handling short of a central system, but the rampaging, competitive development spiral continues, and irreversible environmental damage is being done" (McCall, 1973a).

While McCall sought to portray the situation as a crisis, it became clear as SELUC began to hold hearings that SB 100 was going to be intensely controversial. An authoritative regional planning role for Councils of Governments and the inclusion of specific areas and activities of critical statewide concern generated the most contention. Martin Davis, the Oregon Environmental Council activist, told the senators that OEC wanted more critical areas specified in the bill, something that he had advocated early on to the Macpherson group. He wanted certain private developments added to the list of critical activities to be regulated, including industrial parks, regional shopping centers, and large-scale residential subdivisions (Davis, M., 1973a). OEC's suggestions were supported by Tri County New Politics, a new nonpartisan citizen organization in the Portland metropolitan area. Speaking on behalf of Tri County's Land Use Task Force, Joyce Cohen also suggested that LCDC be required to adopt procedures mandating early citizen input into the development of comprehensive plans and zoning ordinances (Cohen, 1973a). Macpherson asked Cohen to develop specific language that might be included in SB 100 (Cohen, 1973b).

The League of Women Voters of Oregon, which was active on land-use issues at the state level and through the efforts of its local chapters, was a strong supporter of Tri County's position on citizen involvement. Dorothy Anderson, the League's legislative chair, told the senators: "The frightening speed with which development is taking place in many parts of Oregon and the seeming reluctance of many local governments to withstand the pressures for undesirable development dictate fast action . . . We must not continue to despoil our legacy to future generations." The League suggested changes to SB 100 that would mandate more effective participation, including public hearings at all government levels during planning and implementation and a spot on LCDC for someone who was not a member of a special interest group (Anderson, D., 1973a).

George Diel, a coastal activist testifying on behalf of Oregon Shores, strongly supported SB 100. He called on the legislature to ensure that LCDC and OCCDC be given interim permit authority and the power to declare selective moratoria to prevent environmentally damaging development while plans and ordinances were being produced. Also on behalf of Oregon Shores, Steve Schell strongly supported the delineation of critical areas on the coast. Compared with what California voters had adopted in 1972 regarding coastal zone protection, he pointed out, the critical areas in SB 100 were relatively modest. He supported adding lakes on the coast and the lands adjacent to them as an area of critical concern (Diel, 1973a, b; Schell, 1973a, b).

There was some support for regional planning, generally from those involved with active Councils of Governments, Tri County, and the League of Women Voters. Eldon Hout, for example, an elected Washington County official and a leader of Columbia Region Association of Governments (CRAG), strongly advocated regional planning (Beggs, 1973). John Gray, speaking more as a land developer than as a manufacturer, appeared before SELUC to support regional planning and critical areas and activities (Gray, 1973b). Hallock later remembered thinking: "John Gray. He showed up, and I was going like this [clapping], Oh, boy, John Gray of Omark and Sunriver" (Hallock, 2000).

At the same time, Hallock's committee heard criticism about the regional entities. B. J. Rogers, a former mayor of Springfield who was chair of the planning and zoning committee of the Oregon Association of Realtors (OAR), testified that his association objected to Councils of Governments playing an authoritative role in planning processes. More generally, the realtor boards were worried about the loss of local control regarding land-use planning and zoning. Unlike environmentalists and advocates of citizen participation, the realtors were convinced that "no real proof has been shown that the cities and the counties of Oregon are incompetent, uninterested, and not intelligent enough to create land use plans for their respective areas without the intervention of all the various agencies, officials, and clerks, who make up this bureaucratic maze." They could agree that a state agency establish guidelines for local plans, but the plans and implementing ordinances had to be developed by those who would have to live with the results.

Rogers also chastised the bill's sponsors for including an emergency clause, which meant the bill would take effect on July 1 rather than ninety days after the legislature adjourned.

> It is very difficult to understand just what this great emergency is, and what harm will be done if the act doesn't take effect until 90 days after legislature adjourns. In the case of this bill, which at very best is most controversial, it seems to be an affront to the voters of the state of Oregon, who have shown over the years a great desire to retain final control over acts of the legislature through the initiative and the referendum!

OAR was not contemplating action to bring the bill to voters should it pass, Rogers said, but such a course ought to be available (Rogers, 1973).

While testimony was being taken at the state capitol, Robert Logan was discussing SB 100 with Portland Mayor Neil Goldschmidt and the city's commissioners. He reported to Hallock and Macpherson that the city's leadership was generally favorable, but they were concerned that the city might not be represented on LCDC. They also pointed out that including land that was within a quarter-mile of interstate freeway intersections with public highways among the areas of critical statewide concern would mean that the development of much of downtown Portland would be subject to state regulation (Logan, 1973a).

In light of the criticism his committee was hearing, Hallock was persuaded that SB 100 had to be revised if it was to make it out of committee and pass the Senate. At the end of January, he appointed two subcommittees, one to study regional issues and the role of Councils of Governments and the other to examine critical areas and activities. The subcommittees held their own hearings, while SELUC continued to take testimony on SB 100.

Intense opposition to the critical-areas concept continued to surface at the subcommittee hearings. OEC's Martin Davis found himself defending the quarter-mile buffer zone around designated parks and forestlands, for example, because of concerns expressed by two University of Oregon graduate students. Based on their analyses, the students argued, an additional 10 percent of privately owned land would be brought under state jurisdiction if SB 100 passed. Because 54 percent of Oregon was already owned by federal, state, and local governments, the implication was that local governments could ill afford to "lose" an additional 10 percent of taxable land (Zachary, 1978).

Representatives of the League of Oregon Cities (LOC) and the Association of Oregon Counties (AOC) testified that their organizations supported an alternative to SB 100. Their members, who had all the experience there was in Oregon regarding land-use planning and regulation, had concluded that "the basic flaw in SB 100 is that it establishes a very complex procedural relationship among state and local governments before the basic goals have been established . . . [T]he first step in developing a plan is to spell out the basic goals and objectives for the development of the community. Without the goals, no plan can be developed and no implementing regulations can be enacted" (Moore, 1973a; Gordon, 1973). Given their fundamental disagreements with SB 100, the two organizations proposed that the legislature create a new state agency and require it to conduct relevant inventories and to develop statewide goals, guidelines for local planning, and criteria for designating critical areas and activities. The agency would then select critical areas and activities and design a process for coordinating the planning and regulatory actions of state, regional, and local governments. All this would be done in partnership with affected jurisdictions and would include multiple opportunities for citizen participation. The new agency would present its recommendations to the 1975 legislature for adoption (Moore, 1973a).

In his testimony, Bill Moshofsky, a vice president of Georgia-Pacific, one of the largest forest products companies in the region, recommended that the bill not designate areas of critical concern. "In fact," Moshofky said, "including the designated areas of critical concern in the bill at this time (before a state board is appointed and staffed) might itself be considered poor planning." Aligning Georgia-Pacific with LOC and AOC, he supported a go-slow approach. He also stressed the need to avoid overusing zoning and other land-use restrictions to implement plans, especially when the motivation was aesthetic. "Under the police power (zoning and other land use restrictions)," Moshofsky said, "nothing is paid for rights taken, and the extent of the loss to the owner and the public is never known. If a dollar value is put on the taking, and the funds must be raised, everyone knows what's happening." In order to protect property rights and functioning markets, Moshofsky urged the legislators to include guidelines "relating to the use of police power vs. condemnation" (Moshofsky, 1973).

In light of the opposition to SB 100, the Associated Oregon Industries representative on Macpherson's land-use policy group changed his mind regarding the designation of specific critical areas in SB 100. He now argued that the proposed LCDC should develop planning guidelines for localities to follow, and facilitate local action.

> To say that land use in geographic areas of a sensitive environmental nature must be controlled by the state, is to declare that local government is not capable of protecting these resources, and can be entrusted only with those matters of lesser impact. It would seem that a more reasonable approach would be for the state to establish guidelines for the planned use of these geographic areas . . . The solution to past problems in planning land use at the local level should not be to reduce the responsibility of these units of government. It should be found in helping them fulfill their responsibilities by providing financial and technical assistance.

AOI agreed with Moshofsky that "the process of land use planning must adequately deal with the subject of property rights. Without just compensation losses in land value due to land use planning implementation will always raise strong opposition." The association continued to support the idea of a state land-use agency that coordinated the planning efforts of other state agencies through a permit approach to critical statewide activities (Bryce, 1973).

A Critical Turning Point

Hallock was becoming increasingly pessimistic about SB 100's prospects. Drastic action was necessary, he believed, if anything was going to get to the Senate floor. In mid-February, he announced the appointment of an ad hoc group to revise the bill so that it would garner the support of more SELUC members and the legislature as a whole. He appointed Macpherson chair of the eight-person group, which included Martin Davis and representatives of AOI, AOC, the Oregon State Homebuilders Association, and the Oregon Wheat Growers Association. Hallock also announced the creation of a drafting subcommittee, which would report to the ad hoc group. He appointed L. B. Day as chair.

When Hallock and Governor McCall called Day to persuade him to accept the assignment, he agreed subject to several conditions. First, he wanted to select the members of the subcommittee to ensure that it included those whose support would be important for the passage and implementation of the bill. Day also was determined to produce a bill that had teeth in it, one that would include statewide goals and the power to enforce them. He wanted counties to take on more responsibilities and believed they should have sufficient financial support to discharge them. If the final bill didn't have enough teeth in it, Day warned, his union would sponsor an initiative petition to provide the necessary bite. Hallock already had concluded that Councils of Governments would have to be dropped and the role of counties elevated, and he and McCall agreed to all of Day's terms.

Day was a politically astute choice to lead the subcommittee that would draft the new version of SB 100. He appealed to Hallock and McCall because of his legislative experience, his Teamster-related commitment to a strong agricultural economy, his environmental record with the Department of the Interior, and his position as director of the state Department of Environmental Quality. Day embodied a labor-farmer-environmental alliance. After he left DEQ in 1972, the Board of Directors of Oregon Environmental Council voted unanimously to name Day its first Life Member in recognition of his contributions to the environment of the state (Williams, 1973a; "L.B. Day Leaves DEQ," 1972). He also spoke his mind. When Day was DEQ director, for example, McCall had received a letter from a southern Oregon attorney expressing consternation about Day's intervention into a land development issue. McCall's legal counsel had responded:

> The Governor sometimes winces a little when he hears some of the blunt statements made by Mr. Day, but he has thrown his full support behind Mr. Day in his efforts to preserve the environment, including pressure for land use planning . . . Mr. Day says he expects some people to disagree with him and to question his blunt approach. He says he likes to talk plainly so that no one can possibly misunderstand what he means. (Branchfield, 1972)

Day "was a doer, a head-knocker," Hallock said, a mild description compared with what some thought (Hallock, 2000; Walth, 1994). In 1974 he was named one of America's top two hundred young leaders by *Time* magazine—the only labor official so anointed.

The subcommittee included Homebuilders Association lobbyist Fred VanNatta, AOC lobbyist Gordon Fultz, and AOI representative Ward Armstrong, who worked for Weyerhaeuser, one of the largest forest products firms in the region. Hal Brauner, a natural resources adviser to Governor McCall, was assigned to staff the group (Zachary, 1978).

Day's subcommittee delivered a substantial revision a few weeks after getting the assignment. Much to the dismay of environmentalists and their allies, Day reported that "the designated critical areas concept was eliminated from SB 100 as a matter of political reality." Martin Davis objected: "The point of critical areas is more than of local concern because of their nature. Therefore, the state needs to have some power in these areas, and these are the areas which required concentration" (Zachary, 1978).

OSPIRG staff attorney Henry Richmond, in a piece titled "Land Use Bill 'Thrown to Wolves,'" expressed his consternation at the consequences of Hallock's decision to turn SB 100 over to Day and his group. "The heart of original Senate Bill 100," Richmond wrote, "was the 'area of critical state concern'—land areas which needed state regulation." There had been criticism of the role of COGs, he continued, which "came from local officials who didn't like to hear they were doing a lousy job, from a group called the Rural Landowners Association who wanted to be free to sell 'their' land at the highest possible price possible, and from a few ideological types who thought the bill was Soviet-inspired." SELUC had "buckled before this unconvincing parade, and used this so-called 'opposition' to Senate Bill 100 as an excuse to turn the bill over to the paid representatives of the economic interests which opposed the principal features of the bill from the beginning . . . This is a shocking example of legislative abdication of responsibility" (Richmond, 1973a). In Hallock's decision to include lobbyists in the process, Richmond saw yet another example of capture, but Hallock's maneuver appeared to raise few eyebrows among his legislative colleagues.

Day's subcommittee responded to some of the initial criticisms offered by the League of Oregon Cities, especially the notion that goals ought to be developed before substantive and procedural choices were made about implementation. In the revised bill, LCDC was charged with developing a set of statewide goals and guidelines. Critical areas were listed in general terms—land adjacent to freeway interchanges, for example, rather than land within a quarter- or half-mile—and designated as priority considerations that LCDC was directed to take into account when it adopted goals and guidelines and local governments to take into account in their comprehensive planning. Agricultural land made its first appearance on a list of critical areas, while the SB 195-like zoning standards were eliminated from the bill.

Critical activities were now identified as public transportation facilities, public sewage systems, water supply systems, solid-waste disposal sites, energy generating and transmission facilities, and—an addition that reflected a long-standing priority for planners—public schools. Planning and siting permits were still required for those activities. As with critical areas, LCDC was directed to take those activities into account when developing statewide goals and guidelines, as were local governments when writing comprehensive plans. Sponsors of designated activities would apply for permits to county governments, which would decide whether or not to grant them. County decisions would then be reviewed by LCDC for consistency with statewide goals. LCDC was authorized to veto a county's initial decision and require re-examination, and LCDC approval would be necessary before a county could issue a permit.

Regional planning and coordination by Councils of Governments were eliminated as well. Reflecting Day's inclusion in the drafting group of an Associated Oregon Counties representative but not a League of Cities person, counties were charged with coordinating the plans and ordinances produced by the governmental entities in their jurisdiction. "Counties must accept leadership," Day said. "Cities must cooperate with counties and vice versa" (Zachary, 1978). Counties were enabled, though, to voluntarily create regional coordinating agencies. Day's group was concerned that local governments would need some way to gain easy access to the new state agency. In a separate $3 million state land-use agency funding bill, the subcommittee included seven state agency field offices and funding for eight field staff positions, in addition to ten planning staff for the agency's central office. Two-thirds of the appropriation was earmarked for distribution to local governments to pay for planning and ordinance development ("Proposed Budget . . .," 1973). The League of Cities remained opposed to SB 100, while the Association of Oregon Counties now supported it.

The drafting group also proposed to increase the number of state commissioners from five to seven and to require that at least one (but not more than two) be from Multnomah County. Each congressional district would be represented by at least one person. The governor would appoint members of LCDC, subject to Senate confirmation, for no more than two four-year terms, and would be able to remove a member only for cause. These changes were a response to concerns expressed by the City of Portland and advocates for citizen involvement and expressed the commission's desire to acknowledge the diverse regions of the state and the land-use issues those regions confronted. In response to suggestions from Tri County New Politics and the League of Women Voters, the revised version also required citizen involvement during the development of goals and guidelines and established a state citizen involvement advisory committee.

SELUC invited Governor McCall to testify on the new version of SB 100. McCall was impatient. Before the revisions emerged, he had told Hallock: "God damn it, why the hell don't you just give me $500,000, and I'll zone the goddamn state?" (Hallock, 2000). He also had recently "pounded on the theme" to the U.S. Senate Interior Committee that there was a dire need for national and state land-use policies. He stressed both to the U.S. Senate committee and to SELUC their pragmatic nature: "Land use planning does not stop Oregon dead in its economic tracks. It is instead a sure way to protect property values, because it promises compatibility of land uses, and avoids destructive conflicts." In his testimony, the governor told SELUC: "Regarding the protection of our land . . . the lateness of the hour for remedial and preventive moves is almost cause for despair." He said that he was "prepared to announce today" his "support of the substitute bill." Day and Logan had walked him through the changes, and he now felt "that in most respects it is more satisfactory than the original SB 100 . . . and that it also corrects the principal defects in . . . Senate Bill 10."

McCall reminded SELUC that "SB 10 was recommended by one of the traditionally most conservative . . . committees of this legislature . . . Even its conventional thinkers recognized . . . years ago that land resources—particularly the verdant valleys and prairies of Oregon—are finite." SB 10 had given him the power to guarantee that statewide planning and zoning were done, but McCall acknowledged his reluctance to use that power. "Sure, I prodded them to get the job done—and moratoriums against unplanned growth were proclaimed for a dozen areas." The revised version of the bill, however, took that oversight responsibility and gave it to LCDC. He didn't mind at all losing that responsibility, he said. SB 10 was fatally flawed, because while it contained a stick of sorts, it contained no carrots, and the mandates to plan and zone came with no money to facilitate local

government action. He urged SELUC to pay close attention to the companion legislation that would provide financing.

McCall argued, though, that SB 10 had provided "the framework for
land use planning in Oregon . . . [and had] made planning and zoning
clean words . . . The legislature had taken the heat off local officials, several
of whom suffered recall over planning and zoning decisions." His testimony echoed what he had told the U.S. Senate committee about the need
for a new approach to intergovernmental relations in the land-use field:

> The closer you get to the grassroots the harder it is to do these things
> that you can do more easily as a State or . . . as the Federal govern-
> ment, because of the parochialism and whipsawing that comes when
> the neighbors don't want to do this to old Tom, and they all meet
> in the election club and they are all friends. So we need a strong
> sword of Damocles that the Federal government can provide . . .
> When some county commissioners do some things under state law
> that are unpopular, they can blame it on [the Governor], and [the
> Governor] can blame it on the Feds. It is sort of convenient. They
> say this is what they ordered us to do. It gives you leverage in trying
> to do something that ought to be done. (McCall, 1973b)

McCall was deeply disappointed that SB 100 took away the Councils of
Governments' coordination role, but, he argued, the "land use legislation
before you is too important to fall at the hands of a non-essential issue."
He did distribute to SELUC copies of two Local Government Relation Division reports to remind them that some planning issues transcended county
boundaries. One was the Charbonneau case study; the other was about the
implications of a regional shopping center proposed for an exclusive farm-
use zone in Linn County (LGRD, 1973a). McCall suggested that the issue
of compensatory zoning, as well as other implementation issues, might be
studied by an interim committee. "But don't let the suggestion . . . become
a substitute for positive action on SB 100," he cautioned. "The people are
interested in this subject now more than they ever have been. They want
rational land use planning. I urge that the Legislature provide the land use
policy, and the money that must go with it, in this session" (McCall, 1973c).

Gordon Fultz, a member of the drafting group, told SELUC that AOC
welcomed the revised version of SB 100 and would work for its passage. The
association was pleased that local governments would be able to continue

the planning efforts they had already begun. Moreover, Fultz continued, "We feel that counties are prepared to accept the responsibility of being the planning units of the state responsible for the coordination and preparation of comprehensive plans within each county" (Fultz, 1973). The LOC representative, however, believed that the revised bill was fraught with technical and policy difficulties.

> It assigns responsibility for coordinating local and state plans to the county government, which we believe is a step backward. Such a procedure overlooks the experience of cities and the time, funds and effort spent by cities in comprehensive planning . . . Revised SB 100 appears to us to limit city participation to that of turning city plans over to the county and subsequently the state, with only the possibility of making appeals to the state at a later time. We think cities have much more to offer. (Moore, 1973b)

The City of Portland was disturbed by the elimination of Councils of Governments and the prospect of counties playing the coordination role. Lloyd Anderson let SELUC know in no uncertain terms that the county-based approach would "serve no useful purpose in the Portland area." A member of the Portland City Council, Anderson was also on the CRAG executive board. He told SELUC that a regional approach was a necessity in the Portland metropolitan area, although he acknowledged that it might not be appropriate elsewhere in the state. He did not see "how the Legislature can ask for effective land use planning in the Portland area and, in the same breath, destroy CRAG. The counties cannot begin to replace it. They have nowhere near its potential for effectiveness." The new version of SB 100 had to be amended to maintain a regional approach in Portland. "I must speak plainly here," he said. "To have the Board of Commissioners of Multnomah County sit in judgment of the actions of the City of Portland is to sow the seeds of conflict . . . The County staff is neither equipped nor able to make judgments on a great many issues of concern to the City" (Anderson, L., 1973). A Multnomah County representative disagreed and assured SELUC that the county commissioners were up to the task, in part because Anderson had been the county's first planning director and had developed a strong agency (Multnomah County, 1973).

Portland pursued a two-track strategy to achieve its objectives. The City proposed an amendment that would make it, in essence, the state's thirty-seventh county, extracting itself from Multnomah County jurisdiction for purposes of implementing SB 100. SELUC obliged and amended SB 100 to reflect Portland's demands. The City also supported amending SB 769, a bill that CRAG leaders had introduced to enable the establishment of a unique, potentially very powerful regional planning district, to give the new entity the coordination role in the Portland metropolitan area. The regional planning district could designate areas and activities and develop plans and regulations for them with which local governments within the district would have to comply. The amended version of SB 769 passed as well. The district, which was established in 1974, was authorized to play at the regional level the role that the original version of SB 100 authorized LCDC to play at the state level.

The Oregon Environmental Council had to decide where to stand on the revised SB 100 in light of Governor McCall's support for the new bill. The council had never cared much for COGs—environmentalists applied the capture theory to them just as they did to commissions such as OCCDC— but the loss of critical areas and the changes in the way critical activities would be addressed were troubling to them, although Martin Davis was a strong supporter of including public schools siting on the list of critical activities. OEC created Citizens for State Planning to generate support for a stronger SB 100, which, Davis believed, could still include "some critical areas." He drafted an amendment that re-incorporated into the bill some critical areas on the coast and land along the Mount Hood corridor. It also required LCDC to prepare regulations to be applied by all state and local government entities when dealing with development proposals in those critical areas (Davis, M., 1973b). OEC told its activists that the citizen appeal provision had to be defended to enable LCDC to hold recalcitrant local governments accountable. "If you have already written [your legislator] on the original bill," OEC instructed, "you should write or call again giving your full support to the Revised Version of SB 100, and encourage them to put back the section which designates areas of critical state concern" (OEC, 1973).

Other organizations agreed. Dorothy Anderson told SELUC that the League of Women's Voters supported passage of the revised version but that it regretted the elimination of a coordinating role for regional agencies. The League preferred that the bill include specific critical areas, especially on the coast. Anderson was pleased that there were stronger and more specific requirements for public participation, and she also suggested that standing to appeal should be construed broadly to encourage citizen involvement (Anderson, D., 1973b). Tri County New Politics agreed (Cohen, 1973c).

After concluding its hearings, SELUC focused on the Day subcommittee's proposed revisions concerning critical activities. Portland General Electric and Pacific Power and Light, the state's two largest investor-owned utilities, did not want their facilities subject to an additional layer of government approval. Oregon already had the Nuclear Thermal Energy Council, which dealt with issues related to nuclear power, and the utility people were troubled by the requirement that the council had to get a permit from LCDC to site a power plant. The utilities were likely influenced by Bonneville Power Administration's Hydro-Thermal Power Program of 1968, which "presented a schedule calling for two coal plants and *twenty* large nuclear plants to be in operation in the Northwest by 1990" (Pope, 1993). To accommodate those concerns, Ted Hallock moved that energy generation and transmission facilities be deleted from the list of critical activities. The motion passed, with Wingard the sole vote in opposition. Macpherson then moved to add to the list the siting and construction of high-voltage power-transmission lines, except those regulated by the Nuclear Thermal Energy Council. That proposal, which resurrected an aspect of the 1969 session's SB 12, was defeated, with Macpherson and Wingard supplying the only votes in support (Zachary, 1978).

Following that defeat, Macpherson moved that the Day group's proposal be amended to eliminate permitting until after LCDC reviewed a list of activities in the bill and determined whether one or more should be treated as activities of statewide significance requiring a permit. This was another step toward the approach suggested by local governments and supported by Associated Oregon Industries, and it troubled environmentalists. Macpherson's motion, which also authorized LCDC to recommend additional significant activities for legislative adoption, carried unanimously (Zachary, 1978).

In both versions of the bill, SB 100 stipulated that a permit approved by LCDC was necessary before planning and siting an activity of statewide concern. Senator Vic Atiyeh thought it sufficient to require LCDC to review and comment on such plans; his amendment passed, with Macpherson, Hallock, and Wingard opposed (Zachary, 1978). The change introduced a potentially serious obstacle to achieving one of Governor McCall's and

LGRD's major objectives, the coordination of state agency and special district decisions with the plans and ordinances adopted by cities and counties, even if LCDC decided to designate one or more activities of statewide significance.

SELUC also addressed the appeal provisions of the bill. Atiyeh proposed that only those "whose interests are substantially affected" may appeal a local comprehensive plan provision or regulation that was thought to violate statewide planning goals. He suggested that, to be eligible to appeal an order issued by LCDC, a party had either to be "adversely affected" or "aggrieved" by that order. In the original version of SB 100, any person could appeal a provision of an adopted comprehensive plan or an action taken by a regional council (Zachary, 1978). Despite concerns expressed by OEC, Tri County New Politics, and the League of Women Voters, all of whom worried that the new language would make it more difficult for citizens to challenge decisions, SELUC approved the changes.

For OEC, OSPIRG, Oregon Shores, and their allies, the amended SB 100 was a much weaker bill than the original. Larry Williams wrote Governor McCall:

> We have been extremely concerned about the current language contained in SB 100 . . . While we would very much like the areas of statewide critical concern, interim permit authority for coastal planning and a broadening of the language which provides for citizen appeal, we do recognize that this is still a very valuable piece of legislation and we are not willing to risk the future of the entire Bill over these amendments . . . Therefore, we are going to not push for any significant changes in the Bill in the hope that some other pieces of legislation will pick up the deficiencies in Senate Bill 100. (Williams, 1973b)

Macpherson later remembered how grateful he was to OEC for taking that position (Macpherson, 1997). The other legislation that Williams was talking about included a shorelines management act, a bill requiring environmental impact analyses, a bill to reorganize OCCDC and give it interim permit authority, and a bill to regulate the occupational composition of local planning commissions. "We feel that with these additional measures," Williams said, "we will have regained much of what was lost in Senate Bill 100, and possibly even have a stronger hand over statewide control of land use planning than we ever could have realistically expected to have gotten into one piece of legislation." He urged McCall to use his bully pulpit to support the legislation (Williams, 1973b).

Two other significant changes were made to the Day group's proposal that Hallock and Macpherson thought were necessary to get the bill through the Senate. The first, which was expressed in a statement of legislative intent signed by the SELUC members and placed in the Senate *Journal*, differentiated between goals and guidelines. Guidelines were "*not* intended to be a grant of power to the state to carry out zoning from the state level" or to limit "local governments to a single course of action when some other locally conceived course would achieve the same result." They were intended as aids to activate the goals. While the guidelines were "instructive, directional and positive," they would not carry the force of law. SELUC reported that it had made "no effort . . . to further define 'Goals'—preferring the definition to be refined in the process of citizen input, commission approval, and legislative review" (Zachary, 1978). SELUC articulated a performance-standards approach to achieving the goals that LCDC would craft. In line with the changes it had made in the status of critical areas and activities, SELUC was signaling local governments that they would continue to exercise a significant amount of discretion regarding the evolution of the statewide land-use program.

The second change was the elimination of the emergency clause, which had set July 1 as the date on which SB 100 would become effective. Macpherson agreed to the change, yielding to those who argued that citizens ought to have the opportunity to overturn at the polls a law as controversial as SB 100. One consequence of pushing back the effective implementation date of SB 100, however, was that the funding measure that accompanied the bill was taken off the table.

After successfully moving SB 100 out of SELUC, Hallock said on the Senate floor:

> The original SB 100 was voted down in SELUC . . . Senator Burns claims the bill . . . is not strong enough in the areas of critical concern . . . Senator Burns spoke unhappily of the "political art of compromise." I, too, am concerned about the critical areas of concern. However, without the "political art of compromise," there would have been no SB 100 before the Senate today. (Zachary, 1978)

Even though Burns voted "no" on the bill both in committee and on the Senate floor, SB 100 passed.

Hallock told Nancy Fadeley, chair of the House Environment and Land Use Committee, that the bill had to pass through her committee and the House without any changes. He believed that, if it had to go to a conference committee to work out differences, SELUC's fragile agreement and the Senate's approval would unravel. Fadeley, a strong supporter of SB 100, delivered both her committee and the House. Interestingly, a majority of the House Environment and Land Use Committee were women. In the early 1970s, Fadeley remembered, the environment was seen as a women's issue:

> [W]omen could take the environmental ball and run with it because the environment was considered sort of a softy . . . men did things like economic development, taxes, Ways and Means. They really didn't consider these issues substantive or important. So they were willing to leave the environment up to us. There was not a recognition then . . . that environmental lawmaking involves a high level of expertise.

In late 1972, Fadeley had wanted land-use legislation to come to her rather than the commerce or economic development committee, and she had asked the incoming speaker of the House to name her chair of the standing environment committee for the 1973 session. She also asked to have the name of the committee changed to Environment and Land Use. She thought he "got a big kick out of putting all those women on my committee, most of the women in the House" (Fadeley, 1997; Paulus, 1997).

Introducing the bill to the House committee, Hallock told the members:

> Senator Macpherson was the Father of Land Use Planning, L. B. Day was the Godfather, and I myself was the Obstetrician . . . I am here as a political mechanic . . . SB 100 [now] bears little resemblance to [the original] SB 100. It does not go far enough, having critical areas left out, and also relying on the archaic institution of the County rather than COGs . . . The Governor concurs with this evaluation of the bill, but he has accepted SB 100 as a beginning. (Zachary, 1978)

Other Laws and *Fasano v. Washington County*

While SB 100 was the focus of legislative attention during the 1973 session, other laws passed as part of what was known as the Governor's Land Use Package. Macpherson had concluded early on that his legislative approach would include being responsive to the property rights concerns of farmers whose land was zoned for exclusive farm use. A package of explicit benefits was included in SB 101, a companion to SB 100 that revised and extended the farmland preservation incentives the legislature had initiated in 1961. Otherwise, given his understanding of land as a precious resource rather than a pure commodity, Macpherson did not intend to placate those who had what he considered out-of-date views on planning and zoning.

In addition to property-tax breaks, SB 101 included a provision limiting the regulations that could be imposed on farming practices—a "right-to-farm" notion stipulated that land be assessed at farm-use value for inheritance-tax purposes and prevented the imposition of taxes on land in exclusive farm-use zones for projects undertaken by water and sewer agencies. SB 101 also added to the list of nonfarm uses that were permitted, some outright and some conditionally.

A bill mandating changes in the way local governments handled subdivision proposals, an act that evolved from SB 11 in 1969, passed, and separate laws setting occupational requirements for appointments to city and county planning commissions were enacted. Those bills also required city and county governments to adopt the plans they were mandated to produce in the form of ordinances, making them legally binding. The sixth element of the governor's package was a land development-related consumer protection act, which was intended to curb fraudulent practices in central, eastern, and southern Oregon. The bill was extensively amended during the session in response to industry concerns, and it passed both legislative chambers nearly unanimously.

LGRD produced a compensatory zoning bill, SB 849, but it didn't get far. Logan strongly supported compensation in some cases, as did McCall, and they were well aware of deeply rooted property rights sentiments held by many rural Oregonians, including those involved in the farm and forestry sectors. Logan linked "wipeouts" to "windfalls," however, and he thought both losses and gains should be addressed. He was aware, though, of the complexity of doing so and of a national conversation about windfalls and wipeouts that was being led by UCLA law professor Donald Hagman

(Hagman, 1973). SB 849 was intended to introduce the subject to the legislature. SB 100 created a Joint Land Use Committee of the legislature to oversee the implementation of the land-use bills and included a directive to that committee to study and make recommendations on compensation (Logan, 1973b).

During the 1973 session, another drama that would profoundly affect planning and plan implementation in the state was playing out in the Oregon Supreme Court. *Fasano v. Washington County* involved the Washington County Commission's approval of a proposed mobile home subdivision, which was in line with an adopted county plan but which single-family-home-owning neighbors wanted to prevent. Edward Sullivan, the Washington County counsel who argued the case, anticipated that it would be significant for land-use planning practice, and he invited the Oregon chapter of the American Institute of Planners to join him on the brief he submitted to the court (Sullivan, E., 1972a).

Sullivan called the judges' attention to an article in the *Ohio State Law Review* about judicial review of zone changes, which differentiated between legislative and judicial decisions. The argument was that rezoning was a judicial matter and that due process standards that applied to adjudication ought to be used in such cases. Those standards included a meaningful opportunity to be heard before an impartial tribunal, an opportunity to present and rebut evidence, no pre-hearing contacts with zoning authority members on matters to be heard, and a record supporting the findings that formed the basis for the decision (Sullivan, E., 1972b). The Oregon Supreme Court agreed. Based on the justices' interpretation of Oregon statutes, the decision added to that list a public-need standard for a zone change, with the burden of proof borne by the applicant. The court also required the body making the rezoning decision to find that the public need would best be served by changing the classification of the property in question as compared with other available property (Sullivan, E., 1973a).

Sullivan also hoped to persuade the justices that, like their counterparts in other states, Oregon courts were confusing planning and zoning: they thought an adopted zoning ordinance *was* the comprehensive plan. Sullivan argued that "the legislature intended Oregon counties to have a vigorous planning process and for zoning to fall behind" (Sullivan, E., 1972b). The court agreed with that argument, too, differentiating planning and zoning, finding that the comprehensive plan should carry the greatest weight in rezoning matters, and, more generally, ruling that zoning should be consistent with adopted plans (Sullivan, E., 1973a). While in the end the court found that Washington County had failed to adequately justify its action, Sullivan won two much larger battles.

Fasano v. Washington County had profound effects on land-use dynamics throughout the state, especially in rural counties. The procedural rules articulated by the Oregon Supreme Court for quasi-judicial decision making at the local level, especially the necessity for a record that supported the findings and decisions made and the prohibition of pre-hearing contacts with zoning decision-makers about matters to be decided, required county officials to change dramatically their ways of dealing with land-use issues. A legal consultant to the Bureau of Municipal Research and Service at the University of Oregon noted: "Under the *Fasano* rationale it will be much easier to make a successful legal challenge in the courts to zone changes . . . [because] there was a procedural defect . . . [The] possibilities of court reversals . . . could be potentially awesome" (Mattis, 1973).

In its decision, the Oregon Supreme Court indicated that it shared the local government capture theory that was a major motivator for land-use activists. The court justified its decision to reduce the discretion available to local governments to change zoning classifications this way: "having weighed the dangers of making desirable change more difficult against the dangers of the almost irresistible pressures that can be asserted by private economic interests on local government, we believe that the latter dangers are more to be feared" (Oregon Supreme Court, 1973). Sullivan sent a copy of the *Fasano* decision to Fred Bosselman, co-author of *The Quiet Revolution in Land Use Control* and a leader of the American Law Institute's Model Land Development Code project. Bosselman (1973) responded: "I think you deserve an award from the Bar Association for your contribution to the future income of the legal profession." The American Planning Association ranked the *Fasano* case tenth among the top twenty-five cases in planning and environmental law dating back to 1922.

Senate Bill 100 was a complex, far-reaching, and controversial law that had to be implemented in the context of the *Fasano* decision. There was already a good deal of legal contention about land-use issues in Oregon, as there was throughout the United States, and recently enacted national and state environmental laws had generated an increasing amount of such activity. It isn't at all surprising that the combination of SB 100 and *Fasano*

Senate Bill 100 (1973) as introduced and as enacted into law

Major controversies	SB 100 as introduced	SB 100 as enacted
LCDC: Composition	5 members appointed by the governor, 1 from each congressional district (4), 1 at-large. Members serve at pleasure of the governor	7 members appointed by the governor, 1 from each congressional district (5), 2 at-large. At least 1 and no more than 2 from Multnomah County. Members may be removed only for cause
LCDC: Areas of Critical Statewide Concern	Designated critical areas—lands and adjacent lands—in 8 different categories: federal and state scenic waterways; parks and recreational areas; coastal land; estuaries; Columbia River Gorge; freeways and scenic highways. LCDC prepares statewide objectives and regulations for critical areas. LCDC authorized to recommend additional critical areas to the legislature for designation.	No areas are designated. LCDC authorized to review and recommend to the legislature the designation of areas of critical concern. LCDC directed to take the list of areas in the original version of the bill, as well as others, into account when adopting statewide planning goals and guidelines.
LCDC: Activities of Critical Statewide Significance	Designated the following critical activities: airports; state and federal highway systems; mass transit systems; solid-waste disposal facilities; high-voltage power, gas and oil transmission lines; sewerage and water-supply systems; and thermal power plants and nuclear installations. LCDC approval is required before a state agency may either adopt a plan or implement any of those activities. LCDC authorized to prepare statewide objectives and regulations for those activities. -LCDC issues a permit after getting comments from district planning and state agencies. -LCDC authorized to recommend additional critical activities to the legislature for designation.	No activities are designated. LCDC may designate the following as critical activities at its discretion: public transportation facilities; public sewerage, water-supply systems, and solid-waste disposal; and public schools. Section 25 changed language from approval is required before a state agency can act to a state agency can't act without prior LCDC review and comment. Section 27 still described a required LCDC permitting process. LCDC authorized to recommend additional critical activities to the legislature for designation.
LCDC: Public Participation in the Adoption of Statewide Planning Goals	DLCD prepares statewide goals and regulations that are submitted to LCDC within 1 year. No requirement for public participation during that process. LCDC required to hold at least 1 public hearing within each of 14 designated district planning areas.	Extensive public participation mandated during the process of developing statewide planning goals and guidelines. LCDC required to appoint a statewide Citizen Involvement Advisory Committee to oversee the process.
LCDC: Appeals Process	Any person or group of persons may appeal a comprehensive plan adopted by a local government, or an action taken by a district council.	A person or group of persons whose interests are "substantially affected" may be made a party to any review proceeding conducted by LCDC.

Major controversies	SB 100 as introduced	SB 100 as enacted
LCDC: Deadlines and Enforcement	DLCD required to submit planning guidelines to LCDC by January 1, 1975. LCDC goes through the same participatory process as it is required to use for goals and regulations before adopting planning guidelines. The governor authorized to administer plans and regulations for any lands that are not covered by plans and regulations that comply with LCDC adopted goals and guidelines by January 1, 1976. The governor authorized to grant a reasonable time extension in those cases where reasonable progress is being made.	LCDC required to adopt statewide planning goals and guidelines by January 1, 1975. Local government plans required to be in compliance by January 1, 1976. LCDC authorized to play the role assigned to the governor in those cases where local plans and regulations are not in compliance by the deadline.
Coordinating Agencies	14 district council planning agencies are assigned the role of coordinating city and county planning processes within their jurisdictions, and reviewing their adopted plans and regulations for compliance with LCDC statewide goals and regulations before submission to LCDC for compliance review. Most of the 14 district councils are based on existing Councils of Government.	A role for district council planning agencies is eliminated. County governments are assigned the coordination role within their jurisdictions. An exception is made that exempts the City of Portland from Multnomah County coordination authority. The legislature enables the creation of a regional planning district in the Portland metropolitan area (SB 769).
Emergency Clause and Goal/Guideline Distinction	An emergency clause is included; SB 100 would take effect July 1, 1973.	Emergency clause is deleted. SB 100 would take effect on October 1, 1973, giving opponents of the law time to gather the signatures required to submit a repeal measure to the electorate. Senate Environment and Land Use Committee added language published in the Senate *Journal* that distinguished between statewide planning goals that will have the force of law and guidelines that will not be legal requirements.
Funding	Governor's Budget included $300,000 for DLCD. SB 100 does not include an appropriation.	Day drafting committee prepared a $3 million budget request that was taken off the table when the Emergency Clause was deleted. The legislature approved a $100,000 general fund allocation for DLCD, and authorized it to pursue up to $240,000 in federal Department of Housing and Urban Development grants.

would add substantially to the already swelling propensity to attempt to resolve land-use conflicts through legal means.

SB 100 Passes

While everyone was waiting to see whether the 26,656 signatures necessary to put SB 100 on the November 1973 ballot were collected, all activities related to the bill had to be suspended. The deadlines set out in SB 100, however, remained: statewide goals and guidelines had to be adopted by January 1, 1975, and local comprehensive plans and ordinances had to be submitted to LCDC by January 1, 1976 (Logan, 1973c). Even though the ballot measure did not materialize—the signature-gathering effort failed—the $3 million funding proposal was no longer an option.

The version of SB 100 the Oregon legislature passed was more a procedural law than a substantive one, and it set many land-use planning and implementation-related activities into motion. The loss of an authoritative state agency role regulating critical areas and activities and the devolution of coordination authority to the counties meant that local governments would exercise a great deal more discretion than environmentalists thought appropriate, given their vulnerability to capture. As environmentalists had argued before and during the session, there was a need for a new state role precisely because local governments, especially counties, had failed to protect critical natural resources. Excepting a few metropolitan jurisdictions, counties were the least technically proficient unit of government and the most fiscally challenged; they were the unit most likely to emphasize short-term, personal-relations-driven values when making land-use decisions.

As of June 29, 1973, eighteen months after they were supposed to be in compliance with SB 10 mandates, only nineteen of the thirty-six Oregon counties had adopted both land-use plans and zoning ordinances. A very reluctant Governor McCall had given extensions to the seventeen delinquent counties (LGRD, 1973b). Regardless of whether or not plans and ordinances were adopted, as Macpherson had pointed out, the quality of counties' work varied dramatically because no state standards were in place. In addition, counties now had to deal with the *Fasano* decision, and implementing the quasi-judicial aspect was a major political and organizational challenge.

With the passage of the Governor's Land Use Package and the *Fasano* decision, the major structural elements of Oregon's statewide land-use program were in place. Cities and counties were mandated to produce comprehensive land-use plans, and zoning ordinances as well as other regulations and the plans and projects of state and local government agencies would have to be consistent with those plans. Both city and county plans and ordinances would have to conform to a set of legally binding goals that a new state agency was required to adopt and enforce. The new agency, LCDC, was authorized to plan and zone in place of any local government that failed to conform by the deadline. The court had articulated new standards for plan making and implementation. Taken together, the laws and the court decision amounted to a radical transformation of intergovernmental relationships in the land-use field.

Environmentalists, civic and property rights activists, and industry and local government representatives geared up immediately to influence the dynamics this structure set in motion. LCDC would exercise a great deal of discretion; appointments to the commission would be significant. The goals and guidelines that LCDC would adopt, and its choices about the designation of critical areas and activities, would make a great deal of difference. LCDC would influence what happened on the ground throughout the state as it reviewed local plans for conformance with its goals, even though it wasn't mandated to produce and adopt a statewide comprehensive plan or a state land-use map. Enacting Senate Bill 100 was a remarkable accomplishment, an achievement that attracted attention across the country. It was a dramatic step on the path that the Oregon legislature had begun to chart in 1961, but there was a long way to go to achieve the substantive goals the new statewide program was intended to accomplish.

Chapter 4
The Agency: Starting Up LCDC and DLCD

"Any land use planning function directly related to establishing statewide land use policies or programs, or coordination or handling of funds should be immediately transferred to DLCD."
—Land Conservation and Development Commission

The Land Conservation and Development Commission (LCDC) and its staff agency, the Department of Land Conservation and Development (DLCD), immediately confronted many challenges, not the least of which was a deteriorating economic situation. The stock market declined sharply in January 1973, the Oregon economy slid into a deep recession, and the OPEC oil embargo imposed in October 1973 exacerbated the conditions and helped produce what economists called stagflation. DLCD had to secure funds for the remainder of the 1973-1975 biennium, and then for the 1975-1977 budget period.

SB 100 required LCDC to negotiate intergovernmental relationships with established agencies. The Oregon Department of Transportation (ODOT), for example, had to prepare a Willamette River Greenway plan that was subject to LCDC approval. The Oregon Coastal Conservation and Development Commission (OCCDC) had to submit a coastal zone management plan. LCDC could delegate some of its functions to OCCDC, but it was still required to review and approve any actions proposed by the coastal commission with regard to a delegated activity. Both ODOT and OCCDC had ongoing relationships with local governments, and their relationships with private-sector stakeholders would also be affected by LCDC's leadership role. The LCDC-OCCDC relationship was especially important, because federal Coastal Zone Management Act funding for planning was a critical source of money for DLCD.

LCDC also had to work out relationships with the Governor's Office, especially with Local Government Relations, which controlled planning money allocated by the U.S. Department of Housing and Urban Development under its "701" program. The agency also had to provide updates to the Joint Legislative Committee on Land Use; report its recommendations on goals, guidelines, critical areas, and activities; and make suggestions for legislative action in the next session. The Joint Committee, with Ted Hallock as chair, was itself mandated by SB 100 to study compensatory zoning and report to the legislature.

LCDC and DLCD also had to establish themselves in relation to cities and counties and to the Columbia Region Association of Governments (CRAG) in the Portland metropolitan area. There were also school districts; local government boundary commissions; special districts for water, sewer, and other services; county tax assessors; and the Association of Oregon Counties and League of Oregon Cities. DLCD was required to take into account the plans and zoning ordinances that local governments had produced pursuant to SB 10. Its relationships with counties were particularly critical because the department depended on them to play a coordination role in relation to the cities within their jurisdictions. Given the controversial character of SB 100, particularly regarding the nature and extent of discretion that local governments had to produce their plans and implementing ordinances, managing the state-local relationship was a continuing challenge. The governor and the legislature profoundly influenced the dynamics of the relationship by the choices they made about the allocation of limited financial resources, either to DLCD's operations or to local governments' plan-making processes.

The LCDC staff was expected to complete a statewide land-use inventory that local governments would use to plan and zone. Processes for involving citizens were required, both to formulate statewide planning goals and to guide local planning. LCDC also had to design an appeals process, one that would take into account the distinction between legislative and quasi-judicial actions that the Oregon Supreme Court had articulated in the *Fasano* decision. During the 1973 session, environmental activists had strongly supported easy access to appeals as a way to prevent development interests from capturing LCDC and local governments. The attorneys among them looked forward to the role that appeals could play in shaping the statewide program.

LCDC faced a daunting set of challenges, but it was an exciting time. Already established as a leader among states in environmental issues, Oregon was embarked on a path that was unique in the nation. LCDC readied itself to make the land-use planning program a key part of the mix of initiatives that aimed both to manage population growth and to protect the land resource base on which important sectors of the state economy depended.

Budgetary Politics I

Senate Bill 100 provided no appropriation to fund the commission and the department it had created. Governor McCall's budget, which he had submitted at the beginning of the 1973 legislative session, included only $300,000 of start-up money (Uhrhammer, 1973). Interestingly, the budget analysts preparing the DLCD request thought that the general-fund allocation should be supplemented by revenues generated by a real-estate-transaction tax (50 cents on the sale of each $500 worth of real property). Revenues in excess of agency expenditures, they suggested, would be distributed in the form of planning grants to local governments ("LCDC 1973-75 Biennial Budget," 1973). The suggestion was opposed by the real estate industry, and was dropped.

Since the Oregon legislature convened only every other year, an Emergency Board was authorized to allocate money to state agencies during the off years. An alternative method of funding SB 100 was for the House Ways and Means Committee to approve a budget for planning grants to local governments and assign it to the Emergency Board pending the outcome of a signature-gathering effort. After SB 100 passed and was signed into law, Senator Hallock wrote to members of Ways and Means arguing strongly that any money allocated should go to the Governor's Office: "It is feared that those who would like to see SB 100's intent destroyed will make sure that during the interim the Emergency Board does not parcel out monies to the cities and counties as it is supposed to do." He urged the committee to "simply put the money in the Governor's office so that McCall himself can help set priorities if SB 100 is in fact referred" (Hallock, 1973). In the end, Ways and Means approved a $100,000 general-fund allocation for DLCD and authorized it to pursue up to $240,000 in federal Department of Housing and Urban Development grants. The Emergency Board would decide, though, how much the agency would receive if SB 100 survived a referral.

The referral movement failed to gather the necessary signatures, and Governor McCall appointed the first LCDC members in October. Bob Logan from Local Government Relations worked closely with McCall on the appointments, and L. B. Day, who now represented Cannery Workers Local 670 of the Teamsters Union and whom McCall appointed to the commission, likely also influenced the choices. Logan had high regard for Steve Schell, the land-use attorney who had worked with the Macpherson group to draft the agricultural policies incorporated into Senate Bill 101 and with LGRD drafting consumer-protection legislation. Schell later recalled that, on his way into the first LCDC meeting, one of the governor's assistants had said that McCall wanted Schell to nominate Day to chair the commission. Schell did so, and Day was elected chair; Schell was elected vice chair (Schell, 2001).

Jim Smart, a Polk County farmer and county planning commission member, was one of Day's close associates. He had a particular interest in soil conservation and served on numerous agriculture-related state government committees and was board chair of the Willamette Cherry Growers' Association. The governor named Smart to the commission, along with Dorothy Anderson, who was chair of the Lane County Metropolitan Area Plan Advisory Committee and a member of the advisory committee that had developed the Eugene/Springfield 1990 Plan. She also sat on the council that directed the work done under Project Foresight. Anderson had testified several times in support of SB 100 on behalf of the League of Women Voters legislative committee.

The Oregon Environmental Council (OEC) was extremely interested in the LCDC appointments and made its own recommendations with an eye toward securing the appointment of commissioners who would resist capture by land-development interests. Executive Director Larry Williams advocated strongly on behalf of Dr. Paul Rudy, a marine biologist who worked at the University of Oregon's research center on the coast. Rudy was also a coastal county planning commissioner and a board member of OEC and Oregon Shores. He resigned his county position in order to join LCDC (Attorney General, 1974).

From central Oregon, the governor appointed Richard Gervais, who owned lumber, radio broadcasting, and office-supply companies based in Bend. Gervais had been Bend's mayor and had served on the city council. He chaired the local school district's long-range planning commission and was a member of the city's development agency. Gervais also had worked for many years as a manager of Brooks-Scanlon, an Oregon forest products company known for its commitment to local communities and sustainable forest practices.

The seventh member was Albert Bullier, Jr., the president of Bullier and Bullier, which specialized in commercial and industrial property sales and leasing. The firm operated throughout the Pacific Northwest and had been extremely active in the downtown Portland real-estate market. Bullier and Bullier worked closely with the Portland Development Commission on urban renewal projects and generally supported the city's planning efforts. As Albert Bullier, Sr., put it, "Anything that is for the city, we're for" (Bullier, 1982). Finally, Hal Brauner, who had assisted the Day subcommittee, was the Executive Department Budget Division person who would work with LCDC.

All of the members the governor appointed to the commission were supporters of SB 100. They represented diverse stakeholder groups and regions of the state.

Early Meetings and the Budget

The new commission met for the first time on October 24, 1973. They started a search for a director, a position they would not fill until they put a budget in place, and began recruiting applicants for the Citizen Involvement Advisory Committee (Land Conservation and Development Commission, 1973a). Schell suggested they get started planning for citizen participation, and Logan agreed to send a letter to each county about the requirement for a citizen participation plan.

Establishing a budget was a priority, and in November LCDC approved a phase I budget request for $212,000, enough to hire a director, a secretary, and a staff assistant. The commission planned to ask the Emergency Board for additional resources after a director was hired and a work program was developed (Land Conservation and Development Commission, 1973b). At the December meeting, the commissioners learned that the Emergency Board had approved a budget of only $172,000. The salaries they hoped to pay would have to be reduced, as would the amount of office equipment they hoped to acquire. Day told his colleagues that Governor McCall had asked him to meet with state and federal agency people to discuss coordination issues. He had done so and had stressed the desirability of DLCD using studies by those agencies to facilitate its own work (Land Conservation and Development Commission, 1973c).

LCDC began to establish relationships with local governments and to initiate its own citizen-involvement efforts. While county governments were generally pleased with the legislative compromises that made SB 100 politically acceptable, many city governments remained skeptical. They felt that their planning experience and expertise justified a partnership role with the LCDC rather than the subordinate status SB 100 appeared to give them. The League of Oregon Cities adopted a resolution at its November 1973 meeting requesting LCDC to appoint an advisory committee of both city and county officials (Jones, 1973). The commission agreed, and a Local Officials Advisory Council was formed to serve alongside the Citizen Involvement Advisory Committee (CIAC). In early January, DLCD announced the fifteen CIAC members, including representatives of environmental organizations, planners, architects, and civic activists, all of whom were committed to enhancing citizen engagement in public affairs. Ted Sidor, the Oregon State University agricultural extension agent who had played an important role in the adoption of SB 10, was one of those selected. Ward Armstrong, the Weyerhaeuser lobbyist who had been a member of the drafting subcommittee in 1973, and OEC land-use activist Margaret Collins were also appointed. CIAC's charge was to prepare and recommend a program to involve the public in developing statewide goals and guidelines and to make recommendations on how citizens should engage with local governments during planning processes. The committee was also asked to review and comment on the public-involvement programs that local governments proposed to adopt.

Arnold Cogan, Governor McCall's planning coordinator during the late 1960s and a manager at a major planning and engineering consultant firm, began work as DLCD director in February 1974. McCall had appointed Cogan to the Environmental Quality Commission in the early 1970s, where he was vice chair and oversaw the work of L. B. Day, then director of the Department of Environmental Quality. Cogan wrote to Governor McCall after SB 100 was signed into law, and to L. B. Day shortly after the latter was elected LCDC chair, to tell them of his interest in the director position (Cogan, 1973a, b).

Cogan was an attractive candidate for several reasons. He was a leader in the professional planning community and had helped draft the SB 10 goals that were incorporated into SB 100. While working for McCall, he had gained experience securing and administering funds for federal government-financed comprehensive health and law-enforcement planning programs. The governor knew and trusted him. Cogan also had extensive local government planning experience, having worked as a planner for the City of Portland and as director of planning for the Port of Portland. His local planning background was important given the SB 100 mandate that all cities and counties prepare comprehensive plans. In addition, Cogan had economic development experience.

Washington County Commissioner Eldon Hout, a strong supporter of SB 100, was also considered for the position. He was one of the few local elected officials who also supported regional planning by Councils of Government as a key part of the statewide process. He had worked closely with staff preparing the precedent-setting Washington County Framework Plan and had actively participated in the planning work that CRAG was doing in the Portland metropolitan area (Hout, 1973). His support for regional planning councils may have appeared as a political liability to the commission, however, given the opposition that led to their elimination from SB 100. In addition, he wasn't a professional planner. Hout was hired instead to staff the new Joint Legislative Committee on Land Use.

The commissioners also considered Wesley Kvarsten, the planner who had played a key role in crafting Senate Bill 10, for the director position (Kvarsten, 1974). Like Hout, his identification with a regional council of governments likely counted against his selection. Hal Brauner was also considered, based on his work with the Day drafting subcommittee, his experience relating to state budgeting, and his role as natural resources adviser to the governor (Jepson, 1975). Like Hout, he wasn't a professional planner, and the commissioners likely wanted someone with credentials to orchestrate the process of developing and adopting goals with which local government planners would have to conform, one who didn't bring political baggage that would add to what was surely going to be a complex and contentious business.

HB 2607 Interlude

During January 1974, while the commissioners were negotiating with Cogan about the director position, the legislature staged a spectacle that likely influenced the way LCDC members thought about the work ahead:

the repeal of the Land Development Consumer Protection Act. House Bill 2607 was one of the governor's package of land-use-related bills enacted during the 1973 session. The bill had passed by large margins, 55-4 in the House and 28-2 in the Senate, but when the Real Estate Division released the rules and regulations to implement the act, the resultant uproar led the House (by a 44-14 vote) and the Senate (by a 27-3 vote) to repeal it (Sullivan, R., 1974).

LCDC Vice Chair Steve Schell had helped to draft HB 2607, which was a response to concerns in eastern, central, and southern Oregon about illegally subdivided land and fraudulent land sales. Among the requirements in the bill was a years-long rescission period during which a buyer could recoup all money paid if it could be demonstrated that a developer had made material misstatements of fact on a disclosure form. Mortgage lenders feared that with such a requirement buyers would be able to come after them rather than the developer if a problem surfaced (Sullivan, R., 1974).

HB 2607 was set to take effect on January 1, 1974, and the Real Estate Division mailed out the new rules and regulations in the last week of December 1973. Fred VanNatta, the lobbyist for the Oregon State Homebuilders Association, hosted a series of seminars to instruct builders on how to fill out the thirty-page disclosure form. "Many developers are downright irate to put it politely," he reported (Feedback, 1974). Before long, several mortgage lenders and the state Department of Veterans' Affairs stopped approving loans. Eleven Salem realtors took out a newspaper advertisement announcing that they would no longer sell new homes or land in existing subdivisions. The realty board in Corvallis declared that it was in favor of repeal.

The real estate commissioner added fuel to the developing fire when he told a meeting of the Oregon Association of Realtors that "the act was 'very poorly prepared legislation,' but he was going to enforce it." He warned that "'the act gives the consumer a club to beat you bloody dead (and he) can sue your teeth off until it's changed.' Developers who avoid or violate the act' are going to wind up with no hind end" (Feedback, 1974). Homebuilders told the public that residential construction had ground to a halt and repeal was necessary. Local realtor groups brought pressure to bear on legislators. The realtors, homebuilders, and others framed the new regulations as the product of a legislature that had been captured by wild-eyed radicals and a commissioner who was able to exercise too much discretion in implementing the law.

The successful repeal effort galvanized industry groups. Realtors Association lobbyist B. J. Rogers sounded a clarion call to his constituents to prepare for the coming conflicts with land-use planners and their environmental allies. "It took a piece of legislation so poorly drafted, and so obviously biased and vindictive in its intent," he concluded, "that the REALTORS of the state were finally jolted out of their complacency." In passing the legislation, Rogers said, legislators had accepted

> as gospel the word of planners and environmentalists, who have never been a part of the economic system that creates the wealth that sustains our society . . . Most planners have never done anything except go to school and work for the government, and unfortunately the same was true of their teachers . . . Why should they care if their plans bring an entire industry to a halt, and in the process price the average working man out of the market . . . The passing of HB 2607 . . . could very well be the straw that broke the camel's back . . . The result was that these people succeeded in doing the one thing they didn't want to do, they unified the REALTORS of the state as they have never been unified, and they added to their strength by giving them a common purpose with the Homebuilders, Bankers, and Title People. (Rogers, 1974a)

A few months later, Rogers wrote L. B. Day to tell him that the Realtors Association had contracted with Associated Oregon Industries to obtain the services of lobbyist Steve Hawes, who had drafted SB 100 and other Oregon land-use legislation when he was a legislative counsel for the state. Rogers also told Day:

> The attention of our people to the many problems before them has never been higher, and we have the problem of keeping that attention at a high pitch. Quite frankly, planners and planning have and continue to give us the best forum for keeping the attention of our people. I must confess to you that we will probably continue to pick on them in some fashion far into the foreseeable future. If this effort shows them to be too sensitive or too thin skinned, then you may have more of a problem than we will. (Rogers, 1974b)

Rogers's demagogic attacks, Day thought, were out of place in Oregon politics, although he assured him that his own "hide is well thickened" (Day, 1974a).

Fred VanNatta later remembered that repeal of HB 2607 was a watershed moment for the Homebuilders Association; he used the law as a recruiting and organization-building tool. He stressed the need to closely monitor what the legislature and LCDC were doing and to create the capacity to intervene politically when it appeared that one or both were proposing to require something that would, from the association's point of view, increase the cost of doing business (VanNatta, 2008).

In part as a result of HB 2607, LCDC and DLCD began to address their work in a context that included industry groups as well as local governments and environmental and citizen activists who were mobilized and ready for action. Bob Stacey, a University of Oregon law student working with OSPIRG and OEC, observed that "the commissioners' memories go back . . . to the February LCDC meeting, just after the successful repeal, at which Homebuilders Association lobbyist Fred VanNatta assured . . . LCDC that nothing so drastic would happen to . . . a reasonable Commission" (Stacey, 1974a). He wondered: "Will fears of legislative and special-interest reaction affect the content of the LCDC's goals as well?" (Stacey, 1974b). That question was uppermost in the minds of environmental activists throughout the start-up period.

LCDC and its Stakeholders

The LCDC/DLCD start-up process featured a continuation of the politics of the 1973 legislative session in a new setting. After Cogan came on board in February, the commission held a workshop during which representatives of all the organizations that had been active in the session spoke. It was a wide-ranging discussion that included OEC land-use activist Martin Davis telling the commission that his group presumed that

> the order in which the major tasks before the Commission will be attacked is: 1. Establishment of goals and guidelines for activities of statewide significance, followed by the initiation of a permit system for these activities. 2. Establishment of planning goals and guidelines for state agencies, cities, and counties in preparing, adopting, revising and implementing comprehensive plans. 3. Review and

recommendation to the legislature of the designation of areas of critical concern and additional activities of statewide significance.

OEC assumed that, based on a land-use inventory that LCDC was mandated to compile, the agency would develop a statewide long-range plan that would be shaped by an analysis of carrying capacity (Davis, M., 1974). Activists had failed to persuade legislators to keep mandated specified areas and activities in SB 100, so they tried to get LCDC to use its authority to adopt them.

An Oregon Shores activist agreed, and stressed that a permit system to deal with activities on the coast was an urgent necessity. In the face of intense pressure from developers, local governments were refusing to protect fragile coastal natural resources (Bacon, R., 1974a). Ron Eber, a University of Oregon planning student speaking on behalf of the Sierra Club, advocated requiring environmental impact statements as part of permit applications (Eber, 1974).

A representative of Associated Oregon Industries was optimistic that economics and livability could effectively be addressed simultaneously in plan making and implementation. Industry was ready, he noted, for efficient planning. "A new philosophy . . . you will encounter," he noted, "is that land owners are simply stewards of the land and hold the land in that capacity." Land-use planning shaped by that philosophy, though, raised important questions about property rights, taxation, and compensation for landowners, so he asked that the commissioners proceed cautiously (Angstrom, 1974).

Builders just needed to know the rules, Homebuilders lobbyist VanNatta said. Mandating planning could be a good thing if it produced a balanced approach to growth that recognized that people need homes, and he suggested the need for a housing goal, something that wasn't among the SB 10 goals incorporated into SB 100. He worried, though, that power would shift from landowners and developers to planners and wondered whether carrying capacity, which was on the SB 10 list, was a valid basis for planning (VanNatta, 1974a). Urban sprawl was taking valuable farmland out of production, Oregon Farm Bureau spokesperson Howard Fujii acknowledged, but "most farmers consider the appreciation of . . . land as a retirement security . . . Give us flexibility to sell out of farming." While he asked LCDC to educate farmers about the need to "lock" land into agricultural use through exclusive farm-use zones, the retirement-related issue had to be addressed (Fujii, 1974a).

Gordon Fultz, the Association of Oregon Counties lobbyist, wanted LCDC to provide model ordinances. He advocated for financial aid from higher-level authorities for local governments to plan and zone and reminded LCDC to build on the planning work already accomplished. If the goals and the plans developed to achieve those goals were done well, there would be no need to require environmental impact analyses, Fultz argued. He hoped those goals would be sufficiently broad to permit local governments to exercise their judgment to implement them. The problem, the League of Oregon Cities representative said, was that there weren't enough planners to do the work, especially in smaller jurisdictions. Many cities already had, though, complied with the SB 10 mandate to plan and zone, and those products had to be taken into account (Fultz, 1974a; Jones, 1974; Local Government Relations Division, 1974b).

These issues and others, such as the nature and extent of citizen involvement in goal development and local planning, presented LCDC with a daunting set of complex issues. They were both philosophical and pragmatic, and they embodied theories of political economy and human nature that Governor McCall, Senator Macpherson, environmental activists, and planners had introduced into discussions on land use since the late 1960s. Everything LCDC did was closely scrutinized—by the governor and legislature, by state government agencies and industry groups, and by environmental and citizen activists; all worked assiduously to shape how LCDC attended to their priorities.

Budgetary Politics II

The new director's first order of business was to get a budget for his agency. Arnold Cogan later recalled that "the first thing LB [Day] says is: go get Bob Logan's budget" at LGRD (Cogan, 1999). Logan and Cogan, who were good friends, had worked together during the late 1960s in the Governor's Office. Given their relationship, Cogan told Day that he couldn't go after Logan's budget. During a special session of the legislature in February 1974, however, L. B. Day himself did just that. He saw the planning-related elements in Logan's budget as rightfully belonging to LCDC and as central to establishing the commission's authoritative role in Oregon land-use affairs. His effort to capture funds from LGRD was framed by a motion LCDC adopted unanimously that "any land use planning function directly related to establishing statewide land use policies or programs, or coordination or handling of funds should be immediately transferred to the DLCD" (Land Conservation and Development Commission, 1974a).

Cogan then requested twenty-one positions for his department and asked for permission to receive and allocate about a million dollars in local planning grants in the event that Congress passed the National Land Use Act. As Day had wanted, the legislature transferred resources from Logan's LGRD budget, although overall DLCD did not get nearly as much as Cogan had requested. LCDC was authorized to allocate federal Housing and Urban Development "701" planning grants, and nine positions were cut from the LGRD budget. DLCD was given nine positions, and the Emergency Board received $100,000 for the state match of $900,000 expected from the federal government if the National Land Use Act became law (Logan, 1974).

Cogan hired two people from Logan's office, one to be deputy director and another to work closely with local governments. An Oregon Department of Transportation staffer who had been working on the Willamette River Greenway program and the assistant commissioner from the Bureau of Labor transferred to the new land-use agency (Gustafson, 1973a, b; McCall, 1974a).

A few months later, three additional planners joined the DLCD staff; one came from the Central Oregon Intergovernmental Council, another from Buffalo, New York, and the third from the U.S. Department of Housing and Urban Development, which continued to pay half of her DLCD salary. The new DLCD staff was relatively young and had limited local government planning experience, especially in Oregon. Still, they were highly motivated and committed to implementing the policies set out in SB 100, aware that they and Cogan played key roles in an unfolding drama that was unique in the planning field.

The commissioners, led by L. B. Day, made it clear that they would take the lead in setting policy and dealing with the political currents swirling around the agency. Building on his legislative and state agency director background, and his experience chairing the drafting subcommittee, Day met frequently with legislators and with industry and local government lobbyists during the start-up period to cultivate support. The close proximity between LCDC's Salem office and the offices of industry and local government associations facilitated those meetings. Day also encouraged informal meetings between DLCD staff and the industry and local government lobbyists. Day and Cogan communicated frequently with Henry Richmond as well. Commissioners and department staff knew that industry, state and local government, and environmental stakeholders were monitoring them closely. In the context of the political pressures bearing on them, the staff attempted to craft implementation strategies that were in line with legal mandates and professional norms and enabled the commissioners to maintain sufficient political support among key stakeholders.

DLCD, however, was clearly straining to accomplish all of the tasks assigned to it with the staff resources available, which were supplemented to a limited extent by consultants contracted to help develop budget, management, and citizen-outreach programs. Arnold Cogan went before the Legislative Emergency Board in late June with an urgent request for more people. Based on advice from the state attorney general's office on the work DLCD was mandated to do, especially the demands associated with the recently begun effort to develop statewide planning goals, six new professional positions and eleven new staff support positions were required. If DLCD didn't get those positions, Cogan warned, communication and coordination with other state agencies would be severely limited, outreach to local governments would be drastically reduced, and an ambitious citizen-engagement effort would likely have to be curtailed (Cogan, 1974b). The legislature gave DLCD two new positions and assigned one of them to the coastal commission. At the end of 1974, a land-use economist from Kansas joined DLCD.

Bob Stacey reported in *Land Use Oregon,* OEC's newsletter:

> A small committee of state legislators came close to scoring a TKO on Oregon's state land use planning program last month . . . The [LCD] Commissioners were told by Cogan that [State] Senator Boe had based his opposition to the budget request on the fear that an ambitious LCDC program would send local governments and state agencies streaming to Salem to request planning money from the legislature to help them comply with LCDC goals. (Stacey, 1974a)

OSPIRG attorney Henry Richmond wrote Cogan: "the Emergency Board action is a body-blow to Oregon's land use planning efforts" (Richmond, 1974d). Moreover, Congress failed to pass the proposed National Land Use Policy Act, so no funds would come from that source. During the summer, state budget officials became concerned about DLCD expenditures in relation to its severely constrained resources and began to scrutinize the agency closely. Cogan had to allocate staff resources to address those concerns at the same time that he had to begin preparing a budget request and a proposed work program for the 1975-1977 fiscal period (Cogan, 1974c).

Interorganizational Relationships

While LCDC was struggling to fund its own program, it had to establish itself in relation to the Oregon Coastal Conservation and Development Commission and the Oregon Department of Transportation, both of which were mandated to submit plans to the commission. OCCDC had to get LCDC approval to submit an application for planning money to the federal government agency that administered the 1972 Coastal Zone Management Act. In February 1974, Henry Richmond submitted a long memo to LCDC on behalf of OSPIRG, harshly criticizing OCCDC's application: "The Oregon coast is too important to take a chance that this money will be frittered away because the agencies involved have not agreed and clearly stated precisely what is to be done, by whom, how and when in an effort to carry out applicable [federal and state] planning laws." Richmond suggested that it made sense for OCCDC to concentrate on coastal resource inventories and management policies for areas that required special treatment. Those would lead to a future set of LCDC goals that local governments would address in their comprehensive plans ("Intern Report . . . ," 1974; Richmond, 1974a).

Cogan agreed with some of Richmond's concerns, but he believed that the monitoring and coordination that his staff would undertake with their OCCDC counterparts would compensate for the deficiencies Richmond identified. LCDC decided to approve the grant request (Cogan, 1974a). A few months later, LCDC and OCCDC adopted a Joint Memorandum of Understanding intended to guide the coastal agency toward the timely completion of its planning processes in ways that would support LCDC's program. The memorandum incorporated many of the specifics that Richmond had recommended (Ross, 1974).

The OSPIRG intervention—the first clear manifestation of the roles the organization had played during the start-up phase as monitor, enforcer, and adviser—was intended to strengthen LCDC in relation to its coastal counterpart. At about the same time, the federal government established the nation's first estuarine sanctuary—South Slough, an arm of the Coos Bay Estuary—using a process that involved local residents and officials, Oregon Shores members, OCCDC, and LCDC ("South Slough . . . ," 1992; Ross and Hepp, 1974).

Shortly after the memorandum was signed, OCCDC began positioning itself to maintain its autonomy to implement its forthcoming plan. For example, the coastal commission voted to submit a request for a million-dollar budget to carry on its program during 1975-1977, even though it was scheduled to go out of business at the beginning of the 1975 legislative session. A state budget analyst recommended against continued funding and in favor of allocating money earmarked for implementing the coastal plan to LCDC. The OCCDC executive committee voted to appeal the recommendation and to strike references to LCDC in its forthcoming plan; it would refer instead to an "appropriate agency" ("OCCDC okays requests for funds," 1974; Bacon, L., 1974a).

L. B. Day clashed with OCCDC about which agency would play the lead role in shaping the future of planning on the coast. Several OCCDC members were preparing legislation for the 1975 session that would empower a slightly modified version of the commission to implement its plan. While Day thought a regional coordinating organization on the coast would be fine, he strongly opposed an independent state agency that could undermine LCDC's authority to approve the plans and implementation ordinances that local governments were mandated to produce. According to OCCDC's Wilbur Ternyik,

> Day referred to OCCDC as a "coastal folly" at the budget hearing where OCCDC came to protest the state budget analyst recommendation to eliminate its funding, and also said "if it were continued it would result in a 'coastal frolic.'"

No one involved in coastal land-use issues, Ternyik said, wanted LCDC to play an authoritative role (Bacon, L., 1974b).

Day prevailed, and LCDC kept its role as the sole state land-use authority. Governor Robert Straub, who had won election in 1974, refused to include a separate budget for a modified version of an independent agency on the coast, and the Joint Legislative Committee on Land Use resolved that the 1973 legislature clearly had intended "to establish a single state-wide planning agency capable of coordinating land use planning . . . both within and without the coastal zone" ("Land use resolution . . . ," 1975). In an effort to prevent a legislative battle over a proposed new agency while it worked to secure its own budget request during the 1975 session, LCDC hired a former OCCDC member and state legislator who was extremely influential on the coast to help create the regional coordination agency that SB 100 enabled. Nevertheless, tensions between LCDC and the Oregon Coastal Conservation and Development Association (OCCDA)—the new organization that was created—remained high (Conkling, 1975).

LCDC's relationship with the Oregon Department of Transportation evolved in the context of the Willamette River Greenway program, which had been a key feature of gubernatorial politics during the 1960s and was a high priority for Robert Straub. Karl Unthank, a University of Oregon administrator and conservation activist, first developed the program concepts in the mid-1960s. In the 1966 gubernatorial contest, Straub had elaborated on Unthank's proposal and had given it his support; his opponent, Tom McCall, then secretary of state, had endorsed it as well. Both proposals addressed the implications of a growing Willamette Valley urban population and called for protecting riverine resources and creating opportunities for recreational development. Straub's proposal, which was a key aspect of his campaign, heavily emphasized recreational uses (Bauer, 1980; Clucas, 2003).

After he was elected governor, McCall moved the greenway concept forward, focusing on park and recreation development but mindful of farmers' concerns about the negative effects recreation-related uses might have on their operations. In 1967, the legislature created a Willamette River Park System Program, which was limited to state grants-in-aid to local governments to acquire riverfront park and recreation land. The State Park Division of ODOT administered the program, supplemented by grants from the federal Land and Water Conservation Fund. Still, progress on implementing the program was seriously constrained during its first five years.

The Oregon Transportation Commission (OTC), chaired by Pacific Power & Light executive Glenn Jackson, oversaw ODOT. In the early 1970s, with Governor McCall's knowledge and approval, OTC directed ODOT to go beyond the terms of the 1967 law to begin developing state parks along the Willamette River and to acquire additional land for a Willamette River Corridor. ODOT used eminent domain to condemn land for state parks and threatened to use that authority to take land for the corridor as well. Willamette Valley farmers resisted. The Willamette River Greenway Act, passed in 1973, was a response to the farmers and a way for the legislature to discipline ODOT.

The act, House Bill 2497, defined a minimum and maximum greenway boundary and elevated the natural, scenic, and historic-conservation elements of the greenway concept within that area. Farming within the greenway could continue without restriction, and ODOT was mandated to prepare a greenway management and development plan and to submit the plan to LCDC for approval. ODOT could use its power of condemnation to acquire scenic easements for riverfront land when the purchase conformed to plan designations, but it could not use eminent domain authority to acquire easements on land being used for farms unless owners were willing to sell.

DLCD staff was concerned that ODOT's efforts to involve both citizens and local officials had been insufficient and that LCDC members would find them unacceptable. L. B. Day wrote directly to Glenn Jackson: "Before . . . LCDC will be able to approve this plan, we must have clear evidence that opportunity to comment has been offered" to property owners, elected and appointed officials, and interested groups and citizens. The greenway program, Day continued,

> was put in jeopardy because of public confusion, misunderstanding, and lack of involvement. If public officials and other citizens are not given a significantly larger opportunity to have input, there is little chance of the plan ever being successfully implemented. I feel that the Willamette Greenway program is too important to have it lapse into more fruitless paperwork and wasted bureaucratic energy. (Day, 1974b)

LCDC and ODOT agreed to mount an outreach effort that would precede the submission of a preliminary plan in time to meet the legislative deadline established in HB 2497. ODOT's consultant produced a plan that satisfied farmers and local officials, and LCDC indicated that approval of the plan would likely be forthcoming. In late 1974, Governor-elect Straub, however, wrote Glenn Jackson to express his serious displeasure. Straub was concerned that the plan too severely restricted ODOT's authority to acquire land for recreational purposes. He and Jackson agreed that ODOT would not submit the preliminary plan to OTC for approval until after Straub took office and the plan was changed.

Changing the plan set up a confrontation between Straub, Jackson, and ODOT on one hand and L. B. Day and LCDC on the other. Day and LCDC won the battle when the commission decided to develop its own statewide planning goal, and the greenway program shifted away from a recreation-oriented approach toward one that focused on preserving farmland. The plan would be implemented through local comprehensive planning and zoning that LCDC would have to acknowledge as compliant with its goals (Bauer, 1980).

The coastal and greenway planning programs were important learning opportunities for the new agency as it sought, under Day's aggressive leadership, to insert itself into ongoing state agency planning processes and establish its authoritative role. One of LCDC's core functions was evaluating plans and implementation programs produced by state and local agencies, and the coastal zone and greenway planning processes enabled the commissioners and DLCD staff to begin developing concrete notions about how best to do that. Negotiating with OCCDC staff and commissioners—under the watchful eyes of OSPIRG and Oregon Shores activists—permitted DLCD staff to discover what substantive content was important in plans and to learn about the relationship between substantive content and how planning goals ought to be constructed. They also discovered what they valued themselves and what LCDC commissioners thought appropriate regarding citizen-engagement practices.

The coastal zone and greenway episodes also marked the beginning of the tensions that LCDC and DLCD would experience with local governments and other state agencies. Day in particular earned the wrath of Governor Straub, the Transportation Commission, and many local officials on the coast; they would directly challenge him and the program he led.

LCDC and the Joint Legislative Committee on Land Use

One of the entities that SB 100 created was a standing committee composed of members from both legislative chambers to advise LCDC and to make recommendations about land-use matters. During the 1973 session, the chairs of the Senate and House Environment and Land Use committees were specifically appointed as members of the Joint Legislative Committee on Land Use (JLCLU). That meant SB 100 co-sponsor Ted Hallock was a member, and he chaired the committee during the start-up period. While the legislature had frequently empanelled interim committees to explore particular issues, JLCLU was the first permanent body the legislature created to play an oversight role. During the LCDC start-up phase, Hallock and Day met frequently, and Eldon Hout, the committee's executive secretary, shuttled between them. But formal committee meetings "were as infrequent as possible," Hallock remembered. "I wanted [Day] to give a report annually, which was what I believe [SB 100] called for, and he did. No more. There was going to be no more exposure than that" (Hallock, 2000). Hallock also decided against putting much effort into addressing the SB 100 charge to the committee to make recommendations about a compensatory zoning program during the interim. While he provided a buffer between the new agency and hostile forces in the legislature, he was not able to provide much help with the agency's budget.

Chapter 5
Adopting Statewide Planning Goals:
The Grassroots Phase and a New Approach

> *"We're talking about more than preserving the beauty of Oregon.*
> *We're talking about the growth of Oregon and how that growth*
> *can be accomplished in a sane manner. We're talking about the*
> *economy and the environment . . . We're talking about balance.*
> *In short, we're talking about People and the Land."*
>
> —Governor Tom McCall

LCDC had until January 1, 1975, to develop and adopt a set of statewide planning goals and guidelines. It also had to decide whether or not to regulate the activities of statewide significance that the legislature had specified and to recommend the designation of areas of critical statewide concern. The commissioners expected to have eighteen months and enough funding to complete the work; instead, they found themselves in an eleven-month race with far fewer staff people than they needed. Moreover, the legislature had not yet allocated money to help local governments plan and zone, a situation that seriously heightened local concern about how they would implement the SB 100 mandates. As a result, the hopes and fears of all those trying to shape Oregon's land-use revolution were continuously on display during the goal-development process.

Goal Development
In March 1974, LCDC's Citizen Involvement Advisory Committee—influenced by the practices of neighborhood associations in Portland, Salem, and Eugene; the recent experience of the Willamette Valley Futures Forum; and the advice of a local public affairs consultant—proposed an extensive and ambitious public-involvement program. LCDC would host

twenty-eight workshops around the state during April and May, with direct mail and major print and broadcast media campaigns used to attract participants. A primary goal was to involve unaffiliated residents, that is, people who were not members of land-use-related organizations.

Philosophically committed to opening up planning processes to as many people as possible, the committee wanted to downplay the importance of insider knowledge and access to decision makers. They wanted workshop participants to start with a blank slate in the hope that suggestions for goals, areas, and activities would bubble up from below (Collins, 2008; Cogan, 1974k; Rosenbaum, 1977). DLCD would summarize the results of the workshops and disseminate them to participants and others. Then a second round of workshops would be held to discuss what DLCD produced in response to the first round of meetings. Finally, staff would write the goals that would be the basis for public hearings.

Arnold Cogan strongly supported that approach as a way to get new ideas and build political support for the land-use program, especially in rural areas where there tended to be more resistance to planning and zoning. Workshop attendees, he hoped, would have a positive experience with LCDC and tell their friends, neighbors, and legislators about it. During his first public appearance after becoming DLCD director, he told a southern Oregon audience: "This is one program that will be built from the bottom up, not from the top down . . . We look on this . . . as a partnership program—a people-to-people program" (Clay, 1974a, b). Cogan hoped that fifty thousand Oregonians would participate during 1974, "blanket[ing] the state with an aware citizenry watchdogging local governments whose responsibility it is to get SB 100 off the ground and running" (Pintarich, 1974).

OSPIRG's Henry Richmond supported that approach. In OEC's *Land Use Oregon*, he argued:

> Widespread public involvement will help Oregon avoid the pitfalls of other states where members of the land use commission become extremely vulnerable to the political and economic influence of major landowners. Broadening the base for land use decisions will serve to limit the ability of LCD Commissioners to make isolated and arbitrary decisions. (Richmond, Bonnem, Fritts, 1974)

He was articulating the deeply ingrained environmentalist belief that administrative agencies often were captured by the powerful interests they were created to regulate. A combination of specific, fact-based decisions and widespread public knowledge and support was necessary, he believed, to prevent that from occurring (Richmond, 1974b).

The workshops began with an LCDC representative giving an overview of the goal-development process. Attendees were then divided into small groups, where they attempted to reach consensus on the wide-ranging issues the goals were intended to address. One of Richmond's co-authors on the *Land Use Oregon* piece reported on a workshop he attended:

> The meeting . . . reflected LCD's expressed concern that the formulation of goals and guidelines for state land use planning be a "bottom to top" process. There was no parade of slicked-down, briefcase-toting bureaucrats, nor did LCD hand the participants a Xeroxed land use plan and ask them for their "comments." Rather, LCD came prepared and willing to be receptive to the ideas and opinions of all the people as to what they wanted. The meeting was structured to some degree by LCD, but the purpose seemed to be a desire to stimulate active audience participation. (Fritts, 1974)

Of the approximately three thousand people who attended the workshops, 90 percent filled out cards that asked for demographic information. As a group, they tended to be long-term residents of their county and likely to own their homes. Most had college degrees and relatively high incomes. Two-thirds were male. They clearly were not a representative sample of Oregonians. Still, there was some good news for Cogan and the Citizen Involvement Advisory Committee: 51 percent of participants said they were unaffiliated with any group or organization involved in land-use issues (Land Conservation and Development Commission, 1974f; Rosenbaum, 1977). DLCD had made a special effort to send more direct mail to people in eastern, central, and southern Oregon, and the strategy seemed to have worked. One outcome attributable to that effort was noted by involvement committee member Margaret Collins: "Each workshop also resulted in an emphasis on regional differences . . . the people felt that statewide goals and guidelines must be flexible enough to apply to regional needs" (Collins, 1974a).

The citizen workshops were building support, but local government officials were ambivalent about the process. While LCDC members and DLCD staff arranged to meet with local leaders at each workshop location, those meetings did not delve too deeply into details and local officials were not treated any differently than other participants. Local leaders, in fact, were concerned that DLCD had not yet begun to review existing comprehensive plans and zoning ordinances—about two-thirds of cities and counties had adopted plans and zoning ordinances by January 1, 1974—to ensure that statewide goals and guidelines would reflect and build on their efforts. They wanted the agency to give the review of plans as much attention as it was giving public participation (Bauer, 1974). Doing so would be a costly, labor-intensive process, however, and DLCD was operating with a very constrained budget.

Between Rounds

During April and May, DLCD staff members turned their attention to analyzing the workshop materials and distributing their "Report on People and the Land Public Workshops." With its small staff already stretched, the department also began preparing for the second round of workshops, scheduled for that summer. Arnold Cogan urgently requested that the legislative Emergency Board grant a substantial budget increase, but the two new positions that were allocated—one of which was assigned to the coastal commission—were not enough to help much.

Henry Richmond reminded Cogan that state and local government agencies had a great deal of information already available, and the commission's main job—"the identification of the most basic and compelling statewide goals—need not go unsupported by factual documentation despite drastic fiscal constraints." Richmond stressed a point that he would make repeatedly to LCDC during the goal-development process:

> To the extent that statewide goals oblige counties and cities to adopt
> regulations which may appear unusual or restrictive to some courts,
> it is essential that the necessity for such regulations be clearly estab-
> lished—not simply as a reflection of public opinion, but as a result
> dictated by the basic facts of land, water, population and economics.

Land-use regulations, he argued, would be more likely to withstand critical scrutiny by the courts "if there is a solid evidentiary basis" (Richmond, 1974d). Steve Schell shared Richmond's concerns (Schell, 1974a). Environmental activists, especially attorneys such as Schell and Richmond, saw objective, scientifically based evidence as a necessary foundation for land-use planning. That kind of documentation was a bulwark against recalcitrant local government officials and their constituents who owned and developed property and the legal challenges they would mount when constrained by regulations.

For the second round of workshops, the DLCD staff worked on developing thirteen goals and producing information related to the possible designation of areas of critical concern. LCDC thought the number of goals and critical areas would have to be reduced before adoption simply because the staff resources would not be available to develop all of them. The next round would provide important information about which ones to select.

The goals were: (1) agricultural land, (2) forests and forest land, (3) energy sources, (4) estuaries and related wetlands, (5) shorelands, (6) economic development and employment, (7) urbanization/urban development, (8) housing, (9) pollution, (10) freeways and major highways, (11) urban mass transit, (12) content and process of comprehensive planning, and (13) plans of state agencies and special districts. The department presented draft workshop materials to LCDC in late August, just two weeks before the second round of workshops was to begin.

For each of the goal subjects, DLCD staff prepared text that briefly and generally described the problems the goal was intended to address and presented a general goal definition and brief descriptions of possible additional goals or guidelines. The materials triggered an expression of serious concern from Schell. "I have carefully reviewed the goals set out," he wrote,

> and I have some strong misgivings about going to the public with this set of goals . . . The reason is that even from my limited knowledge of a few of these subjects, there is very little attention to either the actual problems or the possible solutions . . . It appears that there is neither a clear understanding of the problem or of the facts involved or of the goal or consequences of that goal. (Schell, 1974b)

While Schell wanted the proposed problem definitions and goal language to contain more technical detail and specificity and expected the staff to provide technically grounded analyses of goal impacts, DLCD staff had concluded that the workshop materials should offer the opportunity for participants to evaluate the impact of proposed goals in the context of their particular geographic areas and to suggest and discuss the impacts of alternative goals that might be more appropriate in those regions (McCal-

lum, 1974). Reflecting their continuing commitment to a bottom-up process, most commissioners and staff, especially Day and Cogan, thought that
such an approach would encourage more active participation and support.

OSPIRG/OEC activist and law student Bob Stacey saw evidence of capture in the design of the workshop materials. He thought that pressure from
industry and local government lobbyists and from state agency people who
were concerned about LCDC's intentions had shaped the choices DLCD
staff made. As evidence, he described a briefing session of "lobbyists from
the Oregon Farm Bureau, Weyerhaeuser, Association of Oregon Counties,
and Associated Oregon Industries . . . for the benefit of a [DLCD] staffer
and the Joint [Legislative] Land Use Committee's Eldon Hout." Stacey said
the lobbyists had described a consensus they had reached on key points:
LCDC could mandate the goals that had to be addressed in plans, but local
governments should be able to choose how to achieve those goals. In addition, if the state did not provide both the data and the funding for local
governments to prepare plans, then the locals should be excused from
complying with SB 100 mandates (Stacey, 1974b). Stacey also reported
that the lobbyists "took advantage of proximity"— the offices of industry
and local government lobbying organizations were very close to DLCD
headquarters— "to share coffee breaks with staff, to buy refreshments for
staff, and to simply stroll through [DLCD] offices unannounced to 'see
what's up'" (Stacey, 1975c). L. B. Day encouraged those interactions as
a way of maintaining support for the program among key stakeholders.
Stacey concluded, though, that the

> staff folded under the pressure . . . [They] had been deliberately
> imprecise . . . the goals were so vaguely stated that it was impos-
> sible for one reading them to guess what consequences might fol-
> low from their adoption. The staff had worked politically rather
> than professionally . . . they had searched for politically acceptable
> solutions . . . they were suffering from their lack of any invento-
> ries or other factual information about the goal subjects . . . When
> there are no real world data to support a precise position, it can't
> be defended against those who are paid to argue the other side. The
> staff's coffee klatsches had taken their toll. (Stacey, 1975c)

At the August 30 meeting, Schell proposed that LCDC initiate a path
parallel to the second workshop round, assigning goal and guideline

development and critical area review to technical committees made up of knowledgeable people from the private, nonprofit, and public sectors. Cogan should assign DLCD staff to support the committees, Schell recommended, and they would report to LCDC by October 1 (Schell, 1974b). The commission adopted Schell's proposal, and he went on vacation.

While Schell was away, Day and Cogan decided that having many small committees would be too difficult to coordinate. Instead, they agreed to appoint one technical advisory committee of twenty-four carefully chosen people drawn from local and state government and from environmental and industry organizations (Stacey, 1974c). When Schell returned and learned what had happened, he "sort of came off the wall . . . saying 'these people are uninformed about the issues. They are political folks who will try to find whatever comfortable compromise they can, and they will not give us the kind of guidance we need . . . and that's not acceptable'" (Schell, 2001). Schell later remembered Day telling him that if Schell thought he could do a better job, he should organize the committees himself.

Schell then worked with DLCD staff to choose technical experts to function as resource advisory people. The technical advisory committee, which had already been appointed, was redirected to serve as a coordinating committee for those advisors, who would write individual goals. The proposed goal subjects were combined into six groups—for example, agricultural lands and forest lands were combined, as were pollution and economic development—and two DLCD staff members were each assigned to work with three of the groups. The groups were asked to refine existing goals or to draft new ones for commission adoption and to base their recommendations on fact-based analyses of problems and the consequences of alternative courses of action. They had twenty days to complete their work (Cogan, 1974l ; Schell, 2001; Stacey, 1974c).

Meanwhile, Henry Richmond pursued an independent track, hoping to influence LCDC efforts. In late July, he wrote Day to tell him about the work OSPIRG interns had done on goal-related projects. Many of the proposals he mentioned would find their way into the goal- and guideline-development process by way of the commissioners, the staff, and the advisory committees Schell established.

One proposal about the preservation of prime agricultural land was grounded in work done by law student David Aamodt. Aamodt, who had grown up on a farm in Clackamas County, sought out Richmond after seeing him on television in 1973 to tell him that soil classifications could be used to identify agricultural land that should be designated an area of critical statewide concern. Richmond was intrigued by the possibilities and set Aamodt to work on an OSPIRG report that was published later that year. Soils classified in categories I, II, and III, the highest quality classifications, by the U.S. Soil Conservation Service, he proposed, should be declared an area of critical statewide concern and subject to state regulation (Aamodt, 1973). In light of Aamodt's assessment in 1974 that "the political chances of an area of critical state concern for prime farm land being created by the Oregon Legislature seems remote," he proposed an approach that LCDC could implement by adopting goals and guidelines. In his proposal, a farmland goal would include a definition of prime agricultural land (Aamodt suggested Classes I, II, III and associated Willamette Valley floor Class IV soils); a requirement that local governments zone such land for exclusive farm use and establish minimum lot sizes appropriate for the continuation of commercial farming; and a prohibition on all development inconsistent with accepted farming practices. Guidelines would permit local governments to address varying agricultural conditions (Aamodt, 1974a). Richmond also outlined proposals to ensure that the most productive timberlands, those in Site Classes I and II, would be rehabilitated where appropriate and managed on a sustained-yield basis. He suggested that LCDC adopt goals that applied to different types of estuaries and require local comprehensive plans to address goals appropriate to the different types.

Another proposal involved an LCDC requirement that all cities establish urban service boundaries, time the extension of infrastructure to lands not placed in agricultural or other natural resource zones to coincide with development in those areas, and establish a procedure to extend boundaries in ways that imposed the least total cost on the public. A boundary goal had an especially important role to play, Richmond thought, until LCDC adopted a statewide growth policy that directed population and economic activity to specific growth centers, perhaps at new locations. He reiterated:

> Rational land use planning decisions about such complex issues as
> the location of growth centers, the pattern of urban development,
> the design of a transportation system, or assisting the maintenance
> of a healthy and diversified state economy require facts. Some of

this factual information bears on degrees of limits which the natural capacity of land, air and water resources can place on human activity. Much of the information which can establish such degrees of limitation is available today, but it is in various formats, on different scales, and from a bewildering variety of sources.

Richmond wanted LCDC to require local and state government agencies to collect relevant data in standardized ways that would become part of a computer-based information system (Richmond, 1974e), a proposal similar to one that Cogan had suggested in 1969.

The Second Round

LCDC partnered with Keep Oregon Livable, a program of the Oregon Department of Transportation, to develop a public relations effort to promote the second round of workshops. Governor McCall kicked off the campaign at a news conference:

I am not asking [you] to take sides, but simply to aid our citizens with the information and knowledge they need to participate in the land use planning workshops, and help spread my message that their participation is enthusiastically solicited . . . We're talking about more than preserving the beauty of Oregon. We're talking about the growth of Oregon and how that growth can be accomplished in a sane manner. We're talking about the economy *and* the environment . . . We're talking about balance. In short, we're talking about People and the Land. (McCall, 1974b)

Major broadcast and newspaper coverage followed the press conference, which the campaign hoped would reach one hundred thousand homes. Questionnaires and information on the workshops were mailed to the three thousand people who had participated in the first round and to an additional ten thousand people interested in land-use issues. DLCD secured a $50,000 grant from the Pacific Northwest Regional Commission to fund the effort ("Description of a Supplemental . . . ", 1974; Fobes, 1974; Gustafson, 1974).

Even with the campaign's efforts and McCall's stirring invitation, attendance at the workshops declined and LCDC got no closer to accomplishing its major tasks. Cogan reported that 1,935 people filled out cards in the second round, significantly fewer than in the spring, and the participants were similar in background to those who had attended the first round. LCDC also added separate, in-depth meetings with about five hundred local officials.

"Generally," Cogan later reported, "people expressed agreement with the drafted goal subjects." Reflecting the bottom-up approach that he and the state Involvement Committee had pursued since the beginning, Cogan also thought "by leaving the goals broad, the participants seemed to feel they were helping the Department make each subject more specific." There was support, he noted, for a statewide standard regarding citizen involvement (Cogan, 1974h).

An OEC activist had a different perception about what people thought about the workshop, describing his "overall reaction . . . as some sort of mild shock . . . we were asked to do far too much . . . with 90 minutes allotted to us we could hardly be expected to say anything very incisive . . . The danger is that LCDC might now conclude that it has reached the people and that it knows what they think (Davis, P., 1974).

The commission was aware that the workshops were not entirely successful. Cogan had also noted that "the lack of specificity caused some concern and provoked comment both at the workshops and in meetings" with local government representatives, and in its report to the Pacific Northwest Regional Commission, LCDC described participants as "frustrated at the lack of specificity in the goal subjects. ... Discussion amplified these frustrations when participants themselves attempted to make the goal subjects more specific." Attendees also struggled to answer questions regarding what they thought would be consequences of the goals, and there were questions about what types of regulations were contemplated for critical areas (Cogan, 1974h; Rosenbaum, 1977).

The goal-development process had reached a low point, and commissioners were troubled by what they saw as the staff's too-slow progress toward meeting their looming deadline. They no longer saw a clear path from a bottom-up discussion of goals, critical areas, and critical activities to products that were administratively, legally, and politically defensible.

Richmond diagnosed the major problem: "LCDC has not had and does not now have staff adequate to carry out the most basic aspect of its land use planning program." He welcomed the addition of advisory committees, but noted that as of late September goal formulation had not reached the point of being either administratively or legally useful. Moreover, several areas that SB 100 had recommended for priority consideration—most of them sensitive environmental areas—had not yet surfaced in the process. SB 100 required LCDC to inventory land uses, but inventories were not getting done. Finally, LCDC had not yet adopted a regulation for conducting review proceedings, including review of local land-use decisions for consistency with the interim SB 10 goals (Richmond, 1974m). Stacey complained that "the legislature ordered a job done and then refused to pay for it." He also warned: "Day has made clear his intention to quit if the '75 legislature doesn't come up with a real land use program. If the money . . . isn't available, all the Commissioners may as well throw in the towel" (Stacey, 1974c).

A New Direction

Things came to a head at the October 11 meeting, where the commissioners considered two very different approaches, one developed by Arnold Cogan and his staff and the other by L. B. Day. Based on his analysis of staff capabilities, workshop results, and technical advisory committee discussions, Cogan recommended that LCDC direct DLCD staff to concentrate on three goals: agricultural lands, forestlands, and urbanization and urban development. Those goals, Cogan advised,

> cover most of the land area, include many of the critical problem areas and activities, and deal with many of the economic, energy and environmental issues. They also represent not only a large, but attainable work load for the staff, and are supported by a sufficient amount of data and expertise to result in well-documented goals.

Agriculture and forestlands were at the top of workshop priority lists. Both privately and publicly owned lands should be covered so that land owned by the federal government—about 52 percent of land in the state—would be included. Urbanization, energy, and economic development also enjoyed significant workshop support, and Cogan argued that

> a goal covering urban development and urbanization will not only deal with economic development, housing, urban containment, growth centers and carrying capacity, but will also affect much of the non-forest and non-agricultural land remaining without goal coverage.

He added that energy and economic considerations would be taken into account as part of each recommended goal, so they did not need to be dealt with separately at this time. Cogan proposed postponing water-oriented goal subjects, such as estuaries and shorelines, until after the Oregon coastal commission presented its work in 1975. He also pointed out that LCDC had the authority to coordinate the activities of other state departments, such as Transportation and Environmental Quality, so separate transportation and pollution goals weren't necessary either (Cogan, 1974g).

Cogan also recommended that the commission "designate only those [critical] areas for which responsibility was ordered by legislative action"—including the Willamette River Greenway and the coastal zone assigned to OCCDC. Local governments, he suggested, should regulate other potential critical areas through their comprehensive plans and implementation actions, and the formal designation of other critical areas should be deferred pending more study (Cogan, 1974i). In addition, the key infrastructure associated with activities of statewide significance, as specified by the legislature, should be dealt with by requiring local governments to integrate them with designated land uses in their comprehensive plans.

Cogan knew that designating activities of statewide significance and establishing permit processes to regulate them required a statewide growth strategy. It would take considerable time, he thought, to achieve consensus about which parts of the state would grow and which parts would be "reduced growth areas" (Cogan, 1974e). The development of a statewide growth policy was a critically important task, Cogan believed, but he did not think LCDC should attempt it during what remained of the fiscal year (Cogan, 1974d).

Day came to the October 11 meeting with his own approach in mind. He wanted LCDC to "reaffirm the goals for comprehensive planning" found in SB 10, because "there is considerable *legislative* pride of authorship" and those goals covered much of what LCDC was mandated to address. He argued:

> By taking the Legislature's own language, while committing to develop a manual for evaluating plans, the Commission and Department are given time to develop a strategy to accomplish the rewriting and improvement of the statutory language based on

what has been learned from the workshops, technical committees and other input.

Day also recommended that a citizen-involvement goal be adopted and that LCDC adopt coastal goals and guidelines based on what OCCDC gave it. "The Commission must avoid the appearance of needless duplication with the coastal planning effort," he thought.

Following his recommendations, Day assured, "is in no way a backing off in the commitment to S.B. 100, but rather is a realization that the process is extremely complicated and must be done correctly for there will be no second chance." Everybody knew that the combination of a delayed start to implementation of the law and the lack of funding had created the difficult situation now confronting the agency. Still, Day concluded:

> To move ahead on the broad LCDC program as currently outlined is to court disaster. There is virtual unanimity of feeling outside the Department that the Commission could well alienate its entire constituency by adopting the current program. The fuzziness of the present work product, if it continues, will cause local government to despair and walk away from the Department's efforts . . . The present inadequate data support for the goal statements is of great concern to the environmentalists and may well be the Achilles heel of the whole program.

He thought local governments would be encouraged to resist LCDC "by those interests who argue for local control where, of course, their access and influence is greater." Acknowledging the significance of goals that the legislature had written and delivering "factually supported, legally defensible goal statements," he hoped, would retain critical political support and prevent capture (Day, 1974c).

The commissioners incorporated some of Cogan's recommendations, but they accepted Day's suggestion—Schell dissented—to work with the existing ten interim goals: (1) preservation of air, water, and land resource quality; (2) conservation of open space and protection of natural and scenic resources; (3) provision for recreational needs; (4) conservation of prime farmlands for production of crops; (5) provision for an orderly and efficient transition between urban and rural land uses; (6) protection of life and property in natural hazard areas; (7) provision of a safe, convenient, and efficient transportation system; (8) development of a timely, orderly, and efficient arrangement of public facilities and services; (9) diversification and improvement of the state's economy; and (10) property development that is commensurate with the character and physical limitations of the land.

LCDC added forestlands, shorelands, and citizen involvement to the list. At a round of public hearings in November, the commission would present standards for preparing comprehensive plans and ask for comments about which aspects should be expressed in a goal and which in guidelines. The commissioners agreed to invite responses about four potential areas of critical statewide concern: the Metolius Deer Winter Range, the Columbia River Gorge, the Willamette Greenway, and federal lands. They would not designate activities of statewide significance but would instead require local governments to address the activities set out in SB 100 in their comprehensive plans. Consideration of coastal issues would be delayed until OCCDC's plan was completed (Cogan, 1974h; LCDC, 1974b; Smith, D., 1974).

While some of the goals added to the SB 10 list were among those being developed by staff and technical advisory committees (forestlands, shorelands, and comprehensive plan process and content), a few that had been specifically under development (energy sources, estuaries and wetlands, housing) would be subsumed under other topics and plans. An explicit carrying-capacity goal made its first appearance on the list, as did goals related to natural hazards, recreation, open space, natural and scenic resources, and public facilities and services.

There was no template for writing land-use goals that would carry the force of law. The process of developing and adopting legally binding goals in Oregon was a lightning rod, attracting opinions from local governments, state agencies, industry groups, environmental organizations, planners, and citizen activists on what goals ought to be included and what their substance ought to be. Not surprisingly, attorneys associated with those interests would monitor the process.

The Road to Goal Adoption

A period of intense activity followed the October 11 meeting, as the commissioners and staff focused on developing goals and guidelines and critical area designations. On October 24, DLCD distributed an eight-page tabloid presenting the outcomes of the commission's deliberations, titled, "Public Hearings on <u>Draft</u> Statewide Land Use Goals, Guidelines, and Critical

Areas." Underscoring "Draft" signaled that LCDC was still in listening mode (Land Conservation and Development Commission, 1974c).

The introduction to the Public Hearings draft contained a set of policy statements to frame the goals, guidelines, and critical areas. Each of twelve goals, not including proposals for citizen involvement and plan process and content, was presented as a statement taken directly from the relevant section of SB 100. For example:

> Carrying Capacity as a Determinant of Property Development. Goal: To insure that the planning and development of properties within the state is commensurate with the character and physical limitations of the land.

A sub-goal statement followed, along with definitions of key terms and the guidelines. Assignments of statements either to the goal, sub-goal, or definitions—all of which would be legally binding mandates—or to the guidelines—which would not be legally binding—engendered intense debate. Four areas of critical statewide concern were also identified for possible designation.

LCDC reactivated and restructured the technical advisory committees in light of its October 11 decisions. Now the commission wanted the technical advisors to react to the goals and guidelines in the Public Hearings draft, address the issue of regionalizing the proposed goals, assess in broad terms the impacts and consequences of the proposed goals, and identify the type and magnitude of potential conflicts among the goals, especially in rural/urban fringe areas and on shorelands. A committee was established to comment specifically on the critical area proposals (Schell, 1974d).

In November, the commission held seventeen public hearings to take testimony on the draft. Commissioners and staff then revised the introductory policy statements, goals, and guidelines and the proposals for critical areas in light of the testimony and the recommendations received from the technical advisory committees. LCDC adopted the revisions on November 30 and distributed "Final Public Hearing on Revised Draft" (Land Conservation and Development Commission, 1974d). The final public hearing was held in Salem on December 13.

Several individuals and organizations that had been active participant/observers during law-making processes in 1973 and goal development in 1974 subjected both drafts to detailed critiques. Association of Oregon

Counties lobbyist Gordon Fultz (Fultz, 1974b, c, d, e), Homebuilders Association lobbyist Fred VanNatta (VanNatta, 1974b, c), and Realtors/ Associated Oregon Industries lobbyist Steve Hawes (Hawes, 1974a, b) were prominent among those providing extensive responses. Washington County planning director Martin Cramton (1974) and City of Eugene planning director John Porter (1974a, b) also commented extensively. Environmental organizations crafted a collective response: OEC's land use committee prepared a pamphlet in cooperation with OSPIRG, Oregon Shores, Northwest Environmental Defense Center, Sierra Club, Central Cascade Conservation Council, and Natural Resources Law Institute. The citizen engagement organization Tri County New Politics collaborated on the effort. Twenty-five people put together the document; thirteen of them served as advisors on various technical committees (OEC, et al., 1974).

In light of the complexity and controversial nature of land-use policy, it isn't surprising that the goals LCDC initially proposed included some vaguely worded ones, some overlaps and conflicts, nor that they might lead to unanticipated consequences. In addition, expressing an exhaustion that many participants may have felt, Eugene's John Porter told LCDC that things had moved too fast.

> I personally have attended every meeting, workshop and hearing in this process and as a professional planner, I have not been able to understand or keep up with what was happening. Receiving this last document [the November 30 tabloid] in the mail on December 10, and trying to get the Eugene Planning Commission and/or the City Council to make some comments, either by today [December 13] or by the 20th [the written comment deadline], in some intelligent manner is virtually impossible." (Porter, 1974)

Nevertheless, LCDC met its deadline to adopt planning goals, guidelines, and proposed critical area designations. The October 24th and November 30th drafts, the responses to them, and the decisions the commissioners made at their December 27th meeting chart the evolution of conflict and compromise about the nature and extent of discretion available to state and local governments and the balance between conservation and development objectives.

Chapter 6
Adopting Statewide Planning Goals: LCDC, Stakeholders, and the Politics of Conflict Resolution

> *"If the . . . goals adopted by [LCDC] are too specific and technical, the commission will be accused of usurpation. If the goals are stated too generally, they will be meaningless because virtually any local planning decision could be interpreted as meeting loose state requirements."*—Register-Guard, *Eugene*

Local government and industry representatives argued during goal development that the Land Conservation and Development Commission's proposals permitted local governments to exercise far less discretion to tailor their planning processes to particular circumstances and to balance potentially competing state and local interests than the legislature had intended in SB 100. In their view, the proposed statewide planning goals were weighted too heavily toward conservation objectives, and they wanted the flexibility to plan for alternative outcomes.

Gordon Fultz was "extremely concerned" that the commission had not followed "the Legislative intent and the workable process by which local government was to prepare comprehensive plans" (Fultz, 1974b). Steve Hawes agreed:

> [S]pecific statements within your proposed goals curb [their] ability to carry on a comprehensive land use planning process applicable to their own jurisdiction. Goal policy statements should not be so specific as to eliminate alternative planning considerations which could be used in different areas of the state under different conditions to reach localized compliance with goals.

Associated Oregon Industries wanted LCDC to know that it was

> supportive of the land use planning effort. However, many of our
> members are concerned with the general preservation direction of
> the goals. Many feel that if a planning body's motivation is towards
> preservation, it could be achieved and easily supported . . . On the
> other hand, if a planning group wishes to accomplish something in
> the development area, it would have difficulty . . . finding justifica-
> tion for doing so. (Associated Oregon Industries, 1974)

State agencies were concerned as well. The Oregon Department of
Transportation, for example, told LCDC: "The more detailed and numerous the guidelines, the greater the likelihood that many valid plans and
projects will be impeded. Certainly a point can be reached at which little
can be accomplished without lengthy delays and/or legal involvement"
(Oregon Department of Transportation, 1974).

State agencies were positioning themselves to deal with perceived
threats to their resources, their missions, and their established intergovernmental and private-sector relationships. Local governments wanted
to make sure they retained their connections and discretion. Industry
groups generally shared the state and local government perspective and
encouraged their members to resist regulations that would increase costs
and disrupt established ties. Everyone acknowledged the difficulties LCDC
faced, but they also wanted recognition for their support during the 1973
legislative session and their participation on technical committees and at
workshops and hearings. They pledged to continue working with LCDC to
achieve the best possible outcome.

Steve Hawes, for example, gave LCDC a political update following
publication of the revised proposals in November: "As you may have
heard following a meeting of the [Realtors] Executive Committee . . .
OAR endorses the legislative concepts in SB 100 but [has] reservations
about specific points covered in your proposed statewide planning goals
and guidelines." While realtors acknowledged that some regulation
was necessary and comprehensive planning would be beneficial both
for individual property owners and the private enterprise system, the
organization wanted to keep government intervention to a minimum.
Hawes assured LCDC, though, that "we are not prepared, and indeed,
have affirmed our position that we will not walk away from this process

if all of our concerns or suggestions are not met in your proposed goals and guidelines."

Environmentalists came at the issues from a different angle. They had supported SB 100 because they believed that local governments exercised too much discretion, which sometimes had environmentally destructive and economically inefficient consequences. That was why a strong state role in planning was necessary in the first place, and they sought detailed, specific language in the goals and clear priorities among them in order to achieve through administrative politics what they had been unable to secure in the legislative arena.

Many Oregon planners strongly supported the goals of environmental activism and they agreed that a strong state role was necessary in land-use planning. Some planners working in local government settings, however, also thought that putting together a plan that their elected officials would willingly adopt required room to maneuver and the ability to respond to local concerns. Local planners whose comprehensive land-use plans had already been adopted reminded LCDC that the commission was supposed to take their work into account. Reopening a recently adopted plan—for example, Washington County's National Association of Counties award-winning plan that environmental activists saw as a generally applicable model—was anathema (Cramton, 1974). Local planners preferred an approach based on performance standards, one that enabled them to tailor their strategies to particular circumstances.

Still, there was some support for LCDC's initial proposals. Bob Stacey at Oregon Environmental Council/OSPIRG, for example, was pleasantly surprised: "The format of the goals and guidelines promises a good deal of clear guidance to local governments and their planners, as well as a sense of continuity from the standards of SB 10 . . . to the new LCDC goals." The influence of an environmentally oriented perspective on the technical committees that Steve Schell had appointed and among commission members and Department of Land Conservation and Development staff was apparent in the sub-goal statements and definitions, but, Stacey observed, "What bugs most people . . . is the question of conflicts and priorities" (Stacey, 1974d). Environmentalists and the planners aligned with them worried that priorities for resolving conflicts between conservation and development goals were simply not clear enough.

In the introduction to its October draft, LCDC had included a section on priorities and conflicts: "LCDC, by developing and adopting goals, establishes priorities. As goals become more specific, priorities become clearer. More specific goals and priorities will be developed in the future" (Land Conservation and Development Commission, 1974c). Until LCDC got to that point, though, planning agencies were told to take specific conflicts into account, such as renewable versus non-renewable resources, non-pollutant versus possible pollutant, and less energy consuming versus more energy consuming. Agencies were to evaluate the economic, social, environmental, and social-cultural effects of their proposed strategies to achieve the goals. Their comprehensive plans should demonstrate that consideration was given to those conflicts and indicate how they were resolved and what priorities were established.

Evaluating impacts would enable LCDC to learn more about establishing priorities and about the extent to which goals should be made more specific. "If the impact is great," LCDC advised, then "the goal may have to be more specific and detailed in order to provide less margin for error." The commission was willing to say that "particular attention should be given to the conflict between rural, i.e., the agricultural, forest and open space land, on the one hand, and urban and urbanizing land on the other." Still, a majority was not willing to go along with a principle urged by commission members Steve Schell and Dorothy Anderson: "carrying capacity and resource capability would be bases upon which the conflicts would be addressed and the goals developed . . . Priority of use for the lands in the state shall be based on the productive capability of the land itself" or an explicit statement that priority be given to preserving agricultural land. The introduction to the first draft also put off specifying regional differences. Statements in the introduction, in any case, were not legally binding.

Two Oregon State University political scientists, the authors of *State Land Use Policies: Winners and Losers*, urged LCDC to include explicit conflict-resolution mechanisms. They were particularly concerned about the conflict between constraints on the supply of land for residential development and the availability of affordable housing. They hypothesized about likely future directions in Oregon based on their studies of other states: environmental groups would form alliances with local citizens who were concerned about the effects of population and economic growth on their social circumstances; developers, realtors, and lenders would oppose them; the stalemate would prevent the emergence of a set of agreed-upon priorities for ten to fifteen years. "Such piecemeal emergence of policies," they concluded, "will favor the organized interests at the expense of the unorganized and especially the lower and lower middle classes."

To prevent that scenario from playing out in Oregon, they urged LCDC to address the conflicts over priorities that the commissioners were avoiding.

> Continued postponement is a luxury which we believe cannot be accepted . . . one of the consequences with land use planning is that it limits the availability of land for development and thereby raises the price of land for housing. Unless this consequence is addressed directly and compensatory measures taken, adequate housing for the lower middle classes may be eliminated.

While dealing with conflicts directly and establishing priorities might appear to be politically riskier than "seeking consensus for the rather vague and often conflicting goals presently articulated" in its initial proposals, they thought it would strengthen LCDC in the future (Godwin and Shepard, 1974).

Although Fred VanNatta generally thought local governments ought to exercise as much discretion as possible, he used the professors' conclusion about the equity aspects of statewide land-use planning to justify calling for the inclusion of housing as a statewide planning goal. VanNatta also wanted LCDC to explicitly prohibit local government moratoria on development, and the commission agreed to include the prohibition in its revised proposals (VanNatta, 1974b).

Environmental activists tried to supply the explicit priorities and related conflict-resolution methods that LCDC had not yet provided. They sought to specify the planning context within which local governments would preserve natural resource lands as well as prevent the equity-related problems the OSU faculty members had identified. In response to those suggestions, LCDC revised its introductory material to identify agriculture as the "most important goal." The commission clearly intended to send an important signal, although the priority still was not binding. The commission also described what local governments should do when it was not possible to apply a goal to a property or situation: justify an exception via a designated process. The exceptions process was intended to be a safety

valve, especially regarding the designation of agricultural land (Land Conservation and Development Commission, 1974d).

VanNatta challenged the new policy declaration: "Shelter equals agricultural land in importance in the citizen's life. Housing merits equal priority treatment with agriculture or . . . all goals should be treated equally and
priority determinations be left to the local jurisdictions." This position was
in line with what most counties and cities wanted to see.

Identifying agriculture as a priority was a positive step, Richmond
thought, but he wanted LCDC to add clear language to that effect in its
proposed Agricultural Lands goal. Given the legal distinction between goals
and guidelines, he argued, "LCDC should accomplish its most important
land use purposes by goals instead of guidelines." After reading the October
draft, he concluded: "The material in [it] under the heading 'guidelines'
contains LCDC's most important comprehensive land use planning provisions. Without the guidelines, the goals are too generally worded to be
useful" (Richmond, 1974o). He strongly endorsed, though, the approach
taken by the Agricultural Lands technical advisory committee and placed
it in the context of LCDC's ability to implement statewide planning goals.
The committee's proposed goal statement said that agricultural lands should
be zoned for exclusive farm use, and agricultural land was designated as
such on the basis of U.S. Soil Conservation Service classifications—classes I
through IV in western Oregon and I through VI in eastern Oregon, as well as
other soils depending on circumstances. "When LCDC receives petitions to
review local government action for compliance with this goal," Richmond
pointed out, "evidence relied on by local government as 'substantial evidence' will be measured by specific, unambiguous language" (Richmond,
1974n). He urged Day to adopt that approach as often as possible.

The legal distinction between goals and guidelines continued to generate controversy. The first public draft had instructed that "where the
guidelines are not used, the responsibility lies with local government to
show that they have met the goal" (Land Conservation and Development
Commission, 1974c). Gordon Fultz told LCDC that his organization "most
violently" disagreed "with the current interpretation of guidelines." He
encouraged the commission to keep the political context in mind:

> There has been a major difference of opinion among many who
> have followed the process as to whether such guidelines should be

directional to provide an easy course of action or should be general and optional to allow maximum local control . . . To erode all options would not gain LCDC and/or the land-use planning process any friends from local government nor would it give them any meaningful support which they desire. (Fultz, 1974c)

Steve Hawes agreed that requiring local governments to justify the choice of an approach that was an alternative to an LCDC guideline was inconsistent with SB 100.

The Eugene *Register-Guard* summed up the political dimension of the conflict confronting those advocating on behalf of conservation objectives:

> If the . . . goals adopted by [LCDC] are too specific and technical, the commission will be accused of usurpation. If the goals are stated too generally, they will be meaningless because virtually any local planning decision could be interpreted as meeting loose state requirements. ("State's dilemma in planning," 1974)

LCDC proposed an administrative rule clarifying the status of guidelines:

> Guidelines are suggested directions that would aid local governments in activating the mandated goals . . . Governmental units shall review the guidelines set forth for the goals and either utilize the guidelines or develop alternate means that will achieve the goals. Comprehensive plans shall state how the guidelines or alternative means utilized achieve the goals. Guidelines or the alternative means selected by governmental bodies will be part of LCDC's process of evaluating comprehensive plans for compliance with goals.

Fultz appreciated the change and told his constituents:

> The definition has been changed to . . . alleviate the burden of proof requirements . . . A local government may use alternatives to guidelines without substantiating the non-use of those guidelines. In justifying compliance with a goal, a local government must indicate the means utilized to comply. The new definition of guidelines lessens the abrasiveness of many guidelines proposed in the initial draft.

At its December 27 meeting, LCDC adopted fourteen statewide planning goals—two process goals, five conservation goals, and seven development goals—and proposed to study the designation of two areas of critical state-wide concern. The commissioners had significantly changed most of what they had presented in October. Their choices reflected efforts to balance the conflicting pressures bearing on them: conservation versus development; state versus local discretion; public versus private interests. They also knew that their decisions at the meeting were just the first step in a continuing process. Additional steps depended on getting funding during the 1975 legislative session.

Critical Areas of Statewide Concern

The designation of areas of critical statewide concern had always been an intensely controversial feature of SB 100. Environmentalists strongly supported designating the four areas that LCDC originally proposed to study: the Metolius Deer Winter Range, the Columbia River Gorge, the Willamette Greenway, and federal lands. Local government and industry representatives opposed designation before more studies had been done and criteria established, and state agencies were critical as well (Oregon Wildlife Commission and Fish Commission of Oregon, 1974). In response, LCDC dropped three of the four areas of critical concern. It was not appropriate, they concluded, to single out the Metolius Deer Winter Range without considering all wildlife winter ranges in the state—about six million acres. A Willamette River Greenway Plan was forthcoming, and it made sense to wait for it, especially since LCDC had final approval on the plan. And federal land issues were sufficiently complex to warrant special legislative attention. Going into the final public hearing, the commission proposed to study just one area, the Columbia River Gorge.

Governor McCall was disappointed. He had specifically asked L. B. Day to designate the Metolius Deer Winter Range as an area of critical state-wide concern because of increasing pressure on county officials there to permit development of home sites. McCall had worked closely with Henry Richmond, who served on the Metolius technical advisory committee, and OSPIRG and OEC were calling for intervention. At LCDC's December public hearing, both McCall and Governor-elect Robert Straub appealed to LCDC to propose the designation (McCall, 1974c; Straub, 1974). The commissioners changed direction again and decided to study designating both the Metolius Deer Winter Range and the Columbia Gorge.

Goals Dropped

The commissioners decided to drop two goals that environmentalists strongly supported: Carrying Capacity, one of the original SB 10 goals, and Shorelands, which had been added to the list. The Carrying Capacity goal stipulated that the character and physical limitations of the land would be a major determinant of development decisions. Hawes, VanNatta, and Fultz—joined on this issue by Oregon Farm Bureau representative Howard Fujii (Fujii, 1974b, c)—argued that the goal should be dropped. Carrying capacity was an umbrella concept that summed up what all of the substantive goals intended to accomplish, they argued, and it needed more study before it could usefully be applied, especially when determining a population limit. While there might be adequate science available to calculate the carrying capacity of a stream or an air shed, VanNatta was skeptical that planners and social scientists had the tools to determine the carrying capacity of people on the land. A representative of the Oregon Water Resources Department told LCDC: "There is such a broad spectrum and scope of alternatives and desires involved in the human element that we feel a specific carrying capacity would be almost impossible to develop" (Wright, 1974).

Planners were divided. Martin Cramton and John Porter, for example, were supportive. Several planners in smaller cities and in rural areas, however, told LCDC to drop the goal because it would be beyond their technical capacity to address it. Some, though, thought it was an important idea, and wanted more specificity about how to work with the goal.

While LCDC dropped carrying capacity as a goal, the commissioners added analyses of the physical characteristics and limitations of the land and natural resources as a guideline to each of the substantive goals. They hoped the change would encourage local governments to incorporate an approach similar to an environmental impact analysis into their comprehensive planning processes.

Shorelands, a goal that the commission also dropped, was initially defined as wetlands and "all lands within the 100 year floodplains or 200 feet from rivers, lakes, streams, estuaries and the ocean, whichever is greater." The sub-goal statement directed that such lands "shall be designated for water-related uses or uses which will cause little reduction in vegetative cover." The statement reflected substantial environmentalist influence in the technical advisory committee and the presence of Steve Schell and Paul Rudy on the commission.

Environmental organizations wanted to strengthen the goal by requiring setback zones on shorelands. The state forester saw it differently: "there are 110,000 miles of Class I streams in Oregon which are those with significant fish populations. Two hundred feet on each side of these streams alone is in excess of 5 1/3 million acres"—about 8 percent of the state's land area. He also reminded LCDC that his agency already regulated activities on lands adjacent to streams under the terms of the state Forest Practices Act (Schroeder, 1974).

The State Water Board also was critical of the definition of shorelands: "In the Willamette Valley for instance, the 100-year flood plain is by and large the entire lower part of the valley and is vastly different than a small strip of land 200 feet from the bed and banks of each stream" (Wright, 1974). Martin Cramton argued that the definition was inappropriate for urban and suburban areas—it included too much land—and that Washington County had already adopted rigorous zoning standards in its flood plains that he did not want to revisit. Steve Hawes articulated the industry point of view that a much more general definition of shorelands was appropriate and that more studies were needed before any specific regulations could be developed. LCDC was persuaded. A revised version dropped the goal statements that directed how shorelands ought to be managed and deleted the numerical standards in the definition. The guideline advising that cities and counties "should establish" setback zones was changed to "should consider."

Environmental activists were very unhappy. The Oregon Shores executive director told the commissioners: "the goal statement LCDC came up with is much worse than none at all . . . As a member of the Shorelands technical advisory committee, I want to disassociate myself completely from the unfortunate wording and thrust of the present draft" (Diel, 1974). The League of Cities, Associated Oregon Industries, and the Homebuilders Association wanted more changes, though, that would reduce the goal's coverage.

In the face of the controversy, LCDC dropped the proposed Shorelands goal entirely. A dismayed Steve Schell told the commission at the December 27 meeting:

> The elimination of the shorelands goal is both a mistake and a tragedy . . . SB 100 mandates us to make the difficult decisions on the conservation and development of broad land areas through the

goal process. For shorelands we have been unable to make these decisions. Thus, this Commission fails in its obligation to the legislature and the state. (Schell, 1974c; 2008)

Environmentalists had other concerns as well. The distinction between urban and rural areas, they thought, was relegated to the guidelines for the Transition and Public Facilities and Services goals, and only weakly addressed there. They urged LCDC to consider an Urban Lands goal and provided a starting point: "Urban land shall be used efficiently and rationally. The use of existing urban infrastructure of roads, sewers, retail centers, industrial activity, utilities shall be maximized. Developed land shall not pass into less active or less intensive use than its optimum capacity and best utilization." The proposed guidelines included ensuring a mixture of residential densities; maximizing housing opportunities, especially for low- and moderate-income households, the elderly, and minorities; preserving historic structures; and providing adequate open space, recreation facilities, and wildlife habitat. They also encouraged compact forms of development in order to minimize energy consumption and maximize the efficiency and quality of service delivery—an effort to cluster "mutually supportive" mixed land uses. An Urban Lands goal did not generate support beyond environmental and planning advocates, but portions of it were included in the adopted Urbanization goal as issues that local governments must consider when proposing to establish and change urban growth boundaries.

The Adopted Process-Oriented Goals

SB 100 required that an officially recognized citizen advisory committee orchestrate citizen involvement in local comprehensive planning processes; but it wasn't clear if planning commissions or city and county elected officials could play that role. Gordon Fultz wanted local governments to be able to designate their own planning commissions rather than create a new citizen advisory committee, and the League of Cities agreed. Martin Cramton pointed out that Washington County's award-winning participation program was based on fourteen functioning community planning organizations, and he thought it a serious mistake to require effective programs to change just to comply with a statewide procedural standard (Cramton, 1974). Fultz also registered the counties' concern that, if LCDC's Citizen Involvement Advisory Committee's suggested approach was adopted as a mandatory goal, it would be financially prohibitive and administratively burdensome for local government to implement.

State agencies were also concerned with the proposal's implications. The State Housing Council and the State Housing Division were critical of much of the citizen participation they had seen in planning efforts. Division administrator Greg Smith argued:

> [T]o a large extent, citizen involvement groups in Oregon have sprung up as a negative force, often to prevent low and moderate income housing from being built in given neighborhoods or communities . . . We are, therefore, very concerned that the Citizen Involvement Goal could become a tool by those elements who seek to restrict housing opportunities for Oregon citizens with modest incomes.

Affordable-housing advocates believed that elected local officials were often more representative of their communities than were the people who had attended the goal-development workshops or who joined local citizen-involvement groups (Smith, M., 1974). ODOT weighed in with its own worries: "We anticipate a staffing problem in dealing with approximately 30 county citizens committees. We also anticipate difficulty relating county committees to our statewide studies" (Oregon Department of Transportation, 1974).

LCDC initially addressed many of these concerns in guidelines. The proposed goal statement required that citizens have opportunities to participate in all phases of the planning process. A stipulation that "the citizen involvement program shall be appropriate to the scale of the planning effort" was an attempt to build in legitimate variation in participatory processes across the state. The sub-goal statement, however, still referred to a required "officially recognized citizen advisory committee" and did not explicitly include the possibility of designating existing planning commissions and elected bodies to fill that role. Following its final public hearing in December, however, the commission added language that permitted local elected officials to assign citizen involvement responsibilities to planning commissions or to assume those responsibilities themselves.

LCDC initially presented Guidelines for Comprehensive Planning that called for fifteen different inventories and kinds of data that should be the basis for preparing plans. Gordon Fultz reminded LCDC that local governments would be unable to complete the large number of inventories without financial and technical support. The State Water Board, articulating a concern shared widely by state agencies, told LCDC: "If the counties are to follow these guidelines, the first thing that will happen is a mass exodus to Salem to request information from state agencies at a level and magnitude never before experienced in state government." LCDC needed to take into account the capacity of state agencies to respond to such requests and to prevent them from being overwhelmed by local governments seeking data all at the same time (Wright, 1974).

Much of what was proposed ended up in the guidelines section of a new Land Use Planning goal. The goal itself incorporated elements of the definition of a coordinated comprehensive plan set out in SB 100, and stipulated that

> Plans shall include definition of issues and problems, inventories and other factual information for each applicable statewide goal, evaluation of alternative strategies for development and ultimate policy choices . . . The plans shall be the basis for specific implementation measures. These measures shall be consistent with and adequate to carry out the plans . . . All land use decisions and actions shall be based on the comprehensive plans of cities and counties.

LCDC also incorporated the exceptions process into the goal. When local governments determined that it was not possible to apply one or more goals to particular properties or situations, LCDC required a report that it had the power to challenge. The commission also responded to a request from Washington County property rights activist Jim Allison by adding a requirement that owners of record within 500 feet of an area subject to a proposed plan or zone change shall receive timely written notice to review the proposal (Allison, 1974). In the end, local government representatives generally liked the way the comprehensive planning standards were set out in the new Land Use Planning goal. They were particularly relieved that LCDC had placed the adoption of a capital improvements plan among the guidelines, rather than as a required part of the goal.

The Adopted Conservation Goals

LCDC did not write an explicit priority for agricultural lands, but placed it first among the substantive goals to signal its importance. As initially stated, the goal was "to conserve agricultural land for the production of crops," with a sub-goal requiring that agricultural land be preserved by adopting exclusive farm-use zones. The definition of agricultural land used U.S. Soil Conservation Service classifications—predominantly classes I through IV in western Oregon and I through VI in eastern Oregon— and included "soil upon which economic farm practices can be undertaken and maintained." This goal came closest to meeting the standards Schell, Richmond, Stacey, and Day had advocated. The most appealing aspect of soil classifications for them was that they were objective. Requiring their use would reduce the discretion available to local officials, which the attorneys hoped would depoliticize planning and zoning processes to a significant extent. In addition, defining agricultural land in that way expressed an understanding of land as a resource that was critically important to the future of the state, something more than a commodity whose value fluctuated according to market dynamics.

The use of soil classifications in land-use planning and zoning was well known in Oregon and elsewhere by 1974. The classifications figured prominently in land-use policies in Hawaii (Callies, 1984; Myers, 1976) and British Columbia. The bill that L. B. Day sponsored in 1967, which was based on a 1965 California law, referred explicitly to soil classes I and II, and Senate Bill 13 in 1969 proposed to give the OSU scientists money to complete soil surveys.

OSPIRG intern David Aamodt was a member of the Agricultural Lands technical advisory committee that proposed the goal statement and definitions. The committee worked closely with LCDC farmer-member Jim Smart, who supported including Class IV soils in the definition for western Oregon as a result of his own experience and his familiarity with the situation of those farming around him. Unlike the adopted Washington County Framework Plan, which used soil classification to designate exclusive farm-use zones, the proposed goal did not specify a minimum lot size in such zones. It said only that a minimum lot size used by a local government "shall be appropriate for the continuation of the existing commercial, agricultural enterprise within the area." "Commercial" was left undefined.

The Farm Bureau's Howard Fujii suggested an amendment to include livestock, based on the contribution livestock and dairy production made to the state's farm economy. He cautioned that "minimum lot sizes should not be related to use of land for agricultural purposes," because some farm operations were feasible on small lots. It would be best, he told the commission, to delete the reference to minimum lot size altogether. Soil classes also should be deleted because conditions varied so much from place to place. He argued that county planning commissions and governments, following the comprehensive planning guidelines and the proposed Citizen Involvement goal, could "use proper judgment to conserve agricultural land" (Fujii, 1974b). Steve Hawes agreed.

Washington County also had a problem with the proposed definition of agricultural lands. "There is no way we can justify Class IV lands," Martin Cramton told LCDC. "Our plan cannot meet the proposed State standards, thereby, it would appear what the County has accomplished in the area of exclusive farm land zoning based upon a comprehensive plan is to be reopened for question."

The environmental coalition evaluated the Agricultural Lands and the Transition from Rural to Urban Land Use goals as a package. Bob Stacey, who served on the Transition technical advisory committee, was especially concerned with a potential conflict between the two goals. LCDC had not articulated any clear priorities that state and local planners could use to resolve conflicts, particularly on the fringes of growing urban areas. He told LCDC:

> The areas included by the goals overlap, and local planners are given no clear criteria for drawing a line or choosing where to grow . . . Giving each community the responsibility for choosing between urban expansion and agricultural preservation, without giving locals any indication of the state's sense of priorities, may lead to numerous appeals to LCDC attacking local interpretations of those goals. (Stacey, 1974e)

The solution, the environmental organizations suggested, was to include a requirement that growth boundaries be drawn around urban areas and to add an Agricultural Transition goal making it clear that there was a greater public need for agricultural products than there was for urban expansion. Local governments and their industry allies argued that such a clearly stated priority would limit too severely local governments' ability to make judgments about the balance between conservation and development.

LCDC added a safety valve to the definition in Agricultural Lands: "except such lands which are presently in or necessary to existing non-farm uses of a permanent nature." The goal statement was changed from "conserve agricultural land for the production of crops" to "preserve agricultural land for farm use" to reflect a broader definition of agriculture. The definition of agricultural land, though, still referred to "economic" farm uses, a term that itself remained undefined.

Realtors still believed, as did the counties, that the requirement that agricultural lands be zoned for exclusive farm use unnecessarily restricted the ability of local governments to preserve small farm ownerships. Realtors urged LCDC to eliminate the exclusive farm-use zone requirements and "insert a new planning guideline directing the use of EFU zones where appropriate" (Hawes, 1974b). Hector Macpherson told LCDC that he liked the approach to defining agricultural land, and believed that exclusive farm-use zoning was the only way to preserve it (Macpherson, 1974b).

While Henry Richmond was pleased that the goal retained its specificity, he told LCDC that it still had some work to do:

> The principal land use problem in Oregon today is the highly adverse economic and environmental impact of urban sprawl on productive agricultural lands . . . With a few modifications, and with vigorous implementation over the next eighteen months, LCDC's agricultural goal and the goal for transition will bring the State of Oregon closer to the overriding objective of stopping destructive sprawl and leapfrog development on the rich agricultural soils of the Willamette Valley, as well as elsewhere in the state.

He recommended deleting the reference to economic farm use altogether. He was convinced that it made the most sense to use soil classifications to define agricultural lands—they were developed by independent experts and were objectively applied by independent observers—and that method "also has the advantage of tying the definition to the productivity of the land resource itself, which is the basic concern" (Richmond, 1974p). Multnomah County's Don Clark agreed and supported setting straightforward priorities among the goals, beginning with the preservation of agricultural land (Clark, 1974).

LCDC dropped the language about "economic" farm use and added a section to the goal statement setting out a required process for converting rural agricultural land to urbanizable land. Among the five factors mentioned was "the retention of Class I, II, III, and IV soils in farm use" (Land

Conservation and Development Commission, 1974e). This was an attempt to respond to the environmentalists' and planners' call for specificity and prioritization, although local governments were required only to consider those factors. In order to convert rural agricultural land to urbanizable land, local governments were required to use the exceptions process in the Land Use Planning goal, which contained its own set of criteria.

Steve Schell saw the adopted goal as a real achievement: "LCDC has stated in clear and unmistakable terms that prime agricultural lands in Oregon are to be preserved and maintained to help feed those who will suffer from a world famine that many regard as inevitable (Schell, 1974c)." Even though LCDC had not explicitly made the Agricultural Lands goal the most important of the fourteen, he believed its placement in the list of goals and the criteria set out regulating the conversion of rural land to urbanizable land indicated its significance. However, the introduction to "Statewide Planning Goals and Guidelines," which LCDC issued after the goals were adopted, explicitly stated "all goals are of equal importance. The order in which the goals are printed does not indicate any order of priority" (LCDC, 1974e).

LCDC did not respond to the concern about the potentially challenging impact the definition of agricultural lands would have on the ability of local government planners to craft plans and ordinances that would both comply with the goal and be acceptable to local elected officials. Agricultural Lands, as adopted, embodied the fact-based detail and specificity that environmental advocates and state-level planners sought, and it is not surprising that implementing it generated immediate controversy. At the same time, the absence of a definition of "commercial" agriculture in exclusive farm-use zones also produced controversy, as local governments adopted widely varying approaches to specifying minimum lot sizes in their plans and ordinances.

Forestlands was the other conservation goal that addressed development issues. LCDC initially proposed that commercial forestland be defined as land capable of producing 100 board feet per acre per year. Such land "shall be retained primarily for the production of wood fibre, but also for other forest uses, consistent with the primary goal." Forest uses were defined largely in terms of the production of trees for forest products and environmental benefits associated with forests. Recreation was mentioned, but only those uses that were compatible with production and the mainte-

nance of environmental values were permitted. The environmental coalition sought to increase the coverage of the proposed goal by lowering the
numerical standard to 50 cubic feet of wood fiber and by requiring commercial foresters to manage their lands on a sustained-yield basis (O'Toole,
1974). LCDC's proposed goal included nothing about forest practices.

Industry and local government representatives opposed a distinction
between commercial and other forestlands. Ward Armstrong—a member
of the Forestlands technical advisory committee—testified on behalf of the
Weyerhaeuser Company:

> [W]e are not yet in a position to state with finality the optimum
> use of all of these lands presently occupied with trees—and indeed
> this should be the task of the county planning commissions . . .
> [They] are in the best position to judge whether our forested lands
> should remain for the commercial production of wood products or
> whether other uses should be permitted or, indeed, encouraged.

He suggested a revised goal statement—"Existing forest land uses shall
be protected unless proposed changes are in conformance with the comprehensive plan" —and supported eliminating a definition for commercial
forestland (Armstrong, 1974). The numerical standard approach based on
specific growing capacities and the way commercial forestland was defined
were at odds with the multi-use framework that industry favored. Industry spokespeople strongly opposed the inclusion of forest management
practices in LCDC goals and guidelines, arguing that the Oregon Forest
Practices Act adequately covered that subject (Armstrong, 1974; Richen,
1974).

LCDC dropped the distinction between commercial and other forestland, and the numerical standard, and revised the definition of forest uses
to include support services related to outdoor recreation. The revised goal
statement included the language that Armstrong wanted, and the commissioners chose not to venture into forest management territory. LCDC also
added a requirement that forestlands be mapped and designated according
to the site classes in a U.S. Forest Service manual, an idea that Richmond
had advocated. Changing forestland uses to another use, though, required
only that the productive capacity of the land be considered and evaluated.
Environmental activists were deeply disappointed and believed that the
goal was seriously flawed.

The remaining conservation goals did not generate nearly as much controversy. The environmental coalition was pleased with LCDC's initial proposal for an Open Spaces, Scenic Areas and Natural Resources goal, as far as it went. The proposed goal required local governments to inventory the location, quantity, and quality of such areas and resources within their jurisdictions; identify inconsistencies between preserving such areas and resources in their original character and other uses; and analyze the economic, social, environmental, and energy consequences of inconsistent uses. The environmental coalition recommended that LCDC add historic areas to the list, as well as several sensitive environmental areas, and urged the commission to explicitly address how conflicts among inconsistent uses should be resolved. LCDC responded by adding historic areas, sites, structures, and objects as well as desert areas and groundwater resources. Recreation-related trails and wild and scenic waterways also became part of Goal 5, now called Open Spaces, Scenic and Historic Areas and Natural Resources.

Forest industry representatives generally articulated a property rights concern in relation to the goal: "Considering the amount of land in the State of Oregon that is now in public ownership, we believe it is the responsibility of your Commission to assure compensation to private owners for any restrictions in the use of their lands caused by open space, natural and scenic resource designations" (Richen, 1974). While property-rights arguments against regulating land use were heard frequently in Oregon and throughout the United States, during the goal-development process they surfaced primarily in relation to the designations in Goal 5.

In an attempt to establish priorities when conflict resolution was required, the commission stipulated that after economic, social, environmental, and energy consequences had been determined for any identified inconsistencies, programs had to be developed to achieve the goal. The commissioners chose not to clarify, though, the ways in which those programs should resolve conflicts.

One of the important sub-goal statements for the initially proposed Air, Water, and Land Resources Quality goal said that discharges from future development, when combined with discharges already occurring, could neither exceed the carrying capacity nor degrade air and water resources. Environmental organizations supported the proposed goal, but others challenged definitions. Steve Hawes noted that "degradation" was not defined in the goal and suggested that the sub-goal incorporate a reference to compliance with pollution-control laws adopted by the federal and state governments. LCDC agreed and made other clarifications suggested by industry and local government representatives to Goal 6.

The initially proposed goal for Areas Subject to Floods, Landslides and Other Natural Hazards also reflected an environmentalist perspective. The sub-goal statement directed, for example, that development "shall not be located in known areas of natural hazards." Hawes suggested instead that local governments be permitted to determine the extent of hazards in their jurisdictions and what kinds of development could safely be accommodated. LCDC followed Hawes's recommendation, permitting development in known disaster and hazard areas if proper safeguards are included. That change, as well as other clarifications suggested by industry and local government representatives, was adopted in Goal 7: Areas Subject to Natural Disasters and Hazards.

The Adopted Development Goals

Some of the development goals met little resistance. Goal 8: Recreational Needs generated no controversy and did not change substantively on its way to adoption. The initial version of Goal 9: Economy of the State, which was intended to diversify and improve the economy in the state, drew relatively few comments. Associated Oregon Industries wanted the language of the goal to more clearly communicate how important it was to encourage economic development by providing sufficient commercial and industrial land in a variety of price ranges (Associated Oregon Industries, 1974). LCDC agreed and added some new language: "Alternative sites suitable for economic growth and expansion shall be designated" in the plans of those jurisdictions that wanted to grow and had underutilized natural and human resources. Commissioners, staff, and many legislators were concerned about the economic decline that was increasingly affecting rural Oregon, and the adopted language, especially the bow to communities wanting to grow, suggested how politically difficult it would be for LCDC to formulate a state growth policy should it be authorized to do so.

Senate Bill 10 had not included a housing goal, and LCDC did not include one in its own initial proposals, but both Fred VanNatta and State Housing Council chair Betty Niven suggested language for a goal and guidelines (Niven, 1974; State Housing Council, 1974). The goal that was eventually added—Goal 10: Housing—required that

Buildable lands for residential use shall be inventoried and plans shall encourage the availability of adequate numbers of housing units at price ranges and rent levels which are commensurate with the financial capabilities of Oregon households and allow for flexibility of housing location, type and density.

The commission intended to address the supply of affordable housing through the language related to price and type, but the requirements to "encourage" availability and allow for "flexibility" regarding location, type, and density remained undefined.

LCDC upgraded a buildable lands inventory from guideline status to the goal statement in the adopted goal and changed the word "design" in an earlier version to "type" to clarify that the intent was to encourage the availability of housing "at price ranges and rent levels which are commensurate with the financial capabilities of Oregon households." In response to industry-expressed concerns, the definition of buildable lands included "availability" along with suitability and necessity for residential use. A guideline suggested that local government plans incorporate the phasing in of public facilities and services in relation to housing development, a provision advocated by environmental organizations. Other guidelines also incorporated their proposals: encouraging increased densities in relation to key infrastructure facilities in order to enhance the efficiency with which urban land was used and coordinating the supply of facilities and services and the dispersion of low-income housing.

The initial version of Goal 11: Public Facilities and Services prompted some disagreement between local government and industry, on the one hand, and environmentalists, on the other. The goal required and defined an "orderly arrangement" as a "plan which coordinates the type, phasing, location and delivery of public facilities and services in a manner which best supports the attainment of desired land use patterns." The intention was to ensure that services and facilities would be supplied in a timely fashion to accommodate the demand for them. Fred VanNatta and Gordon Fultz wanted the word "phasing" deleted because it would lead certain properties to inflate in value, making them more expensive for a builder to purchase. The environmental organizations strongly supported phasing, however, and incorporated it into their proposed Urban Lands goal. LCDC dropped the word "phasing" from the definition, though, and moved the preparation and utilization of a capital improvement program to a guide-line. Revised goal and sub-goal statements did include, however, Arnold Cogan's recommendation that each plan had to address the provision of critical facilities, such as transportation, water, sewerage, solid waste, and schools, and the Association of Oregon Counties and the League of Oregon Cities supported incorporating the provision of key facilities into local planning processes (Fultz, 1974d).

The initial version of Goal 12: Transportation required a balanced system that "avoids principal reliance upon any one mode of transport, [and] reduces and/or prevents the increase of adverse social, economic, environmental and energy costs resulting from undue utilization of any one modal type." Those stipulations clearly reflected an environmentalist perspective on the problems created by a pattern of development depen-dent on automobiles and highways. ODOT did not like the tone of the goal, which in its view stressed the negative—the necessity to avoid, reduce, and coordinate. The goal should include positive contributions, ODOT advised, such as access to economic, social, and recreational activities. The agency also was irritated that the goal called for a balanced system, a phrase it thought was "over-worked and under-defined." It saw a challenge looming to the legal role of the Oregon Transportation Commission regarding the allocation of state and federal transportation dollars to local governments (Oregon Department of Transportation, 1974). Finally, ODOT argued that avoiding principal reliance on one mode of transport might lead to inef-ficient investments and a decline in effectiveness, a position shared by local government representatives and industry spokesperson Steve Hawes, who told LCDC it was entirely appropriate for some local governments to plan for only one mode of transportation.

L. B. Day was unhappy with the ODOT testimony and wrote OTC chair Glenn Jackson: "Attached is an official policy statement depicting the po-sition of your Commission regarding land use planning . . . The net effect of that statement would be to repeal Senate Bill 100. With help like that, who needs enemies" (Day, 1974d). Nevertheless, LCDC incorporated into the goal the "positive" contributions ODOT had suggested, deleted some of the "negatives," and included a new goal statement about meeting the needs of the transport disadvantaged—those, for example, who lacked access to cars for financial or physical reasons. The revised goal statement also reiterated the requirement that key transport facilities had to be addressed and that "principal reliance on any one mode of transport" must be avoided.

While energy conservation was not among the goals initially proposed by LCDC, environmental organizations considered it an umbrella goal: land and other natural resources should be managed to minimize energy consumption. The coalition also wanted LCDC to adopt policy guidelines addressing the siting of power plants and transmission lines as activities of statewide significance. Portland Mayor Neil Goldschmidt, a strong supporter of the environmentalist position, told LCDC: "I am compelled . . . to recommend and request that the Commission include—as part of the goals for land use planning—energy conservation as a major subject." He supplied a proposed goal statement and guidelines, including one that read: "the highest priority in land use planning should be given to methods of analysis and implementation measures which will assure that maximum efficiency in energy utilization is followed." A guideline accompanied the priority: "Land use planning should, to the maximum extent possible, combine increasing density gradients along high capacity transportation corridors and stimulate rehabilitation of older homes and buildings" (Goldschmidt, 1974). The recommendation was similar to what the Energy technical advisory committee had been developing and what the environmental coalition recommended.

LCDC responded by including Goal 13: Energy Conservation, which stipulated that "land and uses developed on the land shall be managed and controlled so as to maximize the conservation of all forms of energy, based upon sound economic principles." Two substantive planning objectives included among the guidelines were to recycle and re-use vacant land and land uses that were not energy efficient, and to "combine increasing density gradients along high capacity transportation corridors to achieve greater energy efficiency." Both objectives supported the Urban Lands ideas suggested by environmental organizations.

The Transition goal was needed, according to LCDC's initial proposal, to "provide for an orderly and efficient transition from rural to urban land use." The goal defined rural, urban, and urbanizable land and stipulated that "conversion to urban land uses shall be based on need for further urban expansion compared with the need and suitability for open land uses." Included in the guidelines were growth boundaries, capital improvement programs—including a suggestion that infrastructure supply be coordinated with population and economic growth—and standards to ensure an adequate supply of housing.

In the revised Transition goal, LCDC elevated boundaries around urban areas to goal status in order to distinguish "land which is necessary and suitable for urban uses from land which is necessary and suitable for rural uses." A series of tests were required to determine if it was necessary to convert agricultural to "urbanizable" land, including a requirement that "the proposed use is compatible with related agricultural land [and] the retention of Class 1, 2, 3, and 4 soils in farm use." Henry Richmond saw a "critical defect" in the revised goal:

> [It] provides standards for converting "agricultural land to ur-banizeable land," but not standards for the establishment of the urban growth boundary itself . . . Hence, if the LCDC really means to face up to the basic issue of urban sprawl . . . two changes have to be made . . . Standards must be set to provide for the establishment of the urban growth boundary, and the question of conversion should deal mainly with the issue of conversion of urbanizeable land into urban land, not rural land into urbanizeable land.

He proposed standards for planning urban growth boundaries that included prioritizing the preservation of agricultural lands, particularly those in soil classes I and II, and ensuring compatibility with adjacent lands in agricultural use (Richmond, 1974p).

Boundaries would not be necessary in all cases, Gordon Fultz argued, although he thought they might prevent leapfrog development and "ranchettes" that would increase demand for services. Urban growth boundaries might also simplify the process of annexing land that was outside a city but within growth boundaries. The Association of Oregon Counties, however, suggested that an approach based on coordinating the supply of services and facilities with the demand for them in urban fringe areas would sometimes be appropriate. The League of Oregon Cities agreed in principle with urban growth boundaries but wanted assurance that LCDC's criteria would apply only when urban growth boundaries were first determined; the conversion of land within designated boundaries would then be regulated according to criteria established at the local level.

Fred VanNatta worried about urban growth boundaries. They "just happen to be the current fad in planning," he lamented, and he offered a cautionary tale. The Council of Government planners in Salem had announced, "with fanfare," that there was more than enough vacant or buildable land within their city's urban growth boundary. Developers determined that there was substantially less land available. "We came to find," VanNatta concluded, that "the planners had included such land as the vacant land around the state penitentiary owned by the state." To avoid that kind of problem, the Homebuilders Association recommended that LCDC define available vacant or buildable land "as land listed for sale, or land with the reasonable likelihood of being listing for sale." The commission incorporated the definition into the Housing goal. VanNatta also

URBAN GROWTH BOUNDARIES

There were several examples in Oregon of the use of boundaries to manage growth in the early 1970s. One was the urban service area boundary established in the Eugene-Springfield Metropolitan Area 1990 General Plan, adopted in 1972 by Eugene, Springfield, Lane County, and the Lane Council of Governments. In 1973, the City of La Grande, in northeastern Oregon, incorporated in its comprehensive plan an urban development limit line based on service areas. In the Portland metropolitan area, the Columbia Region Association of Governments General Assembly adopted in early 1974 an Interim Regional Development Policy, which established priority growth areas based on sewer and water supply. The policy was intended to guide development until a regional comprehensive plan was completed. Between March 1973 and March 1974, under the auspices of Mid-Willamette Valley Council of Governments, the Salem Area Comprehensive Plan, an Urban Growth Policies Agreement, and an urban growth boundary were adopted by the City of Salem, Marion County, and Polk County (Bureau of Governmental Research and Service, 1974). Wes Kvarsten played a major role in that process and promoted an urban growth boundary mandate as LCDC developed goals and guidelines. The Salem-area urban growth boundary was known by some as "Kvarsten's Corset." Norma Paulus, a state legislator who served on the Local Boundary Commission, which was also involved in the process, remembered that the growth boundary was known as "Norma's Iron Ring around Salem" (Paulus, 1997).

suggested that LCDC develop a special guide to boundary development. "It really is the critical pivotal decision that will be made," he said.

The Transition goal underwent a significant makeover, emerging as Goal 14: Urbanization. LCDC answered the question of whether criteria on transition applied both to the initial establishment of an urban growth boundary and to the conversion of rural to urbanizable land. Both the establishment and the change of a boundary, the goal read, shall be based on seven factors, including "retention of agricultural land . . . with Class I being the highest priority for retention and Class VI the lowest priority"; "compatibility of the proposed urban uses with nearby agricultural activities"; and "maximum efficiency of land uses within and on the fringe of

The 1973 Washington County Framework Plan designated Intermediate Urban Growth areas around the cities based on a twenty- to forty-year forecast of population and economic growth and the suitability of various parts of the county to accommodate it—yielding, in effect, urban growth boundaries. As a result of its approach to a growth policy, which was based on carrying capacity, the plan explicitly revised downward the trend-based population projection by 17 percent. In addition, the process of transitioning land uses from Intermediate Urban to Urban and from the other categories to Urban Intermediate was specifically governed by the criteria set out in the *Fasano* decision. Ed Sullivan, the Washington County counsel who argued the *Fasano* case before the Oregon Supreme Court, participated actively in shaping the plan. A policy to establish a monitoring system, based on a requirement for an environmental impact statement and a uniform regional data collection system, was included in the plan to manage land-use transitions.

All of these urban boundary-related programs were aimed at preventing urban sprawl, preserving resource lands, and encouraging compact, contiguous urban development in order to minimize service and facility construction and operations costs. The Washington County Framework Plan also used soil classifications to designate resource lands, an associated minimum lot size standard, and an explicit policy for managing land-use transitions. Overall, that plan provided a model of how LCDC's program could be implemented.

the existing urban area." Boundaries were also to be governed by the need to accommodate population growth and related housing and employment opportunities, provide public facilities and services in a cost-efficient manner, and maintain livability. There was also the ubiquitous requirement to consider "environmental, energy, economic and social consequences." Local governments had to include the results of their consideration of the seven factors in their plan. In the case of a boundary change, LCDC required the use of the Goal 2 exceptions process. While LCDC provided a sense of its priorities, local governments were responsible for arriving at balanced judgments based on their consideration of them.

In response to a long-standing League of Oregon Cities concern about the coordination role SB 100 had given the counties, LCDC added a sub-goal: "Establishment and change of the boundaries shall be a cooperative process between a city and the county or counties that surround it." Another sub-goal statement outlined the process for converting urbanizable land to urban uses. Local governments were mandated to consider the "availability of sufficient land for the various uses to insure choices in the market place" and "encouragement of development within urban areas before conversion of urbanizable areas." The first addition supported the buildable lands requirement of the housing goal. The second criterion incorporated an element of the environmental organizations' proposed Urban Lands goal. As in the case of creating and changing urban growth boundaries, LCDC indicated its priorities in the criteria that had to be considered, but local governments were responsible for striking the balance. The ways in which counties would coordinate the process of designating urban growth boundaries was also left to localities.

Schell was disappointed that the commission "refused to include in the transition goal from urbanizable to urban lands, considerations dealing with the timing of the conversion and population density." The commission had missed an opportunity, Bob Stacey agreed, to prevent sprawl inside urban growth boundaries when it deleted the reference to phasing development in the Public Facilities and Services goal and when it refused to specify densities and require that new development be contiguous to existing built-up areas. "Sprawl can still continue right up to the urban boundary," he warned, and "such . . . wasteful use of land will create pressures to expand those urban boundaries into surrounding farm or forest land" (Stacey, 1974f). LCDC would confront that issue in the years ahead.

The path LCDC was traveling began with a desire to conserve resource lands, and both its attention and the bulk of its political support were oriented to what was and what ought to be happening outside mandated urban growth boundaries. There was not nearly the same level of support for a more directive state agency role inside those lines. Nevertheless, the ways in which Goals 3 and 14 complemented each other was unprecedented. While several jurisdictions in Oregon and elsewhere in the United States had adopted urban limits, often based on sewer service, the Oregon requirement to zone agricultural land for exclusive farm use much more effectively constrained rural residential development and preserved resource lands.

Reflecting on what LCDC had accomplished and what was in store, LCDC's Steve Schell assured people that "we intend to give local government time to assimilate what has been done. With the exception of the Coast and the Greenway, we do not now intend to adopt new goals and guidelines for at least one year." He concluded: "While I have some reservations as to whether we have progressed as far as we need to progress in this first round of goals, I believe that we have kept faith with the words and the noble intent of Senators Macpherson and Hallock. I think there is much in these goals that both developers and environmentalists can be proud of (Schell, 1974c)."

Bob Stacey saw it differently. Generally speaking, he said, "the goals are local in perspective, and fail to adequately express statewide interests." He feared that LCDC's efforts to confront conflicts between conservation and development and to establish priorities in such cases were inadequate. Some land, he thought, would be designated for exclusive farm use, but how much was uncertain. He concluded: "citizens who expected the goals and guidelines to automatically remake land planning in their communities will be disappointed" (Stacey, 1975a,c). Just as they had in 1973, environmentalists geared up for the next round of engagement with LCDC, the legislature, and local planning processes.

The original version of SB 100 reflected, to a significant extent, what environmentalists and planners were advocating at the time, but representatives of local governments, state agencies, and industry groups had insisted that their concerns be addressed in order for them to support the bill. A similar dynamic produced a similar outcome in 1974. There was a good deal of environmentalist/citizen input during the early stages of

The Evolution of Statewide planning goals from SB 10 through LCDC adoption

SB 10 goals	First round workshop goals	Second round workshop goals: SB 10 plus	Final public hearing draft goals	Goals adopted 12/27/74
• Air, land, and water quality	• Pollution	• Air, water and land resources quality	• Air, water and land resources quality	• Air, water and land resources quality
• Prime farm land	• Agricultural land • Forests and forest land	• Agricultural lands • Forest lands	• Agricultural lands • Forest lands	• Agricultural lands • Forest lands
• Transportation	• Freeways and highways • Mass transit	• Transportation	• Transportation	• Transportation
• Carrying capacity		• Carrying capacity as a determinant of property development		
• Rural-urban transition	• Urbanization/urban development	• Transition from rural to urban land use	• Transition from rural to urban land use	• Urbanization
• Natural hazards	• Natural hazards	• Areas subject to floods, landslides and other natural disasters	• Areas subject to natural disasters and hazards	• Areas subject to natural disasters and hazards
• Economy	• Economy	• Economy of the state	• Economy of the state	• Economy of the state
• Open space, natural and scenic resources	• Shorelands	• Open spaces, natural and scenic resources • Shorelands	• Open spaces, scenic and historic areas, and natural resources • Shorelands	• Open spaces, scenic and historic areas and natural resources
• Recreation		• Recreational needs	• Recreational needs	• Recreational needs
• Public facilities and services		• Public facilities and services	• Public facilities and services	• Public facilities and services
	• Housing		• Housing	• Housing
	• Energy			• Energy conservation
• Estuaries and wetlands	• Estuaries and wetlands			
	• Comp plan process & content	• Guidelines for comprehensive planning	• Land use planning	• Land use planning
	• State agency/special district plans			
		• Citizen involvement	• Citizen involvement	• Citizen involvement

goal development, and the initial versions of many of the proposed goals contained a significant amount of substantive detail. However, the same institutional representatives as in 1973 mobilized to influence the process in order to enhance the discretion available to stakeholders at the local level. Knowing that those actors carried a great deal of weight with state legislators and that they needed strong legislative support for a budget, LCDC moved to accommodate several, but not all, of their concerns.

In his year-end report, Cogan, who left DLCD shortly after the goals were adopted to return to private consulting practice, set out DLCD's tasks for the first six months of 1975. The agency would explain the goals and guidelines to government agencies, environmental, business, and other groups, and citizens generally. It would also identify available sources of inventory-related information, including nongovernmental groups such as the Nature Conservancy, develop coastal goals, act on the Willamette River Greenway Plan, and assist local governments through a training program for elected officials, planning commissioners, planners, and citizens. It also had to prepare a report to the legislature on the two areas of critical statewide concern that had survived the goal-development process. A state growth policy that took into account carrying capacity and resource availability was needed. LCDC had to put together a comprehensive land inventory system "in one location," Cogan said. "[A] system to coordinate activities of statewide significance, including the design of a permit and regulations program, must be initiated" (Cogan, 1974j). Clearly, a great deal still had to be done before DLCD got any more resources from the legislature.

Governor McCall was hopeful. "As the official who helped push through Senate Bill 10 and Senate Bill 100 and who appointed this Commission," Governor McCall told LCDC, "no more pivotal appointments have been made by any governor and you and Arnold Cogan have lived up to my expectations in every way—my expectations that you would work hard and wisely to further the public interest, saving everything that is precious about Oregon for today and the future." He suggested that technical resource teams be formed to assist local governments with plan preparation. There are "dozens of people who might joyously leap at an opportunity to serve in this capacity," he thought. "Students, especially graduate students, could be employed." McCall, who was about to step down from the governorship, continued:

In saying thanks and farewell, I also want to assure you I'm not going to live so far away from the center of Oregon activity that I won't be watching and praying for your success. And more than that I'll be working for that success as a volunteer who thinks we have no more significant obligation than to produce for Oregon a land use plan that will be a hallmark of quality for an entire world." (McCall, 1974c)

Cogan labeled 1974 "the year of citizen planning," which it was to a significant extent. In January 1975, McCall announced the establishment of 1000 Friends of Oregon, created to watchdog the implementation of SB 100 and LCDC's statewide planning goals, which aimed to take citizen involvement to another level.

Chapter 7
Watchdog Emerging: 1000 Friends of Oregon

"We are convinced that Oregon now needs a statewide, full-time professionally staffed citizen organization whose sole purpose is to urge state and local bodies of government to make good land use planning decisions."—Henry Richmond

"Every public body needs a counter force and one specializing in land use is most needed at this time."—Hector Macpherson

1000 Friends of Oregon was unique among public interest organizations. A group of full-time attorneys, it was created to watchdog the implementation of a singular piece of land-use planning legislation in one state. The organization and the state's planning program evolved together, and understanding their inter-related development is critical to understanding Oregon's land-use political history.

The emergence of 1000 Friends from the mix of environmental groups active in Oregon at the time—especially OSPIRG, Oregon Environmental Council, Oregon Shores Conservation Coalition, and the Northwest Environmental Defense Center (NEDC)—reflected concerns about the ability of existing organizations to sustain effective participation in the legislative, bureaucratic, and legal arenas that the new land-use laws were creating. Henry Richmond was a central actor in creating 1000 Friends, which would monitor and enforce the implementation of the new laws, educate the growing community of people involved in land-use issues, and promote Oregon's program throughout the country.

When he was hired as staff attorney, Richmond had hoped that OSPIRG would be at the center of and act as the clearinghouse for the Oregon environmental movement. The organization had significant budgetary resources that had enabled it to hire professional staff, but it was also the case that OSPIRG's board of directors was composed entirely of students, which limited its political influence. For the time being, the less well-financed Oregon Environmental Council (OEC) was playing the role that Richmond had envisioned for OSPIRG. He thought that NEDC could be transformed into the sort of entity that neither OSPIRG nor OEC could become—the organization that eventually emerged as 1000 Friends of Oregon.

NEDC was created in 1969, about a year after OEC and just before OSPIRG was incorporated. The initiators proposed an environmental defense fund for Oregon and the Pacific Northwest that would have a staff of full-time attorneys, complemented by attorneys in private practice and by law professors and their students. The organization would coordinate an environmental law clinic at Lewis and Clark College's Northwestern School of Law in Portland and also would develop and promote legislative proposals. NEDC would have two directors: an attorney, and a scientist who would oversee work by medical and scientific personnel. Modeled on some of the national environmental defense organizations then emerging in the East, the first NEDC board included university-based scientists and several attorneys, among them Steve McCarthy and Steve Schell.

With limited funds and a fragile organizational structure, NEDC struggled during its early years. To stabilize the group, its leading activists occasionally suggested collaborating with OEC. In early 1973, OEC began to show some interest, primarily to take advantage of the legal and technical resources the attorneys and scientists associated with NEDC could bring to bear on litigation and on legislative and administrative issues. However, OEC board members who were exploring possibilities heard that "NEDC is not a viable organization at this time." If something with NEDC did not work out, they thought that OEC might develop a less formal pool of attorneys (Roy, 1973).

Despite its struggles, NEDC engaged in litigation. Steve Schell was involved, for example, with a case in Milwaukie, a small city immediately south of Portland. Citizens there, led by Jean Baker, were appealing a decision made by the city government involving a conflict between the local comprehensive plan and a zoning ordinance, a case somewhat similar to Edward Sullivan's *Fasano* case. Baker got in touch with both OEC and NEDC to ask for help. OEC Executive Director Larry Williams wrote Schell to "inquire whether you would be interested in putting together a lawsuit with OEC . . . regarding the Milwaukie Land Use Plan . . . We would certainly welcome working together with you on such a suit." A few days earlier, NEDC had decided that since "Jean Baker was unable to retain a private attorney for this case . . . NEDC would allocate $75 for duplicating so that the suit might be brought up on appeal" (NEDC, 1973; Williams, 1973c). In 1975, Schell and Sullivan, who played an important role in the case as well, won *Baker v. City of Milwaukie*, and the Oregon Supreme Court ruled that a city could no longer allow its zoning ordinance to permit a more intensive land use than was designated in its comprehensive plan. It was an important decision, one that would significantly influence the statewide land-use planning program.

Henry Richmond had started attending NEDC board meetings in the spring of 1973. An attorney affiliated with NEDC had asked him for advice on whether or not the organization should file a lawsuit under the National Environmental Policy Act regarding construction of a sewer trunk line that the Environmental Protection Agency (EPA) had agreed to finance in Jackson County. Responding affirmatively, Richmond noted that "nothing in the EPA's environmental assessment indicates that even passing consideration was given to the urban sprawl impact on prime farm lands the . . . trunk sewage lines will unavoidably cause, even though this is the most obvious, objectionable and significant impact involved" (Richmond, 1974f). On behalf of the City of Medford and OEC, an NEDC cooperating attorney filed suit to halt the project ("The City of Medford . . .", 1975), and the city petitioned LCDC to address the issue.

While he was still at OSPIRG, in late August 1974, Richmond wrote LCDC Vice Chair Steve Schell with a complaint. The Klamath Falls City Council intended to annex 144 acres of agricultural land, and a group called Save Our Soil had asked Arnold Cogan whether the city, "with no comprehensive planning, came under the jurisdiction of your Commission, and if guidelines have been set for such proposed annexations." Save Our Soil had presented the city council with a petition signed by 1,897 people opposing the annexation. Soon after, a DLCD staff member told the organization that LCDC had no guidelines that would help and that the commission "is a tiger without any teeth." It would review the situation, but it had no authority to act.

Richmond sharply disagreed. LCDC definitely had jurisdiction to review a city council action on annexation, he said. SB 100 stipulated that groups of persons who were substantially affected by an ordinance could claim that the ordinance violated one or more statewide planning goals and could petition LCDC to review it. "My concern," Richmond continued, "is that if . . . citizens who are greatly concerned about these annexations had relied on the above statements given by LCDC staff, their legal position would have been seriously, if not irreparably, prejudiced." He wanted LCDC to review the case and made his larger concerns clear:

> In the future LCDC staff should be straining to construe applicable statutes so as to give the public the greatest possible rights and remedies under Senate Bill 100 consistent with reasonable interpretation, instead of exercising discretion in a way which shrinks or eliminates public access to the crucial LCDC review procedures. (Richmond, 1974h)

On behalf of citizens in Klamath County, Richmond petitioned LCDC to review an order by the mayor and city council to annex certain lands. In 1977, the Oregon Supreme Court ruled in favor of Richmond's position in *Petersen v. Klamath Falls.*

These kinds of cases would increase during the months and years ahead, Richmond thought, and citizens and planners were going to face procedural and substantive challenges as they dealt with growth in the context of new laws and new administrative rules and regulations. NEDC's capacity to respond was uncertain, and individual Oregon citizens would be even harder pressed to act. In 1974, Richmond—who was now an NEDC board member—began thinking beyond the cases the organization was litigating to the new world of land-use planning that passage of SB 100 had opened up. In May, writing on behalf of the board finance committee, he outlined a plan to reorganize NEDC (Richmond, 1974c).

The appointment of a finance committee had been triggered by an offer from Allen and Louisa Bateman to donate $5,000 to NEDC "for the purpose of securing full-time legal capability." The Batemans, who owned a resort and tennis ranch, had moved to Klamath Falls from the Monterey peninsula in California, where they had been environmental activists. Governor McCall appointed Louisa Bateman to the Oregon State Wildlife Commission; Allen Bateman was active in the Sierra Club, served as an OEC board member, and was a member of a southern Oregon land-use advocacy group. Based on their experience in California, the Batemans be-

lieved that citizens needed professional legal assistance to protect environmental values in the face of development pressures. They were involved in
the Klamath Falls annexation case.

Given the new governmental context created by SB 100 and the *Fasano*
decision, the finance committee had concluded that NEDC needed full-time
staff. LCDC was discussing goals and guidelines, and Richmond argued that
the commission needed to be pushed to make good decisions and that the
goals would have to be enforced. Monitoring local government planning
processes and products would be critical, which meant more volunteer
lawyers, professionals, and law students. In light of the "environmental
movement's present lack of follow-up and law enforcement capability,"
Richmond wrote, NEDC needed the "capacity to effectively compete with
representatives of development or other anti-environmental interests."

In his role as OSPIRG staff attorney, Richmond was already working
hard on goal formulation and enforcement, and Allen Bateman began a
six-month process of persuading him to accept a full-time role in a larger
arena. The idea for what would become 1000 Friends of Oregon came
initially from Bateman (Buel, 1976; Stimmel, 1975).

NEDC's finance committee offered its board three alternatives for reorganization: a low-cost approach that would buy one lawyer-director and
one office manager-secretary; a mid-range alternative that would add a
staff attorney; and, the most costly option, two more attorneys and two
more secretaries. The committee recommended that the board adopt the
second alternative:

> A two-lawyer, full-time staff is a minimum if NEDC is to develop
> essential continuity in dealing with environmental issues. One
> lawyer simply cannot do the important organizational work, as-
> similate pertinent data and develop critical working relationships
> with agency personnel, while at the same time developing specific
> projects, securing volunteers, and preparing projects for intelligent
> Board consideration.

From this base, the organization would aim to grow over time.

Richmond proposed a membership organization with dues of $100 a
year, which could be paid quarterly. He thought it would be no problem to
recruit five hundred people to fund the mid-range alternative. The "trick"
to the success of the strategy, he said,

is to select the right people and to make the paying process easy but binding. Nor is 500 people an unduly large number of people. In one hour's reflection, I developed a list of 150 people whom I believe would participate . . . I am confident that any NEDC Board member can easily think of 25 persons . . . NEDC should form a special . . . Finance Committee, chaired during the three-month promotional period by Governor McCall.

Richmond also proposed that recruiting be based on county quotas, with the target for each county reflecting its share of the state population. This would create a statewide organization that was positioned to participate effectively at the county level, where the critical planning action would take place. It also would break down recruitment into manageable units.

Among the people that Richmond thought should sit on the finance committee were manufacturer, land developer, and civic activist John Gray; Bill Smith of Brooks Resources, a timber company; attorney Ed Sullivan; and Allen Bateman. The strategy would be to ask Tom McCall to join the new NEDC finance committee. Then "the Committee should send an appeal letter to all prospective members, signed by the Governor." Richmond envisioned a coming-out party for the new organization:

There will be a gala banquet, hosted by Tom McCall, on a certain date in Salem . . . The individual should be told that Ray Atkeson [a well-known photographer] will give a spectacular slide show, displaying the natural resource glories of Oregon, Ken Kesey [an internationally known Oregon author] will read a poem written especially for the occasion, L. B. Day will give a brief update on LCDC, and Tom McCall will give the evening address about the Future of Oregon . . . Spirits will flow, and the food will be good, fun will be had, and in attendance will be Oregon's crème de la crème. Leading politicians and representatives of the media will be guests.

The memo was enthusiastic about the prospect of successfully funding the reorganization.

1000 Friends of Oregon

Within a few months and after discussion within the environmental community, Richmond concluded that a new freestanding organization with a singular purpose and its own board of directors would be a more appropriate way to achieve the objectives outlined in the finance committee's memo. To create the new organization, he decided to partner with Tom McCall. A distinction that he made in that memo, one that he maintained throughout his tenure at 1000 Friends, suggests one reason why he pursued a different path: "Land Use should be emphasized because everyone likes good land use, and not everyone thinks 'environmental' organizations are keen. It should be stressed that a citizens' organization with a core of professionals can be more responsible and less shrill because it will be proposing and not simply opposing."

Land use, Richmond thought, was a broader and less controversial field of action than environmentalism. One manifestation of the broader sweep was that a new organization would take seriously both the conservation and the development dimensions of LCDC's mandate. A board of directors appropriate to the dual mandate would be necessary, and a new organization would be in a better position to attract suitable candidates to such a board. It also would be more likely to attract members and financial support.

Richmond and Allen Bateman made an appointment with McCall, and on August 1, 1974, Richmond wrote the governor to lay out their purpose:

> We are convinced that Oregon needs a statewide, full-time professionally staffed citizen organization whose sole purpose is to urge state and local bodies of government to make good land use planning decisions. The organization would also be capable of seeking judicial review of issues dealing with the proper administration of land use laws. (Richmond, 1974g)

The county-based planning system set up by SB 100, Richmond said, would be "more likely to succeed if an organization exists which is able to give competent legal assistance to people in a given locality who are concerned about a proposed land use action." He briefly described the situation in Klamath County and concluded: "they needed a lawyer."

The failure of Congress to pass a national land-use planning bill, Richmond told McCall, meant that Oregon would not be getting any financial help from that source to support its own planning efforts. Furthermore, the Legislative Emergency Board had recently rejected most of LCDC's budget request to hire professional staff to implement its program. Richmond also reported that "the traditional opponents of land use planning are preparing for serious and effective participation in the land use policy-making process." He was specifically concerned that Steve Hawes, the former legislative counsel who had drafted many of Oregon's land-use laws, was now an Associated Oregon Industries lobbyist.

Given those realities, Richmond argued, the citizens of Oregon needed a lawyer. He proposed the same kind of organization that he had suggested to NEDC: two lawyers funded by $100 annual contributions from five hundred Oregonians. He and Bateman asked the governor for his active support for what they would soon call the Oregon Land Use Project. McCall agreed and told Richmond to indicate his support in the personal solicitation letters.

Richmond then began to recruit members to a board of directors and an advisory board, which McCall would chair. Glenn Jackson, head of Pacific Power & Light and chair of the Oregon Transportation Commission, agreed to serve on the advisory board (Richmond, 1974j), as did J. W. Forrester, publisher of the *Daily Astorian*. Forrester cautioned Richmond about his position on a controversy over a long-term electricity-supply contract that Bonneville Power Administration (BPA) had signed with AMAX, an aluminum company that wanted to build a reduction plant at Warrenton. The Port of Astoria had brought suit against BPA, arguing that the contract required an environmental impact report (Little, A. D., 1974; Springer, 1976; Tollefson, 1987). Forrester told Richmond that "if AMAX satisfies all the environmental requirements I probably will support construction of the plant at Warrenton. If you think that might be embarrassing to your organization I shouldn't serve on your advisory board" (Forrester, 1974). Richmond replied: "I do not believe the differences of opinion on such matters should present any embarrassment . . . My father provided AMAX with its electricity, and so far I have not embarrassed the organization" (Richmond, 1974k).

Eric Allen, editor of the Medford *Mail Tribune* in southern Oregon, also agreed to serve. He advised Richmond that

> there are doubtless 500 Oregonians ready and willing and perhaps eager to make such a pledge [$100 each per year], but there are many more who would be willing and perhaps eager to contribute lesser amounts. John Gray [who agreed to serve on the Advisory

Board] and Glenn Jackson can afford $100 per year; I would find it difficult to do so. By limiting your solicitation this way, you stand the risk of losing the active support and financial assistance of a much larger group of involved citizens. (Allen, E., 1974)

Except for the introduction of a reduced rate for students, the dues structure didn't change immediately. A few years later, though, Richmond took Allen's advice.

Richmond also invited Hector Macpherson to join the advisory board and offered his condolences on the legislator's recent electoral defeat. The SB 100 co-sponsor—a Republican—thought the bill was "only one of several factors that upset the conservative Democrats who make up the eastern half of my legislative district," but he was pleased to join the board: "An organization such as the one that you are promoting is most needed. For years I sat on a planning commission where a steady stream of citizens, each with a special interest, paraded by. Every public body needs a counter force and one specializing in land use is most needed at this time" (Macpherson, 1974a).

Richmond also recruited nature photographer Ray Atkeson; northeastern Oregon wheat and pea rancher Martin Buchanan; Portland conservationist Elizabeth Ducey, who was active on Willamette River Greenway protection; Nani Warren, chair of the Oregon Columbia River Gorge Commission, Republican national committeewoman from Oregon, and a county planning commissioner; and Thomas Vaughan, executive director of the Oregon Historical Society. He had secured commitments from people who were leaders in the different regions of the state and in Oregon's economic, political, and civic life. They conferred instant credibility on the new organization.

The first meeting of the board of directors was held in Salem on September 19, 1974 (Proposed Land Use Organization, 1974). The members present were Allen Bateman; John Frohnmayer, a Portland attorney who had worked for the City of Eugene Planning Commission and chaired the Land, Air, and Water research program at University of Oregon Law School; Elizabeth Johnson, a Portland attorney; Peter McDonald, a Willamette Valley farmer who served on the governor's advisory committee on the Willamette River Greenway; Martin Winch, a central Oregon attorney who had been active in public interest land-use litigation; Alfred Hampson, a Portland attorney involved with tourist-related issues; Wade Newbegin, Jr., a vice president of R. M. Wade and Company and a major OEC supporter; and Joe Kershner, a Portland attorney and accountant. In addition, three others agreed to serve as members: Steven Corey, an eastern Oregon attorney whose family owned a sheep farm; George Thompson, director of a private school on the Oregon coast; and NEDC board member Richard Roy, a Portland attorney active on water policy-related issues. Claudia Burton, who taught land use and environmental law at Willamette University, joined the board shortly thereafter. Newbegin was elected board president, Bateman was named vice president, Kershner became treasurer, and Johnson was secretary.

LCDC chair L. B. Day outlined the commission's program at the meeting, and Richmond reviewed the purpose of the new organization: participation in LCDC decision-making processes; provision of low- or no-cost legal skills to local citizens; publication of a newsletter; creation of a pool of volunteer attorneys, planners, and other professionals; and education for Oregonians to increase support for LCDC. The organization also would be involved with LCDC's goal-related compliance proceedings and work to ensure that legal standing to participate in such reviews was broadly construed. As Allen Bateman said, the "organization will become the expert that the public can turn to." The board adopted by-laws and a policy permitting students to join the organization for $24 per year and agreed to apply for nonprofit, tax-exempt status, even though that would mean the organization could not lobby or endorse candidates. Finally, they agreed to hire Richmond as executive director; he was authorized to hire a staff person for three months to work on the membership drive and to help establish the organization (Richmond, 1974l).

On December 1, Richmond reported that 172 pledges had been received, and he was confident more than two hundred would be in hand by the December board meeting. He hoped the announcement of the new organization that Governor McCall would make in early January would push the pledge total above the three hundred necessary to begin operating. On January 6, 1975, Richmond wrote the membership that the organization

> will be announced and known as 1,000 Friends of Oregon, while retaining the name Oregon Land Use Project for purposes of ex-

isting filings with the IRS . . . While a name is not a matter of overriding importance, Oregon Land Use Project is simply dull and flat—something between a New Deal agency, and a homework assignment for a 7th Grade geography class. In addition, the acronym OLUP sounded something like a Swedish stomach ailment . . . 1,000 Friends of Oregon . . . has the advantage of more zip and spark, as well as the dynamic of a built-in long-term membership goal—1,000 members. (Richmond, 1975a)

Richmond submitted his resignation to OSPIRG in February and assumed full-time duties as executive director of 1000 Friends of Oregon on March 1, 1975, at a starting salary of $12,000 a year. Based on his OSPIRG work, he brought a reputation with him. The Portland *Daily Journal of Commerce* reported that

those close to the land use planning scene in Oregon are gravely concerned when the word was out that their intent was to hire OSPIRG lawyer, Henry Richmond, to staff the new endeavor. OSPIRG generally, and Richmond specifically, has been a negative influence, according to those in the construction industry, on the development of the LCDC goals and guidelines. He has tried on several occasions to write in goals and/or guidelines that would raise the cost of housing substantially across the state, and, in some cases, even prevent its construction.

The *Journal* also was dismayed that Oregon Highway Commission Chair Glenn Jackson and developer John Gray were supporting the organization ("Corvallis spotlights some building woes," n.d.). But Richmond was ready, and he hit the ground running.

Watchdog in Action

In mid-March 1975, Tom McCall received a letter from Laurance Rockefeller, a member of the board of trustees for the Natural Resources Defense Council. NRDC had heard "that your office . . . helped to organize a citizens' organization to defend land use laws in Oregon by the title of '1000 Friends of Oregon'," he wrote. "We would like to have more information about this group" (Rockefeller, 1975). Word was spreading about the new organization.

There were some similarities between 1000 Friends and NRDC, Richmond told McCall:

> Like NRDC, we take our work seriously and do not leap into litiga-
> tion or appeals . . . without careful consideration. We are not out
> to "stop" things. That would be a waste of time. Our purpose is to
> help build a sound body of land use law in a state which the whole
> country will be using as a model within five years . . . Another area
> of similarity with NRDC is the fact that most of the work is done
> by lawyers.

But the two organizations were also quite different from one another:

> [W]e work in one state, and we work on basically one issue (land
> use), though that issue is rather broad . . . I do not think any other
> state has an organization with . . . full-time lawyers working solely
> for environmental progress. There are several national organiza-
> tions, like NRDC, but none limited to a single state. (Richmond,
> 1975i)

Tom Stoel, Jr., a founding member of NRDC whose father was a partner
in one of Portland's leading law firms, once described to a group of industry lawyers the criteria NRDC used to select its cases. The 1000 Friends
Board approved similar selection criteria at its April 1975 meeting: legal
precedential value and impact on agency decision-making patterns; natural resource value; enforcement value; consistency with goals and program
priorities; probability of success; approval of members in the locality; availability of volunteer legal or other assistance; and expense (1000 Friends
of Oregon, 1975a). Stoel also had advised that "both before and after a
lawsuit has been brought . . . [it is] desirable for the industry lawyer to
contact the concerned environmental groups and find out their position
and objectives . . . In short, my advice to you is similar to Mae West's: drop
in and see us sometime" (Stoel, 1975). This was just the sort of relationship
that 1000 Friends wanted to establish with local governments, the staff at
DLCD, and LCDC. The organization also extended the offer to work with
industrialists, homebuilders, farmers, foresters, and anyone else involved
in land-use planning and development.

In January 1975, Peter Herman, the assistant state attorney general
assigned to LCDC, told the commissioners that it was urgent that they

hire a hearings officer to process the cases that were surfacing as local government actions were scrutinized. His office had "already received six petitions," he reported. "And there is good reason to believe that what started out as a trickle, will soon become a flood because of the wide publicity the Department's goals and guidelines have received and because of the former Governor's new citizens committee formed to act as a watchdog on land use planning matters" (Herman, 1975).

Clif and Lois Kenagy, owners of a farm in Benton County and members of 1000 Friends, gave Richmond the opportunity to submit a petition and a brief to LCDC arguing that the county had failed to take into account flood risk when it amended its flood-plain ordinance. In line with the criteria Richmond proposed regarding case selection, he told Board president Newbegin that "the most important issues raised by this petition . . . do not relate to flood plain ordinances, but to precedent-setting procedural issues surrounding the . . . compliance proceedings authorized by Senate Bill 100 . . . [C]itizens are entitled to seek review of . . . zoning ordinances which apply jurisdiction-wide in a city or county."

Richmond planned to give LCDC an opportunity to clarify and protect the state's interest in local planning. He wanted the commission to resolve procedural issues around "standing, the scope of review of . . . LCDC, the degree of proof required of petitioners, evidentiary matters." The hearing on the Kenagy case, he said,

> is the first hearing . . . at which . . . LCDC actually reviewed the adequacy of a zoning ordinance adopted by a local government to determine its compliance with the "interim" goals of Senate Bill 100. Indeed, it is likely that this is the first instance of a state-wide planning agency reviewing a local government zoning [ordinance] for compliance with a state agency land use standard anywhere in the United States." (Richmond, 1975b)

An August 1975 appeal to LCDC of a rezoning action taken by commissioners in Marion County offered 1000 Friends what Richmond considered a classic test case and an opportunity to clarify for Governor Bob Straub the "constructive and absolutely indispensable role which appeals play in the Senate Bill 100 Program." In a long memo to the new governor, Richmond pointed out that administrative appeals enabled all participants in the land-use community to learn while addressing concrete, goal-related issues. The Marion County case involved, among other issues, a local decision to zone land outside an urban growth boundary for an industrial park. 1000 Friends argued that the land should have been zoned for exclusive farm use based on LCDC's Agricultural Lands and Urbanization goals.

Richmond told Governor Straub that appeals had many technical and political benefits for LCDC and the statewide land-use program. DLCD did not have the staff to fully evaluate comprehensive plans and ordinances on its own, and it was crucial that the department's work be supplemented by appeals based on local knowledge. Richmond thought it would be preferable if citizens brought appeals to LCDC rather than have DLCD initiate challenges to local actions. Such appeals, he advised, would "encourage local government sensitivity to goal requirements." He also noted that it was more efficient and effective to address land-use problems within the LCDC administrative setting than in the courts. Although SB 100 permitted LCDC to take over local planning and zoning when a local government failed to conform, "the appeal procedure allows LCDC and local governments to avoid the all-or-nothing, meat axe approach of a full-blown take over, and to focus attention solely on the particular land use policies which are alleged to be in conflict with a specific goal or goals."

Marion County had "one of Oregon's two or three leading county land use planning programs," and the appeal, he urged, should not be seen as a criticism of the county: "The petition is filed because the county's rezoning decision raises important issues under LCDC's key goals, and because the appeal is the most constructive and expeditious means to resolve those issues." In May 1976, LCDC agreed with 1000 Friends that Marion County had violated the goals and ordered the county to re-evaluate its zoning decisions (Dickie, 1976; "East Salem Rezoning . . . ," 1975; Richmond, 1975f). Selecting cases in order to establish precedents, especially regarding procedural matters, made a great deal of strategic sense to 1000 Friends during the early years, but local government planners whose plans and ordinances were challenged were ambivalent about their work being selected to play that role. Planners could appreciate the approach in the abstract. The concrete application of it to their particular places, though, sometimes generated conflict between them and the attorneys, as planners saw their ability to address land-use issues specific to their jurisdictions curtailed.

As the volume of work grew and as he anticipated more to come, Richmond asked the board of directors for more resources. As of April

16, there were 302 membership pledges in hand, and it was time to call in the money. He recommended hiring two third-year law students at the University of Oregon, Robert C. Stacey, Jr., and Richard P. Benner, to help (Richmond, 1975c). A Portland native, Stacey had graduated from Reed College and was a legislative aide to Senator Ted Hallock during the 1975 legislative session. Benner had grown up in Los Angeles, gotten a degree at Princeton, and served as an intelligence officer and commander in the Anti-Submarine Warfare Forces in Virginia. He was a legislative aide to Representative Nancy Fadeley. Richmond had been working with both of them for two years, beginning with supervising the projects they had done as OSPIRG interns. The two men were technically expert and politically astute, and they quickly established themselves as authorities on Oregon planning and land-use law. Hiring them was a financial challenge, though, even at $9,000 per year. Richmond hoped that a portion of their salaries would be paid by the City of Portland using federal funds. When that didn't work out, Stacey and Benner joined 1000 Friends in September with the understanding that they had jobs only as long as the organization could pay them. In the meantime, they dove into the eighteen to twenty cases Richmond had assigned to each of them (Richmond, 1975j).

While he was building staff capacity to monitor and enforce the law, Richmond also was seeking financial support to add the role of educator to the 1000 Friends portfolio. The newsletter was a major undertaking. Aimed at keeping members informed of what the organization was doing, its purpose was also to examine important land-use issues of concern to planners and planning commissioners, attorneys, activists, local elected officials, industry people, and interested citizens. With the newsletter, 1000 Friends hoped to nurture a culture supportive of plan making and implementation that was in line with SB 100 and LCDC goals and to provide a forum where members of the land-use planning community could debate issues and share experiences. The board had approved the publication of 2,500 copies of a four-page newsletter between September and December 1975, but there was no money in the budget beyond that point. With strong support from Governor Straub, the Pacific Northwest Regional Commission funded an increase in the number of newsletters printed to ten thousand in 1976 and sixteen thousand in 1977 (Richmond, 1975g; Richmond, 1977b).

In the cover story of the first issue in the fall of 1975, Richmond framed SB 100 as a state industry policy and LCDC as a key implementer of that policy. He argued that SB 100 and LCDC must be understood as providing critically important opportunities to preserve Oregon's most valuable wealth-producing assets—the state's farm and forest lands—as well as opportunities to economize on the costs of supplying the infrastructure necessary to accommodate growth in Oregon's population and industry. The law and the agency were "as much concerned with dollars and cents . . . as with the quality of life" (Richmond, 1975h).

An old worry surfaced in response to the December 1975 newsletter. Advisory board member Eric Allen forwarded to Richmond a memo he had received from one of his reporters who covered land-use planning issues for the Medford *Mail Tribune*; the critique resonated with Allen's previous concerns about the cost of joining 1000 Friends. He told Richmond:

> You may recall . . . when Friends first organized, I expressed concern that it could turn land use planning into an "elitist" issue. For that reason, as well as simple aesthetics, its latest newsletter and its predecessors concern me. 1000 Friends seems to have gone beyond the elite to address itself primarily to attorneys and professional planners. Virtually all of this issue . . . would be incomprehensible to a layman . . . The point is that 1000 Friends will have to gain widespread support, and can't do so by talking professional mumbo-jumbo . . . The opponents are articulate and plain-spoken enough. (Allen, E., 1975)

The newsletter wasn't the only way in which 1000 Friends sought to play an educator role. Richmond spoke frequently to local government officials about SB 100 and LCDC goal-related topics, often together with Ed Sullivan. Inviting colleagues to a January 1976 land-use planning seminar, for example, the Klamath County planning director noted that Richmond and Sullivan would be featured speakers and that, in his opinion, they "are the most knowledgeable individuals in Oregon" regarding the implementation of LCDC's goals and the state planning laws (Judson, 1976). In June, Richmond started reaching out to planners and homebuilders about LCDC's housing goal, speaking to the annual meeting of the Oregon American Institute of Planners chapter and the Governor's Housing Conference. He stressed to planners the importance of Goal 10 as a way of challenging exclusionary zoning and tried to persuade those directly involved in land development that the goal was "in the interest of the homebuilding industry" (Richmond, 1976b). 1000 Friends, he made clear, was an advocate of appropriate development as well as conservation. A critically important alliance with the Home Builders Association of Metropolitan Portland emerged shortly thereafter.

Fundraising efforts occupied a good deal of Richmond's time. In March 1976, he submitted a proposal to Minnesota-based Northwest Area Foundation for a three-year grant of $189,000 to focus on the implementation of the Agricultural Lands and Urbanization goals in the Willamette Valley. Governor Straub, Tom McCall, Glenn Jackson, and L. B. Day strongly supported the request. Day wrote the foundation that he worked

> closely with 1000 Friends . . . staff attorneys nearly every week. The organization's work enjoys a statewide reputation for being responsible and of high professional quality . . . I know of numerous examples over the past year where 1000 Friends . . . work has provided valuable benefits for local planning programs and for our own program . . . The . . . proposal would be an immense public service to the state of Oregon. I want to do anything I can to persuade the Northwest Area Foundation to approve the request for assistance. (Day, n.d.)

The proposal, which would have covered about half the organization's operating budget during that period, occasioned a board of directors' discussion on the advisability of relying on foundations for funding, especially those located outside Oregon. Some board members worried that 1000 Friends might be attacked as an agent of "outsiders" seeking to meddle in Oregon affairs. Others were concerned that dependence on funding that waxed and waned would create damaging budget instability. A partial alternative, some thought, was to increase substantially the number of dues-paying members. In April 1976, the board voted to limit foundation funding to 60 percent of any fiscal year's financial requirements; Richmond would have to request board approval to go beyond that figure (1000 Friends of Oregon, 1976).

The Northwest Area Foundation gave 1000 Friends a three-year $100,000 grant in June 1976, the organization's first major award. Given its fragility going into 1976, the award was very significant. The next year, Richmond sought to build on the grant with a multi-year $291,000 proposal to the Ford Foundation, but the foundation had decided to phase out of its commitment to the public interest law sector. 1000 Friends did get a grant, but it was not nearly as large as Richmond had hoped to secure. Funding the organization was a continual challenge, and changing the organization's dues structure and attracting more members became a higher organizational priority.

The 1000 Friends attorneys and their environmentalist and planner allies worked hard to modernize land-use planning in Oregon during the 1970s. They never stopped urging state and local planners to base their goals and plans on inventories and other objective data, and to incorporate detailed, specific standards derived from objective sources into their plans and implementation strategies. They sought to enhance the technical sophistication of local comprehensive plans and the technician dimension of the planner role. Richmond and the attorneys he hired quickly established themselves as extremely effective actors in LCDC proceedings, in the courts, and in local trenches statewide where plans and implementing ordinances were created. They initiated and participated in a great many appeals of local and state actions during the early years, and were on the winning side the great majority of the time. The organization played a lead role when the program had to be defended in the legislature and at the ballot box.

A major lesson that land-use advocates around the United States learned from the Oregon experience was the importance of a watchdog (DeGrove, 1994). When disenchanted Hawaii activists sought to initiate a similar organization in Kauai during the late 1970s to watchdog planning there, one of the first things they did was to bring in Henry Richmond to help them launch 1000 Friends of Kauai (Pickard, 1979). Richmond was the keynote speaker at the first annual membership dinner in 1982, and then again in 1983 at the statewide Hawaii's Thousand Friends (Hawaii's Thousand Friends, 2011). The state legislative champion of growth management in Washington State recalled learning in the latter 1980s about the crucial role played by 1000 Friends in the implementation of the Oregon program. He visited with 1000 Friends and then helped to set up an organization modeled on it in Washington (King, 2005). Richmond took the lead in establishing the National Growth Management Leadership Project to exchange information with advocates around the country; nineteen state organizations were members by the early 1990s. He focused on the project after he stepped down from the 1000 Friends executive director position in 1990.

Chapter 8
Governor Straub, the 1975 Legislature, and LCDC

"[T]he Legislature must decide whether it wants to make the down payment for Oregon's future envisioned in SB 100 . . . or whether controlled, sane land use development is worthy of rhetoric, but not dollars . . . Unless this agency is given the resources now to prove itself, Oregon will have lost a priceless chance to come to grips with its future."—The Oregonian, Portland

Adopting the statewide planning goals was a remarkable achievement—a first in the nation—but implementing the commission's program depended on the legislature's willingness to provide adequate funds to the Department of Land Conservation and Development. In 1975, the Land Conservation and Development Commission faced a make-or-break legislative session. Passing its biennial budget was the key, but it was a tough time for the state economy, with unemployment at its highest level since 1950 (Federman, 1975). LCDC needed funding to enable DLCD to complete important work that it had been unable to accomplish in 1973-1975 and to support local governments as they revised their plans and ordinances to comply with statewide planning goals. Without a substantial financial commitment from the state—the situation in 1969 after passage of SB 10—the dynamics set in motion by SB 100 would grind to a halt. Still, land-use advocates were hopeful. For the first time in the twentieth century, Democrats controlled both houses of the Oregon legislature and held the governor's office. Almost one-third of the legislators were freshmen, and many supported land-use planning and environmental initiatives.

Industry representatives, environmental activists, and legislative leaders sponsored numerous competing bills aimed at shaping the implementation of the land-use program. In the months before the session, LCDC sent several ideas to the Joint Legislative Committee on Land Use and to Janet McLennan, Governor Straub's adviser on land-use and natural-resource issues. McLennan, a Portland attorney, had staffed the House Environment and Land Use Committee in the 1973 session and had worked closely with Straub on environmental matters (Cogan, 1974f; Schell, 1974c). Cities and counties pushed for more autonomy and for as many dollars to support their work as they could get. The Oregon Environmental Council (OEC) and Oregon Shores sought new legislation to overcome what they saw as weaknesses in SB 100 and the LCDC-adopted goals. The state Homebuilders Association, Oregon Association of Realtors (OAR), Associated Oregon Industries (AOI), and other business groups lobbied to rein in what they thought was an excessively powerful state agency and to make some basic changes in SB 100.

The Joint Legislative Committee addressed several issues that had been contested in the 1973 session and during goal development in 1974, including compensatory zoning, the coordination of the work of LCDC and the Oregon Department of Environmental Quality, and the continuing challenge of persuading county tax assessors to take seriously the significance of exclusive farm-use zones for property taxation. The Oregon Supreme Court rendered a land-use decision in 1975 that roiled the political waters, and LCDC adopted a Willamette River Greenway goal, its fifteenth.

The DLCD Budget

During the 1974 gubernatorial campaign, Bob Straub strongly supported the statewide land-use program and other environmental initiatives that had been put in place during the McCall years. His platform included support for designating areas and activities of critical statewide concern and increasing the protection of farmland. As a state senator from Eugene in the early 1960s, Straub had sponsored farmland zoning legislation, and as state treasurer he had played a leadership role on coastal resource protection and Willamette River cleanup and recreational development. Given the troubled state of the Oregon economy, however, Straub also had campaigned in support of economic growth that would bring jobs to all parts of the state. Overall, he presented his platform as a balanced approach to conservation and development.

One of the people who worked most closely on Straub's budget was John Mosser, who had chaired the Bob Straub for Governor Committee and was now a general adviser to the governor. Mosser was a Portland attorney and former Republican legislator who had become an Independent, and Governor McCall had appointed him to direct the Executive Department. He had also chaired the State Sanitary Authority, the predecessor to the Environmental Quality Commission. Mosser worked with Stafford Hansell, whom Straub appointed to direct the Executive Department and who was the state's chief budget official (Thompson, W., 1974). Hansell had been a Republican legislator and long-serving member of the Ways and Means Committee. Even though he and his brother had been named Conservation Men of the Year in 1975 for their innovative hog-farming practices—they owned the state's largest hog farm, located in eastern Oregon—Hansell was not particularly interested in land-use issues. Funding for land-use planning had not found much favor in Ways and Means when he chaired it, and he had voted against SB 100 (Hansell, 1983).

In early January 1975, LCDC approved a $6.149 million budget request for the 1975-1977 biennium. The budget was organized into four program areas: conservation and development; assistance and coordination; permits, appeals, and enforcement; and administration and administrative services. Conservation and development accounted for about 10 percent of the request. Building on a concept that had surfaced during the goal-writing process, the staff suggested dividing the state into six regions. DLCD would analyze carrying capacity within each region to inform choices about conservation and development programs at local and regional levels. A top priority, Cogan said, was a "working model of carrying capacity including an inventory and evaluation of all relevant land capabilities and limitations" that would lead to a workable goal and set of guidelines in 1976. A specific target captured what DLCD proposed to achieve with its Conservation and Development program: a 50 percent reduction in the rate of agricultural land loss in the Willamette Valley. The program also would lead to the development of a goal and guidelines for Oregon shorelands.

Assistance and coordination accounted for 68.5 percent of the proposed budget, most of it targeted for grants to local governments to help them produce plans and implementation ordinances. In his year-end report, Cogan wrote: "Of overriding importance to the success of this land use program . . . is the ability of local government to sustain a planning effort.

Substantial state and federal funds will be required to provide assistance for both planning and coordination programs at the local level." Integrating the Oregon Coastal Conservation and Development Commission (OCCDC)'s personnel and products into DLCD's structure and processes was also a key aspect of the program.

The request allocated 12.5 percent for permits, appeals, and enforcement. DLCD would design and implement a system to determine whether or not the plans and implementation actions proposed by cities, counties, special districts, and state and federal agencies were in compliance with LCDC's statewide planning goals and put in place procedures to take appropriate action when they were not. Another target was to have two-thirds of all the counties and one-third of all cities in compliance by June 30, 1977, the end of the biennium. In addition, DLCD would design a one-stop permit system to expedite decision-making processes for all land development in the state. Cutting across all areas addressed in the budget, DLCD would directly involve at least fifteen thousand Oregonians in its programs.

The proposed program budget also included targets that LCDC intended to reach by the end of the decade: the completion of refined carrying capacity analyses for the six regions; a 90 percent reduction in the rate of agricultural land loss in the Willamette Valley; 100 percent of county plans and ordinances and 90 percent of city plans in compliance with statewide goals; an improved real estate development climate; a twenty-year supply of buildable land for housing, including land for low- and moderate-cost housing; and the end of development in estuaries, except where explicitly consistent with statewide goals (Land Conservation and Development Commission, 1975a).

The LCDC staff intended to pick up where they had left off, continuing to refine adopted goals through a regionalization process and adding goals for carrying capacity, shorelands, and coastal zone management. They intended to deliver the financial and technical support that SB 10 had failed to provide to local and regional government planners and to press forward with the critical area and activity programs that SB 100 had authorized them to undertake. LCDC planned to address a potential conflict between conservation-oriented constraints on the supply of land for urbanization and the affordability of housing and to reduce the loss of the state's most productive farmland—the concern that had motivated many political leaders, planners, and environmentalists in the first place.

The Governor's Office significantly reshaped the budget request, proposing roughly the same amount of money—$6.1 million—but shifting a substantial proportion away from funding DLCD capacity building to increasing support for local government planning. The shift in priorities likely reflected Hansell's preferences and Straub's political assessment that a budget oriented toward local government was more likely to receive legislative support. Only half the money would come from the state general fund; the other half took the form of state authorization to receive grants from the federal government. In the event that LCDC was unable to secure the full amount of federal funding, a million dollars was appropriated to the Legislative Emergency Board to make up the shortfall. There was the lingering hope that the U.S. government would pass a National Land Use Policy Act, which would provide planning grants to states. Oregon's economy was in tough shape, and there was a reluctance to commit to a larger amount of state general-fund money.

The governor's budget took money from the conservation and development programs and recommended using existing resources for work related to carrying capacity. While the budget assigned a high priority to a one-stop permit system, the governor did not want LCDC to play the lead role in that process; legislation would be introduced to set it up. In addition, his budget reduced the agency's efforts in citizen involvement, critical areas and activities of statewide significance, implementation of an appeals process, and the use of consultants to enhance staff capacity (Land Conservation and Development Commission, 1975b).

Land-use and environmental advocates were in a difficult position. On the one hand, they wanted more money for DLCD, and they supported many of the elements included in LCDC's budget proposal. They wanted to strengthen the agency's ability to make the best use of the regulatory and other policy tools that SB 100 made available. On the other hand, they were critical of the agency's limited accomplishments. Any criticism of the agency would appear to align them with industry and local government critics of the statewide program, thereby enhancing the influence of those legislators who were disposed to reduce DLCD's portion of the budget (Stacey, 1975b).

The new DLCD director, Hal Brauner, told LCDC that while the governor's recommendations were not exactly what the commissioners hoped to see, the budget would still enable the agency to mount a meaningful program. Brauner was not a professional planner, but he was certainly familiar with SB 100. He had worked with L. B. Day's drafting committee during the 1973 legislative session, had been Governor McCall's legislative assistant for natural resources, and had worked on Willamette Valley Project Foresight. He also had substantial experience working with the Ways and Means Committee, and as a budget analyst in the Executive Department. When they hired Brauner, Day and Steve Schell believed that his background would strengthen the agency's ability to increase legislative support for LCDC's budget request and to manage a substantially larger budget. Eldon Hout was also considered for the position, as was Jim Ross, the OCCDC executive director (Burdick, 1975a; Jepson, 1975; LCDC, 1975b; "The Missing Tooth in Environmental Smile," 1975).

The Joint Ways and Means Committee held hearings on the DLCD budget in early April 1975. *The Oregonian* editorialized: "the Legislature must decide whether it wants to make the downpayment for Oregon's future envisioned in SB 100 . . . or whether controlled, sane land use development is worthy of rhetoric, but not dollars." The newspaper worried that the legislature would be tempted to further reduce funds allocated to DLCD for appeals and for critical area and activities projects. "It would be far better," the editorial concluded, "not to fund this agency at all than to give it a token appropriation which will not allow its mechanisms to work . . . Unless this agency is given the resources now to prove itself, Oregon will have lost a priceless chance to come to grips with its future" ("Bill to shape future," 1975).

Some of the conflicts that had characterized the 1973 legislative session and the 1974 goals-development process resurfaced during the hearings. Property owners came to Salem from southern Oregon and the coast to challenge the agency, the law that created it, and the state planning goals. A representative of the Multnomah County Farm Bureau wanted the committee to eliminate the agency altogether because its goals were "interfering with the ability of the farmers he represents to sell their land to speculators at a good price . . . 'They seem oblivious to the fact that their goals may cost people millions of dollars loss in property values.'" Willamette Valley farmer Lois Kenagy, however, who 1000 Friends was helping appeal a county zoning ordinance, told legislators: "I think there are many farmers who support the LCDC goal on the preservation of farmland." Oregon Shores supported full funding ("Conservation budget stirs pros, cons," 1975) and OEC urged that funding for DLCD be increased by $350,000 so the agency could design and implement programs on critical statewide areas and activities (Hemingway, 1975a).

Land-use and environmental advocates expected some property owners and their organizations to continue to challenge the statewide program on what they saw as ideological grounds. They were outraged, however, when Steve Hawes, testifying on behalf of OAR and AOI, said that not only did the groups he represented want DLCD's budget cut significantly, especially for work related to critical areas and significant activities, but he also urged fundamental changes in SB 100. OEC's lobbyist, who was close to the Straub administration, told members, "LCDC has not yet begun its first enforcement action," but "its opponents are already trying to portray it as a power-mad agency out of touch with reality so that it will never be able to get the funds it needs to get started" (Hemingway, 1975b). L. B. Day was incensed. In his opinion, the amendments that OAR and AOI proposed—embodied in a bill that wasn't even before the Ways and Means Committee—"call for the repeal of SB 100 . . . What's good for the realtors in this state isn't necessarily what's good for the state of Oregon" (Burdick, 1975b; Collins, 1975).

On behalf of the professional planning community, American Institute of Planners (AIP) President Larry Frazier told the committee that planners enthusiastically supported funding at the recommended level but they preferred the allocation proposed by LCDC. Studies of carrying capacity and areas of critical statewide concern were the two most important programmatic elements the planners wanted to see accomplished. The amount of grant funding proposed by LCDC was sufficient to enable local governments to make an effective start on revising their plans. Further, the information and guidance resulting from LCDC's work would be necessary if local planners were going to be able to produce plans that complied with the statewide planning goals (Frazier, 1975). Representatives of the League of Oregon Cities and the Association of Oregon Counties liked the governor's proposed allocation of funds and indicated their relative satisfaction with the ways in which their relationship with the state agency was evolving (Collins, 1975).

The governor's budget recommended forty-five DLCD positions; the legislative committee recommended forty-four. Those numbers represented a significant increase, but the legislators added a major twist by reallocating the positions to more than double the number of staff assigned directly to assist local governments. The committee decided to phase in the new positions, which cut the DLCD budget by $169,000, all of it from the general fund. While it substantially increased the state investment in local coordination, the committee recommendation meant a further reduction in the amount of professional staff time DLCD could assign to carrying capacity, critical area and significant activity studies, citizen engagement efforts, and evaluation of local government plans.

The Joint Committee's budget notes to LCDC's allocation were not legally binding, but they were taken seriously as expressions of legislative intent. The committee wrote: "The recommended budget provides 13-1/2 professional positions for the local coordination effort. It is the intention of the Legislature that these positions be physically assigned and based throughout the state in order to assist local government with the development of comprehensive plans." The committee also acknowledged that the amount of money budgeted for local government grants was significantly less than what would be required to complete plans and ordinances. It recommended that LCDC implement a decision rule to allocate the limited funds: "those local jurisdictions which can certify to LCDC the demonstrated ability to commit local resources to comprehensive development which, in conjunction with the state grant, could reasonably be expected to produce an approved or improved plan" should get top priority (Joint Committee on Ways and Means, 1975).

Given the trying economic times, passage of a $6 million budget for DLCD would be a major accomplishment. Straub's willingness to support that amount was profoundly important to the survival of the program, and the willingness of the Joint Ways and Means Committee and most of the legislature to support the budget was just as significant. That said, the revisions to the LCDC request set the state agency on a different path than the one the commissioners and their staff and wary allies wanted it to take.

The changes in the budget decisively turned DLCD away from a role that emphasized its own planning and regulatory responsibilities and toward one that was oriented largely to local facilitation, enforcement, and appeals. The Joint Ways and Means Committee had responded both to industry concerns about potentially excessive state power and to local government concerns about the amount of resources they would need. The result was a DLCD budget that seriously constrained the department's discretion and its capacity to implement some of the provisions of SB 100.

The creation of a set of county-based coordinator positions—field staff hired by the counties but funded by the state—also made the relationship between DLCD and local government planners more complex. DLCD staff wanted the coordinators to adopt a state-centered point of view and to defend that perspective to the local governments in their jurisdictions; they sought to prevent the county coordinators from "going native." Local governments, for their part, wanted their county coordinators to exercise as much discretion as possible to tailor goal-compliance efforts to reflect local conditions. The counties saw the coordinators as their advocates. Rural jurisdictions in particular wanted coordinators to convey to DLCD their respect for the ways counties engaged citizens and the weight they assigned to citizen wishes. The coordinators clearly faced conflicting expectations.

Proposals to Change the Statewide Land-Use Program

While developing the statewide goals, LCDC created a subcommittee staffed by Arnold Cogan to develop ideas for the 1975 legislative session. The members of the subcommittee worried that local governments might not be able to effectively evaluate large-scale development proposals, so they suggested revisiting one of the OEC-endorsed American Law Institute Model Land Development Code ideas that had not been incorporated into SB 100: the regulation of developments with regional impacts. Regulations would apply to shopping centers, recreational second-home projects, and industrial parks beyond a certain size. The subcommittee also wanted the legislature to give LCDC the authority to designate the location of power-generating stations and transmission lines. Developers of large-scale projects that promised state or regional benefits, they thought, should be allowed to appeal a local government's denial to LCDC, which should be authorized to reverse the local decision.

The subcommittee also recommended enabling legislation that would allow local governments to establish transfer of development rights programs, and they outlined a wipeout and windfalls policy, with windfalls funding wipeouts. The land-use decision-making processes had to be simplified, they thought, and they proposed one-stop permitting centers, with LCDC specifying procedural rules. Because tax policies had a large and sometimes contradictory impact on what land-use plans attempt to achieve, the subcommittee called for restructuring property tax assessments to make them consistent with plans and zoning ordinances and studying whether it made sense to shift the property tax burden from buildings to land. They concluded that the absence of a state growth policy was a problem. One proposed solution was for LCDC to designate growth areas after consulting with state and local government agencies and completing a comprehensive analysis of environmental, economic, social, and energy impacts. Other state agencies, such as the Oregon Department of Transportation (ODOT) and the Housing Division, would rearrange their investment priorities to support the growth-area designations, and local governments would designate industrial zones accordingly. The subcommittee also recommended that Oregon take advantage of recently passed federal legislation to create a new-towns program. LCDC would designate sites, and other state agencies would cooperate to implement the program. A bond-financed land bank would enable local governments, subject to LCDC approval, to borrow money so they could acquire and hold land in advance of development (Cogan, 1974d).

The list of potential legislative proposals, some of which had first been put forward in the late 1960s, was an ambitious one. It included many ideas being discussed by planners, attorneys, and land-use and environmental activists around the country—ideas that had not been incorporated into SB 100. Containing investment and incentive approaches in addition to regulatory programs, they aimed to strengthen LCDC's capacity to implement its conservation and development objectives.

Many of the subcommittee's ideas were embodied in bills introduced during the 1975 session. Two bills were proposed at the request of the Joint Land Use Committee—one authorizing local governments to establish transfer of development rights programs to implement their plans (SB 27) and another creating a division in the Department of Commerce to establish a one-stop permit process (SB 122). Committee chair Hallock also introduced bills that added to the list of activities that LCDC could designate and regulate—for example, the authority to designate the siting of power plants and transmission lines and to approve proposed plans and actions related to certain large-scale private developments (SB 91; SB 968). Other bills he sponsored directed LCDC to establish one-stop permitting processes for private development proposals (SB 838) and enabled LCDC to accept applications for major development proposals and to issue permits that would bind other agencies (SB 949). At Governor Straub's request, Janet McLennan wrote a bill authorizing LCDC to resolve conflicting permit requirements (SB 903) and creating a new division in the Executive Department where project proponents could apply for state and local permits. Through these legislative initiatives, the Governor's Office, the Joint Land Use Committee, and Senator Hallock were attempting to facilitate large-scale investments during a severe economic downturn and to give local governments tools that enhanced their flexibility to implement plans.

Another set of bills called for a state growth policy. HB 2304 proposed the creation of a Governor's Council on Oregon's Future; HB 2334 established a Population and Growth Advisory Commission; and HB 2639 required LCDC to prepare a growth policy for the state. Incorporating a concept embodied in many of the LCDC-adopted guidelines, a House Joint Resolution declared that a legislative policy on growth should take into account energy, the environment, the economy, and social considerations (HJR 45). On a closely related topic, HB 3012 required LCDC to study the potential development of new towns in rural areas. Several bills addressed financial aspects of the land-use program. HB 3026 introduced a windfall-wipeout approach to dealing with compensatory zoning issues, and a pair of bills changed the responsibilities of county tax assessors for assessing land in farm and forest use zones established pursuant to LCDC's goals (HB 2621; HB 3015).

All of this proposed legislation reflected concepts discussed by LCDC and its staff, and much of it embodied a desire to strengthen the agency's ability to coordinate state and local conservation and development actions. LCDC decided early in the session, however, that it would actively support only three bills: HB 3015 on property tax assessment; SB 210, to strengthen the state role in relation to federal government agencies that owned land in Oregon; and SB 638, which required the filing of all plans and implementation ordinances and mandated title insurance companies to insure plan and zone designations.

Environmental advocates wanted to push the statewide land-use program well beyond where it was. A bill was introduced at the request of OEC to add review authority for major development proposals (HB 2829); another (HB 3021), supported by OEC and Oregon Shores, provided the specific kinds of shorelands protections that LCDC had declined to adopt in 1974. HB 2885 established a real estate transfer tax designed to discourage speculation. OEC also supported one of Hallock's bills, SB 91, which added to the list of activities of statewide significance.

Senator Vic Atiyeh came at LCDC from a different angle, one that challenged what SB 100 and LCDC had produced thus far. SB 346, strongly supported by OAR and AOI, required the legislature to review and approve LCDC-adopted goals and guidelines. Another bill, sponsored by both Atiyeh and Senator Michael Thorne, was introduced at the request of the Oregon Landowners Association and its leader, Jim Allison. SB 497 amended the farm-use zone statute to permit outright nonfarm-related single-family homes and related structures on lots created before farm-use zoning was established. It also added several nonfarm uses to the list of those allowed in farm-use zones subject to county approval, including personal-use airports and helipads, and limited the application of exclusive farm-use zoning. Atiyeh also sponsored SB 309, a bill that would repeal the regional planning district that had been created in the Portland metropolitan area in response to SB 769 (1973). Oregon AFL-CIO, concerned that goal-related regulations might unreasonably constrain job and income growth, requested a bill that would require an economic impact report whenever there were proposed zoning and land-use changes (SB 630).

While the 1975 legislature was in session, the Oregon Supreme Court rendered a landmark decision in *Baker v. Milwaukie*. Steve Schell argued the case on behalf of plaintiff Jean Baker. AIP and OEC had asked Ed Sullivan, now legal counsel to Governor Straub, to submit a brief on their behalf because the case involved the nature of the relationship between a comprehensive plan and a zoning ordinance, as *Fasano* had. The two organizations wanted the Oregon court to continue along the path charted in 1973, when it found that comprehensive plans and zoning ordinances were distinct documents and that zone changes were subordinate to and had to be consistent with adopted plans. The court took the unusual step of asking Sullivan to argue before it.

The *Baker* decision held that when a comprehensive plan designates a less intense land use than what is permitted in a zoning ordinance, the plan prevails. The decision, rendered just as the building season was getting underway, triggered a determined effort by the Oregon Homebuilders Association, OAR, and AOI to secure a legislative remedy to an outcome that they thought would lead to moratoria on land development. Fred VanNatta and Steve Hawes argued that landowners and developers depended on zoning codes, which were much more detailed and specific than comprehensive plans. According to VanNatta (1975),

> The majority of comprehensive plans are much too general, impre-
> cise, and unclear to take the burden placed on them by the "*Baker*"
> case. Read a comprehensive plan. See if you can determine the
> boundaries between the colors on the map. See if you can deter-
> mine in any given area if you can build a house, an apartment,
> or start a business based on the comprehensive plan. Maybe you
> can tell, and maybe you can't . . . This chaos created by the *Baker*
> case . . . may set land use planning back a decade in this state. An
> initiative measure with broad support may well be the result.

VanNatta and Hawes met with Ed Sullivan, Janet McLennan, L. B. Day, and city and county representatives to craft a compromise. The cities and counties believed they could resolve conflicts on their own and did not think legislation was necessary. VanNatta and Hawes argued that a period of time should be established during which existing zoning ordinances would prevail over plans. Sullivan resisted their argument, and no agree-ment was reached.

VanNatta and Hawes sought amendments to SB 122, one of the bills introduced at the request of the Joint Land Use Committee that had been referred to a committee co-chaired by Vic Atiyeh. Sullivan urged caution in a summary of the *Baker* case for the senator: "The whole statutory scheme of planning and zoning places the comprehensive plan in a superior posi-tion to the zoning regulations"—a position strongly reinforced both by SB 10 and SB 100. "Since *Fasano*," Sullivan continued, "neighbors have come to rely upon the comprehensive plan as the standard upon which rezon-ings . . . will be judged—this legislation would leave no standard during the gap so that high-powered developers could push through a rezoning with virtual immunity" (Sullivan, 1975). Atiyeh's committee voted, however, to amend SB 122 as VanNatta and Hawes had proposed. Steve Schell argued vigorously that the amended bill was not needed and that it was "unfair to citizens who have participated in developing comprehensive plans and have relied on those plans for determinations of land use in their areas . . . What some short-sighted developers want is 'just one more development' based on antiquated zoning ordinances before newer comprehensive plans are applied to them" (Schell, 1975).

Only a few of the proposed land-use bills passed during the 1975 session: the federal lands-related bill and an amended version of the county tax assessment bill that LCDC supported; an amended version of the permit-center bill submitted on behalf of the governor; and an amended version of the bill that Atiyeh and Thorne introduced about nonfarm uses in farm-use zones. The federal lands bill was largely symbolic. Oregon governmental entities could not require federal agencies to act in ways that were consistent with state or local regulations. The county tax assessment bill, as introduced, required the assessment of real property at its value under existing zoning designations. The version that passed told assessors to take into consideration existing plans, zoning designations, and other land-use restrictions. It took time and additional effort to bring county-level assessment practices in line with what advocates of farmland preservation sought to achieve. Amendments to the bill to create a permit center made participation by local governments optional and eliminated LCDC's conflict-resolution role. Amendments to the Atiyeh/Thorne bill eliminated the section permitting nonfarm-related single-family homes and related structures on lots created before farm-use zoning was established. It also eliminated some of the non-farm uses proposed for the list of those allowed in farm-use zones subject to county approval. Personal-use airports and helipads remained in the bill.

Overall, industry groups and local governments successfully resisted the expansion of LCDC's authority and the adoption of new conservation-oriented land-use initiatives. Planning and environmental advocates, in turn, parried significant challenges to SB 100 and LCDC and efforts to advance development-oriented policies. OEC's lobbyist noted that the legislature "seemed ready to give land use planning a chance to work" and that money allocated to DLCD "should give it the opportunity to hire the staff necessary to get on with the job for which it spent all last biennium 'gearing up'" (Hemingway, 1975c). Bob Stacey, about to start working as a 1000 Friends of Oregon staff attorney, agreed that "LCDC finally has money—not much in its own operations budget, but . . . it is no longer weak; land use planning proponents will begin to demand action . . . and start constructively carping at the results" (Stacey, 1975c).

The Joint Legislative Committee on Land Use

The Joint Land Use Committee reviewed three key issues that remained unresolved: relations between the state land-use and environmental-quality agencies, which was part of the larger question of whether or not LCDC should designate activities of statewide significance and institute permitting processes; the prospects for compensatory zoning; and the behavior of county tax assessors in relation to the land-use planning program.

DLCD and DEQ. In November 1975, 1000 Friends Attorney Richard Benner urged LCDC to designate the planning and siting of sewerage facilities as an activity of statewide significance. His request was triggered by a letter from L. B. Day to the Environmental Protection Agency recommending that the agency not require an environmental impact statement on a sewage project in Lincoln County, on the Oregon coast. Benner was concerned that the approach the state Department of Environmental Quality (DEQ) used to make decisions about the land-use effects of such projects was inadequate. That approach, adopted in March 1975, involved a "sign-off" procedure in which local elected officials stipulated that "they have reviewed the project and find that it does not violate applicable land use plans of the county and meets applicable statewide planning goals and guidelines and laws." DEQ did not inquire further into the situation, because doing so was not part of its legislated mandate and it lacked the time and expertise to examine land-use impacts in any case. Benner was concerned that the size and location of the Lincoln County project would trigger a sprawling pattern of development on the coast and frustrate local and state efforts to plan for a more compact form of urban growth.

In the spring of 1975, 1000 Friends urged DEQ to deny septic tank permits for a subdivision proposed for lands that, according to LCDC's Agricultural Lands goal, should be zoned for exclusive farm use. Because there was no plan or zoning ordinance in place for the property, 1000 Friends told DEQ that the agency was required to apply the goal directly to the permit application and issue a denial. DEQ resisted, but DLCD director Hal Brauner supported the watchdog's interpretation (1000 Friends,1975b).

In light of the 1000 Friends initiatives and testimony from an OSPIRG researcher on the implications of sewer projects for land-use planning, L. B. Day wrote the Oregon Environmental Quality Commission requesting that it "delay taking action on the recommended priority list for sewage construction grants until your next meeting and that you request your staff to review their recommendations with the LCDC staff" (Day, 1975). DLCD staff prepared a memorandum of understanding with DEQ, but neither commission took formal action. After a hearing on the issue in July, the Joint Land Use Committee concluded that effective coordination between DLCD and DEQ was critically important to the success of both their missions and that the issue of sewers had to be addressed. "The size and location of sewer lines," the committee noted, "is now regarded as the prime factor affecting urban growth nation-wide." The sign-off procedure implemented by DEQ was "inadequate to assure real compliance with local comprehensive plans and LCDC goals and guidelines. It resulted in *pro forma* statements of compliance, not supported by specific findings." The committee asked the two agencies to agree as soon as possible on a coordinated approach to sewer facilities and land use. DEQ and DLCD promised that an agreement was forthcoming (Joint Legislative Committee on Land Use, 1976).

While the two agencies were negotiating their relationship, an LCDC subcommittee chaired by commissioner Richard Gervais explored alternative ways of addressing activities of statewide significance. DLCD staff were directed to work with University of Oregon planning faculty and students to develop case studies of the impacts of activities that LCDC was authorized to designate. In their August 1976 report, the UO team recommended that public transportation facilities be designated an activity of statewide significance but that the other activities be handled through the planning and review processes associated with existing statewide planning goals. Taking those recommendations and the OSPIRG study on sewer and water facilities into account, the subcommittee decided not to designate any activities or to establish a permit system. Instead, it recommended that DLCD review local comprehensive plans and determine whether or not they adequately addressed impacts (Carter, 1975b; Gervais, 1975; Lake, 1976). 1000 Friends wanted more. They continued to believe that

> the most efficient long range solution is LCDC designation of location of sewerage facilities an activity of statewide significance. It would remove a burden which DEQ is unwilling to carry and put it in the hands of the agency with the information necessary to review projects quickly and effectively. (Benner, 1976c)

The commissioners declined, though, to change the local plan review path they had chosen to pursue.

Land Use and Tax Assessment. During the 1975 session, the legislature attempted to align property tax-assessment practices with land-use plans and zoning decisions. In August, however, the Joint Legislative Committee on Land Use learned about county tax assessors continuing to value properties based on the assumption that zoning designations were likely to change to permit more intense land uses. A key issue for the committee was that, in light of the *Fasano* and *Baker* decisions, tax assessors had to understand that changing plan and zone designations to accommodate land-development proposals would be a much more complex, time-consuming, and uncertain process than in the past. Current designations, not possible future designations, had to govern assessments for tax purposes.

The committee learned that the Department of Revenue had not issued an administrative rule implementing HB 3015, although an educational program about new assessment procedures was in place. The committee wrote the director of the Department of Revenue praising the educational effort but also urging him to issue an administrative rule to address those cases where assessors were not yet implementing the new approach (Kafoury, 1975). Joint Committee staff drafted a set of guidelines, which the Department of Revenue adopted and promulgated in early 1976, but citizen groups in Clackamas County reported that "the county assessor simply refused to recognize the law in this area." Because the guidelines did not carry the legal force of rules, the committee drafted legislation for the next session (Joint Legislative Committee on Land Use, 1976). The bill failed to pass in 1977, and re-orienting county assessment practices remained a challenge.

Compensatory Zoning. SB 100 required the Joint Committee to study the issue of compensatory zoning and make a recommendation to the legislature. Oregon courts had adopted the beneficial-use test, the committee concluded, as had state courts around the country:

> A taking occurs only when planning and zoning leave the landowner with no beneficial use of his property . . . So long as the most restrictive portions of local plans and zoning ordinances center around farm use designations for prime agricultural land, the beneficial use test will be complied with, and the question of taking will not be successfully raised.

The committee staff heard UCLA law professor Donald Hagman describe a possible windfall/wipeout scheme, but he "said he was not sure that his plan could feasibly be applied in the real world." The Bureau of Government Research and Service at University of Oregon had issued a comprehensive report on compensatory zoning in January 1975, and a faculty group at Oregon State University had National Science Foundation funding to study the topic. The Joint Committee decided that more information was needed to make a good decision and recommended against moving forward with any proposal: "A hastily adopted scheme could cost the state or local governments enormous sums, and could bankrupt the land use planning effort. More work must be done in Oregon and around the country to determine whether windfalls and wipeouts can or need to be dealt with legislatively" (Joint Legislative Committee on Land Use, 1976). When the OSU group issued its results in 1977, they agreed with the Joint Committee's assessment. While the sort of system outlined by Hagman, in theory, might improve equity and efficiency, "the most serious area of concern is the ability of our property assessment system to accurately identify and measure land value changes caused by zoning actions. Without substantial new funding the task is probably impossible, and even with such funding it is not to be envied" (Ervin et al., 1977). The Joint Committee was loath to plunge into a policy domain fraught with such uncertainty and was unwilling to recommend allocating resources to reduce the uncertainty involved.

A Willamette River Greenway Goal

In late 1974, Governor-elect Straub had written Glenn Jackson to express his serious displeasure with the ways in which ODOT's consultant had revised the preliminary Greenway plan in response to LCDC concerns about too little local government involvement and the potential negative impacts on farmers. Straub was concerned that the plan too severely restricted ODOT's authority to acquire land for recreational purposes. Straub and Jackson agreed that ODOT would not submit the preliminary plan to the Oregon Transportation Commission (OTC) until after the new governor took office and the plan reflected his priorities.

The Greenway Plan was changed in early 1975 to enhance ODOT's role in relation to LCDC and local governments, removing references to the commission and local government plan making and implementation.

The plan also incorporated authorization for the state to acquire property beyond the purchase of scenic easements. OTC scheduled a public hearing on the new plan in late April. At the governor's request, Janet McLennan prepared and the House Environment and Energy Committee sponsored two bills reflecting his ideas on the Greenway; and Straub hosted boat and air trips for Fadeley, the committee chair, and other members during which he elaborated on his vision (Colby, 1975; Roby, 1975a, b). Despite a challenge from farmers who had been galvanized into action by L. B. Day (McLennan, 2009), OTC approved the plan and sent it on to LCDC. The bills introduced at Straub's request did not pass: one never emerged from committee, and the other was narrowly defeated on the House floor.

LCDC agreed to hold a public hearing in September to consider the Willamette Greenway Plan that OTC had approved, along with several implementation approaches DLCD was considering: adoption of the proposed plan, coordinated planning in the context of the adopted statewide goals, the adoption of a new Greenway goal, and the designation of an area of critical statewide concern (Land Conservation and Development Commission, 1975a). A fifth alternative emerged before the hearing: the resurrection of the preliminary plan developed in 1974 by the ODOT consultant and tentatively approved by LCDC (Land Conservation and Development Commission, 1975d). Local governments strongly supported the last alternative, as did farmers and others who participated in the hearing (Greenleaf, 1975a). At a public hearing in the Willamette Valley during October, yet another approach surfaced that included a new statewide planning goal, the interim adoption of the Greenway boundaries set out in the 1974 plan until permanent boundaries and land-use designations were established by a joint ODOT-local government planning effort and approved by LCDC, and a requirement that the boundaries and use designations be incorporated into local comprehensive plans that LCDC would acknowledge (Bauer, 1980). LCDC rejected the OTC-approved plan and endorsed the integrated approach.

In December, LCDC adopted a fifteenth statewide planning goal and a preliminary Willamette River Greenway Plan. The plan contained interim boundaries and restricted land-use changes within them to protect the Greenway until a final plan was approved. In line with earlier adopted goals, urban and rural area requirements were distinguished and an exceptions process was included. After the interim period, though, the Greenway goal required a compatibility review for proposed changes in both urban and rural areas, a new twist to local plan implementation. Existing land uses were permitted to continue, and farm uses were not affected.

The approach adopted by LCDC transformed the Greenway program by enhancing the authority of LCDC and local governments in relation to the state transportation agency. While ODOT would still be able to acquire property under certain circumstances, recreational and other development possibilities would be determined by local government comprehensive plans and implementation ordinances that were subject to LCDC approval. LCDC's emphasis on conservation in rural areas would constrain Greenway recreational development alternatives, as well as public access to the Willamette River. A zoning-based regulatory approach overshadowed the acquisition-oriented effort that ODOT and Straub wanted to pursue.

Local governments generally were pleased. The Yamhill County planning director wrote the Joint Committee: "It is our belief that . . . LCDC has spent considerable energy and time in developing this goal and that the process of adoption is to be commended for the numerous opportunities for people to become involved and for the ability of . . . LCDC to consider the impact of the proposed goal on the local governments" (Greenleaf, 1975b). McLennan, however, thought the Greenway goal was "incomprehensible" (McLennan, 1976d). Henry Richmond wrote 1000 Friends Advisory Board member J. W. Forrester, Jr.:

> I have shared the same concerns you expressed . . . about a possible clash between the Straub administration and LCDC on greenway goals . . . I agree with you that the most important step is to preserve farmland in the greenway . . . the farm community now appears to be in support of what . . . LCDC is doing and this is an essential ingredient in the success of . . . LCDC objectives for the Willamette Valley . . . I have told L. B. Day and Janet McLennan that I think the Agricultural Lands goal is more important than . . . recreation . . . and if pushing hard right now on the greenway threatens the agricultural lands goal, then I am inclined to back off a little bit. (Richmond, 1975l)

Day agreed with Richmond's position, and he successfully oriented the goal and the plan to address the concerns expressed by LCDC's key farmer and local government stakeholders.

LCDC clearly had won the confrontation with Straub and Glenn Jackson's state transportation agency, but the governor was still looking for ways to insert his priorities during implementation. In an article about the Willamette Greenway for the 1,000 Friends newsletter, Governor Straub struck a cautiously optimistic note about the LCDC-adopted plan and goal (Straub, 1975). Straub and McLennan also began to rethink Day's role on LCDC as a result of their Greenway-related conflict, a process that intensified during the commission's even more controversial effort to adopt a set of statewide planning goals for the coast.

Chapter 9
The Agency, the Watchdog, and the Dynamics of Local Planning

"The work can't all be done at once. LCDC needs to give some direction on what should be done first."—Henry Richmond

With the Department of Land Conservation and Development budget approved, much of the agency's attention for the remainder of 1975 was focused on putting in place a process to give state money to local governments. Proposed plans and ordinances had to be submitted to Land Conservation and Development Commission for review by January 1, 1976, or local governments had to show evidence of satisfactory progress toward meeting the statewide planning goals. First, LCDC had to define what "satisfactory progress" meant, taking into account the priorities the Joint Ways and Means Committee had articulated in its budget note. Working closely with its Local Officials Advisory Committee and an ad hoc group of local planners, DLCD staff began to craft a feasible allocation process. Planning advocates worried that the commission might be reluctant to state clearly how satisfactory progress should be measured, and 1000 Friends of Oregon mobilized to prevent the goal displacement they saw looming ahead.

In mid-June, the Local Officials group presented its allocation recommendations to LCDC. They proposed a point system with five criteria, the weightiest of which addressed the Joint Ways and Means Committee's concerns about local progress and commitment. The criteria also took into account growth and development pressures on a jurisdiction, ability to pay, willingness to share resources with other local governments, and size of population and land area. That system would be used to rank requests for time extensions and money. DLCD asked local governments to evaluate the progress they had made in planning and implementation in light of LCDC's goals and report what remained to be done. The legislature's mandate that LCDC evaluate local government work done pursuant to SB 10 thus became a requirement that local governments evaluate their own progress. The Local Officials group incorporated into its proposal a review role for itself regarding the prioritization of requests for funding (Carter, 1975a).

At Henry Richmond's request, two professional planners at Skidmore, Owings and Merrill reviewed the group's proposal. "In its present form," they reported, the plan "does not address the most basic issue facing Oregon's cities and counties—i.e. —what does it take to comply with LCDC's goals and guidelines. Unless compliance is clearly defined now, the next two years could be a planning nightmare for LCDC." LCDC needed to articulate a procedure for evaluating and improving local plans already adopted and in process and to describe what local governments would have to do to comply with the statewide goals. The two planners also developed a workbook to guide local planners through their compliance efforts (Crandall and Diemoz, 1975).

Richmond had another concern: "The grant criteria are applied to *who* the applicant is, rather than *what* the applicant proposes to do with the grant money . . . planning grants should be used as a tool to effectuate state land use policies and to secure compliance and satisfactory progress as defined by . . . LCDC." He told L. B. Day that LCDC ought to explicitly establish priorities for the next biennium, because everybody knew that cities and counties would not be able to comply with all of the goals during that period. "The work can't all be done at once," he concluded. "LCDC needs to give some direction on what should be done first." Program priorities should vary by region, he thought, with money tied to specific standards related to goal compliance. The priority for Willamette Valley cities, for example, should be the designation of urban growth boundaries, required by the Urbanization goal; Willamette Valley counties should focus on implementing the Agricultural Lands goal outside those boundaries. "Such a framework for local planning," Richmond said, "will enable LCDC to give the 1977 Oregon Legislature a meaningful and persuasive status report: e.g. 'x' thousands of acres of Willamette Valley farmlands have been identified on maps and protected by implementation of LCDC's Agricultural Lands Goal" (Richmond, 1975d). He urged Day to consider making growth control a priority in the Willamette Valley, reminding him about the continuing loss of farmland there and the availability of soil information that could be used to designate agricultural lands (Richmond, 1975e). The LCDC chair, however, was reluctant to take an action that might appear to give one statewide planning goal a higher priority than any other.

DLCD staff members met with local planners at the end of June—the first time such a meeting was held—to discuss "operational" issues associated with implementing the statewide program. They wanted to get responses to drafts staff had prepared about the nature of local comprehensive land-use plans, criteria for evaluating those plans for compliance with statewide laws and goals, and the process for requesting time extensions. Several challenges to getting local planners' attention and getting them on the same page became evident. The DLCD staff member summarizing the meeting noted, "for many of these [local] planners, their frames of reference are short range; they have invested little or none of their time in conceptualizing about the development and operation of the state's planning program." He was also dismayed to learn that "several individuals were skeptical of the ability to actually produce a single plan for a city or county," and that "most appeared to be unwilling and unable to voice an opinion about our description" of a comprehensive plan, which involved modifying the notion of such a plan so that "it will become the central guiding land use blueprint for his jurisdiction." In addition, "it was apparent that a number of those present have little or no idea about how to achieve or meet the coordination responsibilities expected of them," although the DLCD staff member acknowledged that "achieving coordination is an area that we really have not thoroughly addressed in-house," and added that the agency should begin to focus on that quickly, especially in the context of training the county coordinators who would be hired and DLCD's own field representatives. Local planners also wanted better coordination with state agencies, and access to state agency data, and wanted clarification about the level of detail in their inventories that would be expected of them (Knight, 1975).

In August 1975, DLCD presented a revised approach that set out criteria for getting a planning assistance grant and for receiving either an extension based on satisfactory progress or a temporary extension for more time to demonstrate satisfactory progress. In both cases, evidence that the local government had designated a citizen involvement body and had established a coordination mechanism figured prominently. Several planners told LCDC that the latest draft from DLCD staff was complicated; it would take too much time to complete, called for subjective judgment, and would not produce documentation of necessary facts. "If this material is used as the basis of LCDC's grant program," four of them concluded, "we predict that confusion, wasted effort, and costly delay will result. We realize that LCDC is anxious to proceed with its grant program. We feel, however, that time spent now in establishing a valid and workable program framework will result in . . . future savings in time and money" (Cramton, et al., 1975; DeBonny, 1975; Greenleaf, 1975a; Land Conservation and Development Commission, 1975c).

DLCD staff sought to chart a path to goal compliance in the context of the continuing argument over state-set priorities and the role of objective data on the one hand and local discretion on the other. In November 1975, following a round of comments by local governments and after two weeks of intensive work by staff and members of an ad hoc group of planners, LCDC distributed the *Oregon Land Use Handbook*. Local planners were asked to assess the extent to which they had done goal-related inventories of agricultural and forest lands, for example, and the extent to which they had considered social, economic, energy, and environmental needs. They also were asked to assess the extent to which they had identified and resolved potential conflicts between, for example, resource-protection and development-oriented goals and to supply goal-related quantitative baseline data on such measures as the number of acres the jurisdiction had designated as agricultural and forest lands. Local planners were also asked to describe their citizen involvement programs. The *Handbook* laid out procedures for applying for money and for preparing a schedule for the work that remained to be done to comply with each goal. It also contained descriptions of successful citizen involvement programs and concluded with a discussion of alternative approaches to preparing and presenting comprehensive plans. The example was the Washington County framework plan.

The intent of the *Handbook* was to provide information that would enhance the rationality of LCDC decisions about extensions and grants. The commission leaned heavily on local governments, many of which, especially among the counties, had limited analytical capacities, to evaluate how well they had complied with a large number of interrelated plan-making and implementation requirements. DLCD staff would look closely to see that local planners had identified and addressed internal contradictions in comprehensive plans, and they would evaluate the relationships between facts, policies, and implementation choices. Some county planning directors who worked in jurisdictions that were committed to a strong land-use program shared the more state-centered approach that recognized the importance of objective information as a basis for decision making. However, all local planners foresaw technical and political challenges they would face when responding to the information requests in the *Handbook* and in preparing their requests for extensions, funding, and acknowledgment of compliance.

Of 277 jurisdictions in Oregon, 247 submitted a request by the deadline (Collins, 1976), and processing the requests became a massive undertaking. By early April 1976, LCDC had approved 82 requests for extensions, 46 of which were temporary. Thirty-five of the 36 jurisdictions that received planning extensions were granted funds. LCDC had not received all of the federal money it had anticipated, however, so the reserve fund administered by the Emergency Board had to be tapped. A handful of jurisdictions had sent their adopted plans and implementation ordinances to LCDC seeking formal acknowledgment; but knowing that their responses would create precedents, the staff proceeded cautiously (Gassaway, 1976).

When the City of Eugene submitted its acknowledgment-of-compliance request on March 1, 1976, it included fifty documents that comprised its Comprehensive Plan. The *Oregon Land Use Planning Handbook* had made it clear that there were several acceptable approaches to preparing and revising comprehensive plans, so DLCD staff members were anticipating variations, but they were not expecting such a large number of documents. The absence of an overview of the Eugene plan and the process used to produce it, and the lack of a volume that clearly related each document to the statewide goals made it still more difficult for DLCD to review the Eugene submission. Eugene planners, led by director John Porter, clearly intended to send a message to the state: the city had been planning for some time with a staff that was more experienced than the DLCD staff, and LCDC should take whatever the city wanted to give it. In the end, DLCD requested an additional thirteen documents from Eugene and did not complete its analysis until February 1977.

In September 1976, two southern Oregon cities, Medford and Central Point, were the first to be acknowledged for their comprehensive plans as they applied within their city limits. Full acknowledgement awaited agreements between the two cities and Jackson County on their respective urban growth boundaries. LCDC's field representative had coordinated the assistance that local planners had received from federal and state agencies, and several commissioners had visited the cities to work out potentially troubling details. Hal Brauner was encouraged and optimistic about the future. "Following current projections, given continued financial and technical assistance from the State," he predicted, "all cities and counties will have adopted comprehensive plans that fully comply by mid-1980" (Department of Land Conservation and Development, 1976).

Experiences elsewhere, though, suggested a more troubling forecast. Planners for the City of Gresham, at the eastern edge of the Portland metropolitan area, were not sure whether to apply for an acknowledgment of compliance or for a planning extension. When they asked for advice, DLCD's Jim Knight told them that they needed to do more work before the state could acknowledge the comprehensive plan. He identified issues that would surface in many other cases:

> We found your plan to consist of a collection of broad, sometimes conflicting community objectives spanning a variety of topics . . . [S]upporting materials (inventories, special studies, etc.) were referenced but could not be clearly traced to adopted decisions. So far, we have been able to isolate neither the policies nor the reasons for their adoption.

There was also no evidence, Knight said, that Gresham had coordinated its plan with the policies and projects of other agencies and special districts. Further, "specific requirements of the goals appear to have not been followed closely . . . it is not possible to know if the goals have in fact been carried out in your plan." Knight's tone was cordial as he thanked the city for its support and praised its efforts thus far: "For me, the opportunity to work with a city considering acknowledgment is proving very valuable in learning to balance our requirements with the needs and circumstances of the community" (Knight, 1976a).

It wasn't long before the long-serving Gresham city manager left his position and the mayor made public statements that were critical of LCDC and its program. The local newspaper editorialized against SB 100, and Knight learned that the city would delay seeking a planning extension until after the forthcoming SB 100 repeal effort was settled. He initiated conversations with a Gresham city councilor who was also on the Columbia

Region Association of Governments board, and who "recognizes that our position is not being adequately represented in the press or in the Mayor's comments." Knight offered to "meet with Gresham leaders, and to bring a commissioner if requested, to discuss all aspects of the Gresham-LCDC relationship" (Knight, 1976b). This kind of political dynamic characterized what happened in many other jurisdictions as well.

Even though there wouldn't be any state money allocated for local planning until 1976, the January 1, 1976, deadline for the submission of local plans and ordinances remained in effect. LCDC made it clear that requesting one of the two types of extensions would satisfy the legal requirement, and that it was well aware that it would take many jurisdictions several years to complete the process. However, SB 100 authorized the agency to take over local planning and zoning if it deemed a jurisdiction was not making satisfactory progress. In addition, McLennan noted that tension between the state agency and local governments occurs when "LCDC makes judgments about the propriety or diligence of local agency planning. The fact that LCDC wields a big stick in the form of grants of money only exacerbates the tension" (McLennan, 1976a).

Twelve jurisdictions were given one-year planning extensions at the first LCDC meeting in 1976. Eleven of those local governments told LCDC that it would take between ten months and six years to fully comply with all of the statewide planning goals. The twelfth, Lane County—the only county that would have to comply with all nineteen of the goals that LCDC adopted—said it would take ten years to complete the job. Bob Stacey saw a ray of hope in the willingness of the commission to state program priorities as it gave one-year extensions. "Day and the rest of the Commission minced no words in asserting the protection of agricultural lands as the first order of business," he wrote in *1000 Friends of Oregon Newsletter*. He reported that LCDC required the cities to designate urban growth boundaries and the counties to protect agricultural lands with exclusive farm-use zones as soon as possible (Stacey, 1976a).

A few months later, however, Stacey was dismayed to learn that LCDC had given Lane County a new three-year planning extension, which allowed the county to take until mid-1979 to finish zoning agricultural lands for exclusive farm use (Stacey, 1976b). It was an example of a broader conflict between DLCD and counties over priorities. While DLCD wanted to prioritize drawing boundaries and zoning for exclusive farm use—although LCDC still hadn't formally designated priorities among the goals—many counties wanted to defer those controversial tasks as long as possible. In June 1976, following a meeting during which the commissioners processed 110 requests for extensions, 1000 Friends filed a petition asking LCDC to impose minimum conditions on those jurisdictions that received extensions. Stacey told the Joint Land Use Committee that the demands of processing cases on LCDC and DLCD were resulting in "the granting of loosely drawn compliance schedules that stretch out over several years." Those extensions created lengthy periods during which agricultural lands, especially in the Willamette Valley, were at risk for urbanization. "Counties will apply their existing zoning ordinances to these lands," Stacey warned. "No county has a formal policy of directly applying the LCDC goal standard to a building permit application in farmland, and many existing ordinances allow one to five acre homesites in agricultural areas." Moreover, a great deal of agricultural land in the Willamette Valley still was not zoned at all. 1000 Friends wanted LCDC to mandate that those counties receiving an extension adopt an interim ordinance requiring immediate compliance with the Agricultural Lands and Urbanization goals (Stacey, 1976c).

LCDC did not initiate the new approach that 1000 Friends wanted to see. Shortly after the organization filed its petition, L. B. Day resigned from LCDC and Governor Straub announced that he would not reappoint Steve Schell and Paul Rudy. A November ballot measure repealing SB 100 loomed ahead, and there was a great deal of conflict between DLCD and coastal jurisdictions over the adoption of coastal goals. The Governor's Office attempted to diffuse these linked crises by changing the composition of LCDC and signaling to local government and industry critics that it would contemplate amendments to SB100 during the 1977 legislative session.

Changing Commissioners and Surviving a Ballot Measure Challenge

In early July 1976, Governor Straub discussed with reporters Day's decision to resign. The governor had spoken at town hall meetings around the state, he said, and he concluded

> that there had built up a lot of personal resentment toward L. B. Day. I want to say it was because of his success with which he operated as chairman that this criticism was stirred up. I also felt that

when I saw that the opponents of LCDC would get their measure on the ballot . . . that it was extremely important that we not permit any personality to interfere with the success of the LCDC vote in November. (Straub, 1976b)

Day had antagonized a number of local government officials when coastal goals were being written and had been "hanged in effigy before a hearing" in Florence. Day had responded, the *Oregonian* reported, by saying that "the city officials [in Coos Bay] are the biggest bunch of irresponsible asses that ever walked the earth." Such "frankness . . . earned Day many enemies and caused many attacks on himself" (Church, 1976).

Day also tangled with local governments about what he saw as their inadequate response to the Oregon Supreme Court's *Baker* decision. The *Capital Journal* reported that Day complained that "'it is inexcusable that local governments throughout the state have not acted . . . Every governing body should be acting right now to resolve these conflicts.' And Day backed his criticism with the threat of action by . . . LCDC" ("Day rips local governments," 1975). He also had criticized Salem city officials about what he saw as their limited response to *Baker*, and the Association of Oregon Counties and the League of Oregon Cities had protested LCDC's creation of an ad hoc committee to evaluate the City of Salem's planning process (Bennett, 1975; Olson and Carruthers, 1976). Day believed, as did many land-use and environmental advocates, that "'most local governments would be incapable of standing up to the local interests out there. They can't stand up to them without the LCDC backing them up'" (Robinson, 1976).

Day certainly could be abrasive in his dealings with local officials, but under his leadership the commissioners and staff had worked hard to respond to local government concerns. He may have been reviled on the coast, but the interests of officials there had been accorded a great deal of weight during the coastal goals development process. Day also had frequently expressed his strong support for job-creating local economic development efforts on the coast and throughout the state.

Straub clearly wanted to avoid the November ballot measure becoming a referendum on Day's leadership, but he had another reason for wanting to see him leave the commission: their conflict over the Willamette River Greenway program. Straub had been deeply disappointed that LCDC had successfully challenged his vision for the Greenway during the 1975 legislative session and the Greenway goal development process (McLennan, 2009, 2008).

After Day made his resignation from LCDC public in early July 1976, Henry Richmond told him,

> I think you have done an excellent job and made an absolutely tremendous contribution to the state. I believe *no one* in Oregon could have brought LCDC from where it was in February 1974 to where it is today except you. Your land use priorities have been right all along, and you have protected the agency from its enemies . . . I am most grateful to you for making yourself available to me over the past two years to discuss the program." (Richmond, 1976a)

L. B. Day felt similarly about 1000 Friends' contribution to the program he led, telling a Portland publication a few months before he resigned: "They've made our process work, made it mean something." Day was back in the state legislature as a senator representing Marion County in 1977, and he would work closely with 1000 Friends for several years.

Straub told reporters that John Mosser would replace Day as chair of the commission. Janet McLennan strongly supported him, as did Henry Richmond; and she worked hard to persuade Mosser to accept the appointment (McLennan, 1976c). In addition to his prior service as a legislator and agency leader, Mosser was also a student of land-use planning, who had taken a sabbatical, from fall 1975 to the next spring, to travel in Europe, primarily in the Netherlands and in France, to study the planning that was going on there. He was also familiar with land-use initiatives in the United States (Mosser, 1990; Uhrhammer, 1976). Mosser was reluctant to step into the LCDC position, though, because it was so controversial. He believed that L. B. Day "had made enemies almost everywhere in the state by going around telling local officials that they had to do this and that and had built up a great deal of resentment"—unnecessarily, Mosser thought. He also was troubled by what he perceived as serious organizational problems: "The program appeared to me to be totally disorganized. The staff was chaotic . . . They had some good people on the staff, but they had sort of grown like topsy and they were one big family. The world was out there against them and they were going to save the world" (Mosser, 1990). The *Oregon Times* reported that Mosser was "expected to be no less committed to land use planning [than Day], but a lot quieter" (Scharf, 1976).

While Mosser was highly regarded by his LCDC colleagues, Governor Straub's early public mention of him as the new chair generated some concern among continuing members. Under SB 100, the commissioners were supposed to elect their own chair, and the governor appeared to have taken that responsibility from them. Commissioner Albert Bullier, Jr., weighed in with his belief that "in view of the existing concerns of land use planning and the LCDC, the most qualified member of the Commission to serve as Chairman" was Richard Gervais, who had extensive experience as a locally elected official. He "expressed his concern for the way in which the chairmanship was announced," because "he felt it is time for the Commission to disengage itself from the politics and concentrate on the acceptance of this program statewide." Gervais "shared Commissioner Bullier's displeasure with the manner in which the appointment of a replacement for Commission Chairman was made" and "emphasized that the Commission is not run by the Governor's Office but by the members of the Commission." In the end, however, Jim Smart nominated Mosser for the position, and he was elected unanimously (Land Conservation and Development Commission, 1976b).

Straub and Janet McLennan also replaced commissioners Steve Schell and Paul Rudy, both of whom were strong advocates of coastal resource protection. Conflict continued to surround the adoption of coastal goals, and the governor anticipated high levels of support for the November ballot measure among coastal residents. Schell was disappointed at the change, but he thought that "'it was a politically wise move on the governor's part . . . L. B. was regarded by many as a tough dictator,' and many coastal residents regarded Schell 'as a wild-eyed environmentalist'" (Roby, 1976). McLennan urged the appointment of Anne Squier to replace Schell. A biologist, Squier was a founding member of Oregon Shores and chair of the state's Water Policy Review Board. She joined LCDC as it moved forward on the coastal and Willamette Greenway goals (McLennan, 1976c, d). Straub replaced Paul Rudy with J. W. Forrester, publisher of the *Daily Astorian*, a member of the 1000 Friends advisory board, and an advocate for economic development on the coast.

Mosser made it clear that the LCDC role and the size of the DLCD staff should get smaller over time, as more and more local government plans and ordinances complied with the statewide goals. Mosser "said the LCDC mission is primarily to get local jurisdictions to complete their own comprehensive plans as soon as possible—then fade from the limelight" (Hayes, 1976). Hal Brauner at DLCD shared some of Mosser's views. He told an *Oregon Times* reporter that his staff did not necessarily "know much about the practical political problems with which localities have to cope" and that "the naivete of the state planning staff is already being made an issue by the repeal forces. Brauner figures if his staff grows much beyond its present scope that it will mean the state is doing things it has no business doing" (Scharf, 1976). He also pointed out, however, that the DLCD staff was doing an enormous amount of work under intense pressure, putting in enough hours on a voluntary basis to equal four full-time positions (Hayes, 1976).

Mosser helped lead the effort to defeat Measure 10, the initiative on the November ballot that called for the repeal of SB 100. Fellow LCDC member Dorothy Anderson joined him on the steering committee of Citizens to Save Oregon's Land, which was created to spearhead the opposition to the measure. Janet McLennan, Henry Richmond, Hector Macpherson, John Gray, Larry Williams, labor representatives from the building trades, and other civic activists were also on the steering committee. According to the group, Ballot Measure 10 was supported primarily by "landowners, farmers and conservative groups who view LCDC and state-wide planning as an infringement on private property rights, loss of local control, too much governmental bureaucracy and dictatorship of appointed officials." More than 80 percent of the signatures gathered to place the measure on the ballot were obtained from a handful of counties that had coastal jurisdictions, two southern counties, and the two Portland metropolitan-area counties that had a substantial amount of rural land—Clackamas and Washington (Citizens to Save Oregon's Land, 1976). Governor Straub put the repeal effort in a larger context:

> Powerful national forces have reportedly boasted that they can raise a campaign warchest of $250,000 to repeal SB 100. I'm not surprised—nor is their strategy difficult to discern. If land use planning can be defeated in Oregon—its major stronghold—then it can be defeated in any state in the Union. The opposition is looking to complete a devastating one-two punch against the sensible and sensitive management of our land resources. The scuttling of the National Land Use Act was the left hook . . . Measure 10 in Oregon would be the lethal right cross—*the knockout.* (Straub, 1976a)

Citizens to Save Oregon's Land planned a sophisticated, wide-ranging approach to defeat the measure. "The issue," they concluded, "boils down to those who say that LCDC is going to take away your property vs. those who say we are trying to protect Oregon for the children and grandchildren" (Citizens to Save Oregon's Land, 1976). In August, an Associated Oregon Industries leader reported that one poll found

> strong support for the concept of land-use planning in the metro-politan area, which he expects will defeat the ballot measure . . . A lot of noisy action is coming out of Roseburg [in southwest Oregon], but it takes more than Douglas County to repeal the LCDC . . . it would be chaos if Ballot Measure 10 passes and the Land Conservation and Development Commission is disbanded.

AOI leaders continued to think that land-use planning was necessary ("Oregon Industries . . . ," 1976) and the rumored national campaign did not materialize.

Even though major business groups did not support the measure and it appeared headed for defeat, Governor Straub continued to indicate that he would be willing to consider amendments to SB 100 during the upcoming legislative session. Hallock wrote the governor to express his concerns:

> I believe that the time has come to cease being gentlemanly regarding the subtle and most clever attempt to set-up Senate Bill 100 for psychosurgery in the 1977 session . . . So far, to "stave off repeal" . . . we have given the enemy the head of L. B. Day. Surely that should suffice as a goodwill offering . . . I am well aware of the fact that you and Mosser . . . have lived your lives based on the "diplomacy wins friends" precept . . . It comes to me that we just might be involved in the beginning days of a war . . . and if that's the case, victory can't possibly belong to the generalists, the cliché peddlers, the selfish . . . If you concur that it's time to really punch (I mean you personally, not the campaign), then I hope you will . . . really *lead* the current campaign to prevent repeal, but, of probably even more importance, to prevent erosion or emasculation come next January. (Hallock, 1976)

Wade Newbegin Jr., president of the 1000 Friends board of directors, wrote Governor Straub to express his concern "about your willingness to support amendments to Senate Bill 100 . . . without insisting on specific evidence of problems in the legislation," especially regarding citizen appeals to LCDC. Newbegin thought appeals had been useful both to LCDC and local governments. He concluded:

> I know many businessmen who support Senate Bill 100 for the same reason I do: it will not only help take care of the special qualities that make Oregon a wonderful place to live, it is beginning to give badly needed, long-term protection to the rich agriculture and timber lands which are the foundation of Oregon's ability to create wealth. Let's not weaken a program which is effectively making headway toward these goals unless there is ample justification. (Newbegin, 1976)

But Straub thought there were modest changes that might enhance the effectiveness with which SB 100 was implemented (Straub, 1976c). He told Ted Hallock:

> I am spending a lot of my time trying to defeat Ballot Measure 10. It is difficult for me to strike an aggressive posture, as you recommend . . . Perhaps, if I thought I could make an unequivocal . . . case to the people that not one word and not one comma should be changed, that would be the course I should select. However, I cannot find it in my style to make that case with conviction.

Ballot Measure 10 received only 43 percent of the vote in the November election. The margin of defeat was 2 percent greater than in 1970. The measure was successful on the coast, though, where LCDC was still developing four new planning goals. Similar initiatives would fail in 1978 and 1982, and in each case an organization similar to Citizens to Save Oregon's Land would be created to oppose it.

The continuing stream of legislative challenges and ballot measures created turmoil for LCDC, as the agency's existence, its programs, and staff positions were continuously contested in an intensely politicized atmosphere. DLCD staff experienced the tension on a daily basis; they bonded tightly in response to it. The agency during the early years was a mostly flat organization; the relative absence of hierarchy engendered a sense of solidarity among staff members and between staff and agency managers. The personal values of staff members were aligned with the work they were doing. They took a great deal of pride in the statewide land-use program and their roles in it. There were often sharp disagreements within DLCD about particular issues, but the feeling that their work was critically important for Oregon's future, and that planners, activists, and officials elsewhere were watching, gave them a long-term perspective on the program, kept them talking through their internal conflicts, and sustained them.

A consequence of the turmoil was that the many local officials who were reluctant to plan and zone—for reasons ranging from the overwhelming nature of the tasks they faced to their opposition to LCDC's goals—delayed or moved slowly to implement SB 100. 1000 Friends and its allies, who were watching the horizon of acknowledged plans and ordinances recede, intensified their efforts to monitor and enforce the law. They sought to ensure that the goals were directly applied to land-use actions until the acknowledged plans and ordinances were in place, sometimes in cooperation with and sometimes in opposition to state and local planners.

DLCD staff were in the middle between 1000 Friends and local planners and officials; county coordinators were often aligned with local actors as well. They were also in the middle between local planners and officials and groups opposed to the state land use program. A complex relationship between DLCD staff and county planning directors evolved over time. Sometimes county directors quietly told DLCD they knew the state agency had, for example, correctly identified a problem with their proposed plan or ordinance, but they were unable, for local political reasons, to fix it. The county planners wanted DLCD to order them to address the problem, thereby strengthening their position at the local level. A similar "good cop/bad cop" routine, along the lines Tom McCall earlier described to Congress, emerged in the relationship between DLCD and 1000 Friends, and in the relationship between county planning directors and 1000 Friends. County planners would sometimes tell critics of a proposal that planners thought was required by a statewide goal that 1000 Friends would very likely appeal if something contrary was put forward to LCDC. DLCD staff sometimes leaned on 1000 Friends in a similar manner in their relationships both with local governments and their commissioners. Planners and the watchdog were aware of the mutually interdependent nature of the roles they were playing, but serious strains sometimes emerged as a result of the intense conflicts that often enveloped state and local planners.

The political and economic forces shaping state, special district, and local land land-use decisions continued to operate during mandated local comprehensive planning processes, subject primarily to the coordination constraints imposed by SB 100 and LCDC goals. Jurisdictions continued to compete with one another to attract private and public investments, and public and private investors continued to exert influence on state and local planners and decision-makers to facilitate their projects. Long accustomed to undertaking land-use-related actions, state agencies saw SB 100 requirements and LCDC proposals as opening up long-settled practices to negotiation both with local governments and LCDC. The resulting tensions made coordination problematic.

Local comprehensive plans and ordinances made explicit who were winners and losers among property owners and developers. For some participants, particularly state-level planners and the state officials who supported them, explicit plans and ordinances would lead to a more stable environment for private and public investors; the more certain the future of land uses, the more investment there would be. Explicit outcomes emerging during planning processes, however, increased conflict, which severely challenged local planners to complete plans that reflected professional norms, were technically feasible, and were in line with legal mandates. Local planners sometimes wanted flexibility to craft politically feasible outcomes when confronted with conflicts; they wanted to solve problems specific to their places.

Mindful of the political pressures bearing on planners, 1000 Friends sought to prevent local planners, especially county planners, from being captured by governmental and private sector advocates of development, and to prevent DLCD planners from being captured by their local level counterparts. Problem-solving behavior by planners often appeared to the public interest attorneys as evidence of capture. 1000 Friends also worried that the demands of processing large numbers of local government requests would distract DLCD staff from focusing on achieving the statewide planning goals. That is why the attorneys leaned so heavily during the early years on appeals to LCDC and to the courts, to counterbalance the pressures bearing on planners at both state and local levels. DLCD staff members were acutely aware that the findings they were writing about particular issues would serve as the basis for legal proceedings when there was a challenge; that disposed them toward a legalistic approach when dealing with local counterparts.

While most state and local planners generally supported what the watchdog was trying to accomplish, when 1000 Friends challenged an exercise of discretion that it felt transgressed a statewide planning goal— when planners were told they had to follow the rules and enforce the law—the political conflict that resulted made the practice of planning very complex, especially about rural issues.

Chapter 10
The Coastal Goals

"Politically we have a situation in which no one is happy. The local leaders and government officials who invested time and pride in OCCDC feel their work is being shunted aside. The environmentalists . . . find the draft goals full of political compromise and too vague to be enforceable. They allege with merit that the goals may well fall short of meeting the federal standards."—Janet McLennan

The four coastal goals that the Land Conservation and Development Commission adopted in December 1976 were shaped by the requirements of a federal law as well as the availability of federal money. LCDC leaned heavily on planning grants from the federal Office of Coastal Zone Management (OCZM) to fill out its budget. When the Oregon Coastal Conservation and Development Commission (OCCDC) finally delivered its products in early 1975, the commission hoped to adopt goals by June and submit them as the core of a grant application to the federal agency for implementation funds. That spring, Department of Land Conservation and Development staff distilled nine draft coastal goals from the forty-two policies OCCDC adopted and invited comments. Conflict between LCDC and local coastal governments about their respective roles dogged the goal adoption process from beginning to end.

Along with the preservation of agricultural lands in the Willamette Valley, the protection of fragile coastal resources was a major area of concern for 1000 Friends of Oregon. In March 1975, Richmond submitted a lengthy memo to LCDC criticizing the recommendations OCCDC had delivered to the legislature and the commission. He argued that the OCCDC policies failed to designate areas of particular concern in the coastal zone and to specify permitted uses within them. OCCDC had also failed to complete coastal shorelands inventories, identify coastal shorelands boundaries, classify shoreland resources and specify permissible uses within those boundaries, and classify different types of estuaries and specify uses permissible within those types. All those elements were required, Richmond argued, given the real threats to coastal resources. Furthermore, that information was needed to obtain federal approval for implementation funding. He recommended applying for another planning grant and taking the time to get it right (Richmond, 1975d).

Based on Richmond's concerns and comments at public hearings, LCDC decided to apply for another planning grant and appoint technical advisory committees to revise four basic coastal goals; the new target adoption date was March 1976. Acknowledging a concern expressed by several OCCDC veterans, L. B. Day announced that the committees would be asked to evaluate the economic consequences of proposed goal revisions, and he promised that testimony from the forest products industry in particular would be sought ("OCCDA will elect . . . ," 1975). Richard Benner chaired a committee to write a goal for shorelands, and Bob Stacey was named a member of an estuaries and wetlands goal committee.

The technical committees worked through the summer and produced drafts that addressed the issues Richmond had outlined in his memo. The estuaries committee, for example, took a classification scheme that OCCDC had recommended local governments adopt and made it part of a revised goal, thereby transforming the scheme into a mandatory element. Uses permitted in the different classifications were included, but local governments would assign estuaries in their jurisdictions to particular classes. The shorelands committee defined boundaries in terms of distances from different bodies of water, listed five possible use priorities, and permitted uses for different kinds of shorelands. Again, local governments would assign priorities in their jurisdictions.

In December 1975, LCDC held a public work session to consider the goals developed by the technical advisory committees and DLCD staff. The commission also entertained the recommendations proposed by the Oregon Coastal Conservation and Development Association (OCCDA), the group of coastal city, county, and port officials that LCDC helped establish. At the end of the session, LCDC decided to eliminate six of the nine goals it had originally proposed because the existing goals adequately addressed those issues. DLCD staff was directed to continue working on planning goals for estuaries, beaches and dunes, shorelands, and the continental shelf, although LCDC leaned toward the OCCDA's recommendations rather than those suggested by the technical advisory committees regarding the character of those goals. As Andy Zedwick, the OCCDA chairman, said: "Our organization definitely came out on top, compared with LCDC's technical advisory committees." LCDC told DLCD staff to write goals that would give local governments on the coast more flexibility to plan for development (Hayes, 1975). In addition, the commission directed that the draft document should include both goals and guidelines, unlike the Willamette River Greenway goal, which had no guidelines. The reintroduction of the goal-guideline distinction generated the same sort of conflict that had occurred earlier.

A tabloid titled "Draft Land Use Planning Goals and Guidelines for the Coastal Zone," presenting a second set of goals, was widely distributed in early 1976. The introduction noted the impact of the major policy decision LCDC had made in December: "the draft goals as presented here are less specific than earlier drafts, but will provide sufficient standards to assure prudent use of coastal resources in specific applications in local comprehensive plans" (Land Conservation and Development Commission, 1976a). Neither OCCDA nor land-use and environmental activists, however, were pleased with what DLCD staff had proposed. Summing it up for Governor Straub, Janet McLennan said:

> The published goals are extensive, complex and confusing. Politically we have a situation in which no one is happy. The local leaders and government officials who invested time and pride in OCCDC feel their work is being shunted aside. The environmentalists . . . find the draft goals full of political compromise and too vague to be enforceable. They allege with merit that the goals may well fall short of meeting the federal standards.

In addition, the commission was running out of time to qualify for federal implementation funds (McLennan, 1976a). LCDC scheduled hearings and two public work sessions to review the testimony.

The Joint Legislative Committee on Land Use considered a resolution challenging the approach embodied in the draft goals. The committee said they understood and appreciated LCDC's desire to "permit local governments the broadest discretion consistent with protection of statewide interests," but implementation by local governments had to be "clearly reviewable" by LCDC. Because the draft goals "place clear and precise statements of permissible uses and priorities among uses only in guidelines," LCDC would not have the authority the federal government required to review local decisions. In its proposed resolution, the committee urged LCDC to "include clear and reviewable statements of uses which the state deems permissible together with statements of priority among such uses in particular areas, in the text of the coastal goals" (Joint Legislative Committee on Land Use, 1976).

Steve Hawes submitted comments to the committee on behalf of Associated Oregon Industries, challenging the argument that the federal legislation required the coastal goals to include the detailed elements called for in the resolution. If those elements were necessary in order to comply, however, Hawes said that the appropriate course was for LCDC to recommend to the legislature the designation of the coastal zone as an area of critical state concern:

> To suggest . . . that LCDC can now alter the philosophy of SB 100 and establish a critical area without prior legislative approval is a not too subtle attempt to overcome the progress made to date in land use planning. It also assumes that local governments are incapable of providing proper protection for estuarine and other coastal areas . . . LCDC intent, in interpreting the limits of SB 100, has been to allow as much local discretion as possible . . . We should not bend our land use program for a few dollars to meet a broad national program not designed with Oregon's SB 100 in mind. (Hawes, 1976)

On behalf of the Homebuilders Association, Fred VanNatta reinforced Hawes's points (VanNatta, 1976).

The government affairs manager for the Weyerhaeuser Company added his opinion: "Compliance with this resolution would . . . threaten the success of the land use planning effort on the coast as it would undoubtedly create a groundswell of resentment and opposition from Oregon's coastal community" (Conover, 1976). The *Daily Astorian* editorialized that "[Senator] Hallock said he proposed the resolution 'because I don't trust those coastal counties,'" and he "stirs residents of the coastal counties to white heat by his inference that non-coastal residents should dictate use of the resources of the coastal counties" ("Give us time to think," 1976).

Richard Benner urged the committee to adopt the resolution. SB 100 did not contemplate leaving "unfettered planning authority in the hands of local governments," he argued, and the goals were intended to articulate statewide interests. He also pointed out that "strong, clear standards are very much in line with the Oregon land use planning program. The two goals which will have the greatest beneficial effect on the state . . . the Agricultural Lands Goal and the Urbanization Goal—are the two goals with the clearest, most specific standards." Compliance with federal requirements wasn't just a matter of money, he said. It also meant implementation of the federal consistency clause, which, given the major presence of several federal agencies in the state, meant a good deal to Oregon (Benner, 1976a).

The Joint Committee agreed and adopted the resolution. The chair's statement announcing the action said:

> While the committee hopes that adequate protection will be provided for estuarine and shoreland areas, its intention is not to limit in any way the healthy economic development of the Oregon coast . . . The proposed goal changes, particularly with regard to estuaries, should help in this effort, allowing concentration of limited development resources where they will do the most good. (Kafoury, 1976)

Based on conflict that surfaced during public hearings—McLennan (1976b) referred to them as "wild" —L. B. Day urged the commission to postpone goal adoption until the end of the year. His colleagues agreed and directed DLCD staff to revise the draft coastal goals in light of the hearings. A third draft, distributed in June, distinguished between goals and guidelines and placed the estuary classification system, shorelands-related boundaries, and specified permissible uses and priorities in the guidelines rather than in the goal statements. With a grant from OCZM, LCDC mounted an educational program that featured more than a hundred meetings between DLCD staff and coastal officials and residents during September and October. Another set of hearings was held on the coast in November and early December (Hildreth and Johnson, 1985).

OCZM itself solicited comments in September and October on the draft Oregon Coastal Zone Management Program, which was based on the proposed goals. Benner submitted a lengthy critique of the program. The proposed goals, he wrote, "are unreviewable and unenforceable because they do not contain clear standards . . . The Oregon program includes 'permissable uses' and 'priorities of uses.' But they are merely suggestions for local implementation." He concluded that the Oregon approach was "inconsistent with the requirements and intent of the Coastal Zone Management Act." On behalf of 1000 Friends of Oregon, he recommended that "the Office of Coastal Zone Management urge the Oregon Land Conservation and Development Commission to make the changes in the current proposed program necessary to receive [implementation] funding" (Benner, 1976b).

The Natural Resources Defense Council challenged the draft Oregon program on the same grounds that Benner had (Beers, 1976). Maradel Gale, a former Oregon Environmental Council president, who had been one of the six gubernatorial appointments to OCCDC in 1971, testified that the draft goals would permit each local jurisdiction to classify estuaries and permissible uses as it saw fit. "What is likely to occur at the local level," Gale worried, "is that short-term economic interests will prevail, and even in estuaries not remotely within the realm of economic development, there will be a push to classify certain segments or areas for future development." What was missing was a region-wide comprehensive classification of estuaries that took into account that some estuaries should have no development at all (Gale, 1976).

LCDC was set to adopt coastal goals in mid-December. In late November, Benner wrote the OCZM director to express 1000 Friends' concern that LCDC had not yet heard about whether or not there were any problems with its program that might jeopardize federal funding. "LCDC must be notified," he wrote, "as soon as possible of OCZM concerns about the Oregon program if the current efforts are not to be wasted." Benner reiterated his earlier criticisms and pointed out that "LCDC has still not amended the draft goals to include use and priority standards." Benner copied the letter to new LCDC chair John Mosser, Hal Brauner, and DLCD coastal program staff (Benner, 1976d).

DLCD coastal specialist Edward LaRoe wrote to the commissioners before a scheduled public work session in early December to "clarify the stance of the Office of Coastal Zone Management regarding our program" in light of the concerns Benner raised. LaRoe was in a good position to do so because he was an employee of OCZM on loan to DLCD and was aware of the agency's latest thinking. He was also the federal coastal program staff person who had toured South Slough in 1974 when OCCDC and LCDC were considering nominating it for estuarine sanctuary status. LaRoe pointed out that "standards must be sufficiently substantive and specific to allow for administrative review and enforcement of compliance." He also noted that "as long as the state legislature allowed LCDC some . . . discretion, OCZM should not second guess the state, so long as the process for decision making is adequate, the input to the process is adequate, and the state can enforce its findings" (LaRoe, 1976).

Led by Anne Squier and James Forrester, the commission decided to make the goals more specific. They would classify estuaries to retain diversity, an approach Benner had recommended in 1973, and the Beaches and Dunes goal would prohibit residential, commercial, and industrial development on active foredunes and other specific areas. The Shorelands goal would include a specified minimum area within which resource inventories were required for planning purposes, although the commission also decided to limit the spatial extent of the goal to shorelands that are unique to the coast and directly linked to coastal resources.

Richmond and Benner, however, saw deficiencies in the revised Shorelands goal and suggested some changes. The revised goal, they worried, still did not contain "standards according to which particular kinds of shorelands can be classified. These are included in guidelines and are thus unenforceable suggestions which may be disregarded at will." Similarly, the suggested list of priorities for the use of coastal shorelands remained in the guidelines. Richmond and Benner told the commissioners that in 1975 the technical advisory committee on shorelands—Anne Squier was a member of that committee—had recommended that a classification system be included in the goal statement and noted that Washington State's coastal program, the only one in the country approved by OCZM, included a classification system and a list of priority uses. They recommended that the "structure and approach of the coastal Shorelands Goal should be the same as the Agricultural Lands Goal. The difference—an important one— would be to have four resource classifications instead of one, and four sets of permissible uses instead of one" (Richmond and Benner, 1976).

At its December 18 meeting, LCDC adopted four goals that became the foundation of Oregon's coastal management program. In the Estuarine Resources goal, LCDC committed itself to developing a system in which each estuary would be assigned to a particular class based on the most intensive development and alteration permitted in the waters and wetlands of that estuary. The commission adopted, effective in October 1977, classifications that identified twenty-one of the twenty-two estuaries in the coastal zone as natural estuaries, conservation estuaries, shallow-draft development estuaries, or deep-draft development estuaries. Local governments would develop management units within each classified estuary in their jurisdictions. Natural-area management units were required even in those estuaries that were classified for development. The Coastal Shorelands goal included ranked priorities for the use of shorelands, a definition of a coastal planning area, and a specified interim boundary within it. It differentiated among urban, urbanizable, and rural areas and set out permissible land uses for shorelands development. The goal would apply to shorelands within the interim boundary as of January 1, 1977.

Presenting the proposed coastal management program for LCDC review, DLCD Deputy Director James Ross said, with regard to permissible uses and priority of uses in the zone, "Our revised coastal goals address these uses, and their priorities, with greater specificity than earlier drafts." He also noted that some reviewers had questioned whether or not the commission had sufficient authority to implement the proposed program. DLCD was "in the process of identifying the standards contained in our goals and in the supporting statutes" to document that ability, and "the final revisions to the coastal goals greatly assisted this identification by explicitly establishing standards" (Ross, 1976).

Richmond was pleased with the proposal and even suggested that Governor Straub compliment the commission "for completing an enormously difficult job, with great competence and political tact" (Richmond, 1977a). Andy Zedwick of the Oregon Coastal Zone Management Association (OCZMA)—which succeeded OCCDA—disagreed both with the way in which LCDC had amended the goals and the substance of those amendments. He urged the National Oceanic and Atmospheric Administration (NOAA)—the Office of Coastal Zone Management was a unit within NOAA—to "intercede for the postponement of approval of Oregon's Coastal Management Program by the Office of Coastal Zone Management until the concerns of local officials have been addressed." OCZMA had petitioned LCDC to delay adoption of the coastal goals in December: "Without paying heed to elected coastal officials . . . LCDC, an appointed body, adopted a revised version of the Coastal Goals . . . Although the adopted goals are significantly different from the previous drafts, no public hearings on the finalized Goals were conducted." Zedwick also charged that

> LCDC has consistently ignored and circumvented the efforts of [OCZMA] . . . While . . . LCDC is hurriedly attempting to comply with . . . the requirements of the Coastal Zone Management Act . . . to justify its budget requirements to the State legislature, it is in effect hampering and endangering the very Program that is so extremely important to coastal residents by ignoring coastal input, alienating coastal officials, and in fact, undermining the potential effectiveness of the Program. (Zedwick, 1977)

Zedwick failed to persuade OCZM to postpone action, and Oregon's coastal program was approved in May 1977. During fiscal years 1977 and 1978, OCZM granted $3.35 million to Oregon for implementation, funds that were critically important to the continuation of the statewide land-use planning effort.

Still, relations between many coastal officials and LCDC remained tense. One of the planners who had moved from OCCDC to LCDC in 1975 and had worked on the coastal management program told commissioners shortly after the goals were adopted that "local governments at the coast are . . . grappling with . . . tasks they perceive to be of such magnitude that it's just creating a lot of trauma." Addressing the fourteen goals adopted in 1974 presented a major challenge to planners on the coast, and adding the four coastal goals made the prospect of comprehensive planning even more daunting (Coenen, 1977).

Epilogue
Oregon's Unquiet Land-Use Revolution Unfolds

> *"The prospects seem bright that Oregon's SB 100 goals can and will mature into the Nation's most complete and effective State urban strategy."*—John DeGrove and Nancy Stroud

Ironic twists abound along the winding path to Land Conservation and Development Commission approval of the first generation of local comprehensive plans by the mid-1980s and the evolution of the statewide program beyond that phase through 2009. Some of the ironies evolve from the legislative compromises embedded in SB 100 and the politics of the LCDC budget in 1975. Others stem from the decisions made by LCDC about goal-related definitions and the question of priorities among them. Ideas and proposals initially rejected or inadequately appreciated re-surface in different settings. Unintended consequences emerge from the ways in which contentious issues were addressed during the early years. Oregon's unquiet land-use revolution unfolds in relation to those consequences through legislative mandates and administrative agency actions taken in the context of continuing conflict and cooperation among land-use program stakeholders.

Critical Areas
While the legislature declined to incorporate specific critical areas in SB 100 and LCDC did not recommend the designation of the Columbia River Gorge and the Metolius Deer Winter Range as critical areas, several goals and key pieces of federal legislation nevertheless functioned in similar ways. The goals that applied to the Willamette River Greenway and the coastal zone were regional in nature and more specific than other substantive goals, as was the way in which agricultural land was defined in Goal 3. In those cases, LCDC had taken advantage of the detailed inventories that were prepared

by other state and federal agencies and had adopted goals that would shape local government regulations. The legislature had carved parallel paths for the Greenway, the coastal zone, and exclusive farm-use zones, creating a favorable context for LCDC action on those goals. In 1986, Congress passed the Columbia River Gorge National Scenic Area Act, which embodied a critical area approach that built on LCDC goals and on a gorge commission previously established by the legislature. Richard Benner left 1000 Friends of Oregon to direct the Columbia River Gorge Commission and to lead its effort to adopt a land management plan for the scenic area (Abbott et al., 1997). During the 2009 session, LCDC returned to its December 1974 decision and recommended that the legislature designate the Metolius River Basin an area of critical statewide concern, the first time a critical area had been recommended for designation since 1977, when the agency did so for a sensitive natural area on the coast in response to an Oregon Shores request (Herman and Hull, 1981; Ouderkirk, 1992; Rindy, 2004).

An ironic reversal regarding the role that critical areas should play emerged early on among program supporters and critics. While he strongly supported the designation of critical areas in SB 100, Henry Richmond argued in 1977 that requiring local governments to complete their plans first had some significant advantages. "The justification for further state incursion in the local government domain to regulate critical areas . . . may be less when local planning programs comply with the state's basic land use regulations" (Richmond, 1977b). Bill Moshofsky, the Georgia-Pacific lobbyist who had testified against designating critical areas in SB 100, began in 1976 to advocate getting LCDC out of the business of regulating local comprehensive planning and restricting its mandate to designated critical areas (Moshofsky, 1976). A property rights organization he helped found, Oregonians in Action, continued unsuccessfully to urge the legislature to make that fundamental change.

Comprehensive Plans, Zoning Ordinances, and Resource Lands Conservation

SB 100 and LCDC in 1974 interposed local comprehensive planning between the state-level definition of agricultural land based on soil classification and the adoption of exclusive farm-use zones by local governments. LCDC refused to explicitly prioritize Goals 3 and 14, and most Oregon local governments were not applying the statewide goals directly to the land-use decisions they were making about, for example, whether or not to change an existing zoning designation or to annex land to a city. In May 1977, however, LCDC decided to stop allowing local governments to design their own planning work schedules and to require them to sign an agreement that they would either adopt adequate interim measures to protect agricultural lands in accordance with Goal 3 by the end of September or adopt exclusive farm-use zoning by the end of March 1978. LCDC also required cities and counties to sign an agreement by the end of September 1977 committing them to collaborate to produce urban growth boundaries and stipulating a date by which the boundaries would be adopted (Brauner, 1977; Land Conservation and Development Commission, 1977). While it took several years before local comprehensive plans were in compliance with all statewide goals, the LCDC action sped up implementation of Goals 3 and 14.

By mid-1980, 84 percent of the privately owned land in the Willamette Valley that LCDC had expected would be designated exclusive farm use was zoned that way; statewide, the comparable figure was about 67 percent. A report to the National Agricultural Lands Study in 1981 concluded that Oregon's farmland protection program was "the most fully integrated and comprehensive in the country" (Coughlin et al., 1981). At the same time, however, just 34 percent of all local government comprehensive plans—17 percent of county plans statewide, including one Willamette Valley county plan—were in compliance with all statewide goals by the end of 1980, six years after the goals had been adopted. The difference between the proportion of land zoned for exclusive farm use and the percentage of local governments with acknowledged comprehensive plans reflects in large part the LCDC decision to prioritize the implementation of Goals 3 and 14.

A world-class wine industry did, indeed, emerge, right where the two vintners told Governor McCall in 1973 it would if given a chance.

Oregon's approach to dealing with requests to exempt property from exclusive farm-use zones differed from the approach used in Hawaii and British Columbia. State and provincial agencies in those places created processes to respond to requests for zone changes from landowners and local governments. The procedure in British Columbia for refining the boundaries of agricultural zones, for example, included a provincial acknowledgment that errors had occurred during the adoption period because of decisions made hurriedly and the use of inadequate information (Garrish, 2002/3; Pierce, 1981; Pierce and Furuseth, 1982; Runka, 2006).

Oregon local governments had available the Goal 2 exceptions process if they wanted to exempt particular rural parcels from an exclusive farm-use zone. There was a great deal of variation in the extent to which and how well counties used the exceptions process; it was rigorous, and both DLCD staff and 1000 Friends watched it closely. Many agricultural landowners likely believed that they would still be able to sell or develop their land whenever they thought it was time to do so, and they wanted the tax benefits in the meantime. If a parcel of agricultural land was not given an exception during plan making, however, the Goal 3 definition of such land and state and watchdog scrutiny made it difficult to change. Early on, there was no legitimate, state-level process of "refinement," as there was in British Columbia. A significant and continuing level of tension resulted as county planners and officials confronted disappointed property owners and constituents, and sometimes it appeared to local actors that insistence on the continuing utilization of objective standards produced irrational farmland zoning decisions.

By 1979, Hector Macpherson had developed some sympathy with that local point of view. He told the Joint Legislative Committee that "[i]ncreasingly the courts have put a high burden of proof on local governments that would use the exceptions process to legalize actions demanded by their constituents," and expressed his concern that legal decisions were "fast turning planning into a technical process in which public desires cannot be accommodated even when local officials attempt to apply the goals in a reasonable way . . . [S]ome re-interpretation of the exceptions process is badly needed" (Macpherson, 1979).

The continuing tension spilled over into the legislature in two ways: first, legislators frequently added to the list of nonfarm uses that were permitted either outright or conditionally in exclusive farm-use zones; second, they attempted to modify the definition of agricultural land and to define "commercial," a term left undefined during goal development that related to the use of minimum lot sizes in farm-use zones. During the 1980s, 1000 Friends contributed studies of decision making by counties in exclusive farm zones in which the watchdog alleged that in many cases local officials had failed to follow required procedures and had permitted uses in those zones that were at odds with what was legally mandated. County decisions, 1000 Friends worried, were undermining the state's efforts to preserve the land base for the economically crucial agricultural sector. While DLCD and some county planners critiqued the watchdog's methods and conclusions, DLCD acknowledged that it had limited capacity to monitor the situation and did not have a clear idea of what was happening on the ground in rural Oregon (Rohse, 1985). The absence of information about the cumulative effects of local land-use decisions was an ongoing concern that kept 1000 Friends and DLCD staff vigilant.

Continuing controversy about the rationality of objective standards used to define agricultural land and commercial farming, rising real estate prices, and an influential property rights movement spearheaded by Oregonians in Action that was increasingly influential in the state legislature but frustrated by gubernatorial vetoes in the mid-1990s, led to the passage of two ballot measures that challenged core aspects of the statewide land-use program (Abbott et al., 2003; Howe et al., 2004). While Ballot Measure 7, which passed in 2000, was invalidated by the Oregon Supreme Court on procedural grounds, the passage of Ballot Measure 37 in 2004 persuaded the state legislature and the governor that it was necessary to take a "Big Look" at the program as a whole, something that had not happened since the mid-1970s. The task force that began meeting in 2006 struggled with many of the same contentious issues that had surfaced earlier.

A 2005 survey suggested that passage of the measures in 2000 and 2004 reflected a firm belief among a majority of Oregonians in the importance of protecting individual private-property rights. At the same time, most people supported protecting resource lands, especially farmland, and believed that land use should be determined by public planning processes rather than market-based decisions. Two-thirds of respondents to the survey believed that growth management had improved the state's quality of life (CFM Research, 2005). In 2007, Ballot Measure 49 passed, substantially reducing the potential land-use impacts of Measure 37. Oregonians appeared to be of two minds regarding the statewide land-use program, reflecting both the continuing importance of land-use priorities established in the 1970s and newer political and economic circumstances.

In the end, the legislature adopted relatively modest changes to the statewide program in 2009. Counties were authorized to review lands designated as farm and forest for "mapping errors" that might have occurred when their plans and zones were originally acknowledged. Amendments had to be based, in part, on an analysis of the carrying capacity of the land for the proposed nonresource uses. In addition, the legislature also authorized a transfer of development rights program—a bill to do so had been introduced in 1975—and DLCD is implementing a pilot effort to test different approaches in forested areas.

LCDC and Other State, Local, and Regional Governments

The budget and policy direction that LCDC had received from the Governor's Office and the legislature in 1975 and the defeat of several bills that would have enhanced DLCD's capacity had set the Land Conservation and Development Commission on a limited, largely reactive path. John Mosser supported an agency focus on getting local comprehensive plans and ordinances approved, as did Governor Vic Atiyeh, who defeated Bob Straub in 1978. The commission would not be producing a statewide growth policy or regionalizing goals within the context of carrying capacity. LCDC's lack of resources to regionalize the statewide program during the early years, however, reinforced resistance to the mandates to plan and zone in conformance with the statewide goals, as a sense that the state agency was imposing a "one-size-fits-all" approach took root. The absence of an explicit statewide growth policy and LCDC's decision not to designate activities of statewide significance made it difficult to coordinate investments by state agencies and special districts that significantly influenced the pattern of land development.

Another consequence of the choice to shift resources away from DLCD and to local governments was to reinforce LCDC's reliance on the goals to achieve growth-management objectives, and dispose the agency to clarify and elaborate in policy papers and administrative rules what many of the goals required in light of what LCDC was learning through processing cases. Local governments sometimes interpreted those initiatives as "moving the goalposts," and the resulting sense of regulatory unreasonableness reinforced local dispositions to challenge the state. LCDC frequently felt it necessary to resort to legal means to force compliance with its goals.

Macpherson also noted that LCDC's choice early on to withhold acknowledgement until plans and ordinances fully complied with all applicable goals exacerbated state-local tensions. When he and his group were formulating SB 100 they understood clearly that "planning was an ongoing process," and, in retrospect, he now believed that "[n]o greater error in judgement was made in the original legislation than to assume that the entire process of conforming the [local] plans . . . to the goals could be compressed into one year following the adoption of the goals." He thought it would be appropriate for LCDC to tell local governments submitting plans for review that some goals were adequately addressed while others weren't. LCDC would require improvements in those areas needing work during a scheduled plan update; however, "only very serious deficiencies would cause plans to be totally rejected." Macpherson wanted LCDC to "accept plans with minor deficiencies," in order to "ease the planning tensions around the state" (Macpherson, 1979). Many DLCD staff members and 1000 Friends opposed formally adopting that strategy, though.

In line with the good cop/bad cop dynamic that Governor McCall had described to a congressional committee in 1973, Macpherson said he expected that "solid requirements adopted at the state level would cause consternation somewhere in the state. The steam generated would be safety valved in Salem, protecting local officials who were conscientious in applying goals." However, Macpherson saw that a "wave of recall movements against local officials despite the safety valve undermines their ability to cope. Obviously we can't protect every official from attack," and he now worried that "[t]he adversary relationship between the LCDC and local governments that I see developing around the state is the most destructive force on the horizon." He felt it necessary "to remind ourselves that planning is a political process and that local officials need some room in which to maneuver." The nature and extent of room for local officials to maneuver had always been, of course, at the center of contention, and 1000 Friends and its allies were vigilant in their continuing efforts to reduce the amount of room available as much as possible. Indeed, everyone involved in land-use issues was well aware that planning was intensely political, and they worked assiduously at state and local legislatures and administrative arenas, in the courts, and at the ballot box to shape both planning processes and substantive outcomes.

An authoritative planning role for regional agencies was the first casualty that SB 100 had sustained during the 1973 legislative session. The politically pragmatic response to harsh criticism from local government associations and their industry allies had led to an elevated role for county governments. The institutional structure of planning in the Portland metropolitan area, however, evolved into nearly a full-blown manifestation of the original version of SB 100. Enactment of SB 769 in 1973 and legislation in 1977 that enabled area voters to establish the nation's first—and still the only—directly elected regional government in 1978, created a regional entity authorized to adopt and maintain an urban growth boundary and regulate the land-use, transportation, and other planning done by the city and county governments in the context of the statewide planning goals. The Metro Council deals with the same sorts of political challenges as county governing bodies do, but it has far more technical and financial resources available to plan and shape implementation. While Metro leans on DLCD to create a supportive political context in which to address complex regional planning issues, the state agency leans on Metro to demonstrate how to address important growth management problems within the context of the statewide land-use program.

Critical Activities

The ways Goals 3 and 14 were written, and the priority assigned to implementing them, kept the state agency on a path toward achieving its resource-lands conservation objective. In another ironic twist, LCDC also began to create critical activity-like frameworks for local and regional planning inside urban growth boundaries to enhance the prospects for achieving larger growth-management aims. The legislature provided support. LCDC moved to address the supply of affordable housing inside urban growth boundaries by elaborating on the requirements for Goal 10: Housing in a set of policy papers that intended to prevent exclusionary zoning and to require attention to types of housing in addition to traditional single-family homes (Kartez, 1982). Goals 3, 14, and 10 were intended to be mutually reinforcing. Prodded, supported, and complemented by 1000 Friends, DLCD and the watchdog took actions to confront explicitly the potential conflicts among those goals, and many builders joined them. The resulting package of rural and urban strategies persuaded the authors of a 1980 report for the National Academy of Public Administration that "the prospects seem bright that Oregon's SB 100 goals can and will mature into the Nation's most complete and effective State urban strategy" (DeGrove and Stroud, 1980).

In 1981 the legislature designated affordable housing as a "matter of statewide concern," and defined "needed housing" types that local governments would have to plan for and zone land to accommodate within their jurisdictions. LCDC also adopted a Metropolitan Housing Rule that stipulated minimum residential densities that city and county governments within the Portland area would have to plan to achieve. The American

Planning Association (APA) gave Oregon's statewide land-use program a national award in 1982.

LCDC supplemented its Goal 10 efforts inside urban growth boundaries with its Transportation Planning Rule, adopted in 1991, which amended Goal 12: Transportation. APA gave the rule a national planning award in 1993. The rule required cities with more than twenty-five hundred residents, counties with more than twenty-five thousand residents, and metropolitan area planning agencies to prepare transportation system plans that prioritized the reduction of principal reliance on any one mode of transport—the automobile—and in the Portland metropolitan area to require local governments to reconsider adopted land-use plans and zoning ordinances in order to achieve that objective. Many of the housing and transportation goal-related changes incorporate proposals made during 1974 but placed into guidelines. LCDC has continued to address growth boundary management issues and development inside boundaries since then.

Learning from Oregon

Other states that have established growth-management programs learned a good deal from the Oregon experience. Among the key features of the Oregon approach that have been debated elsewhere are: consistency between statewide goals and local plans and ordinances; growth boundaries; resource lands protection; affirmative affordable housing strategies; and certainty as a consequence of plans and regulations. 1000 Friends—a key role for a watchdog organization was widely acknowledged—promoted the Oregon program enthusiastically during the 1980s; well-received analyses of the program done by 1000 Friends influenced growth-management legislation adopted in Florida and New Jersey, for example, in mid-decade. Maine, Rhode Island, and Vermont in the later 1980s, and Washington and Maryland in the early 1990s, discussed the Oregon approach, borrowed, tinkered, and adopted different aspects of it in line with their varying circumstances (DeGrove, 1994). The legislative champion in Washington State, for example, recalled a meeting he had had with Stafford Hansell during which Hansell advised him to limit state mandates to plan to those jurisdictions that met some growth threshold, rather than, as in Oregon, require all jurisdictions to plan and zone in conformance with state goals; Hansell thought that would reduce the level of conflict Washington would experience. The advice was incorporated into that state's program (King, 2005).

SB 100, other land-use laws and court decisions, the agency and its statewide planning goals, and the watchdog's intense scrutiny all grew out of and built on earlier local, state, and national initiatives. Together, they produced revolutionary changes in the structure and dynamics of plan making and implementation in Oregon. In 1999, APA declared SB 100 a National Planning Landmark, and presented Hector Macpherson its Distinguished Leadership Award for a Citizen Planner. But the transformed relationship between state and local governments seriously disrupted land-use institutions and practices at all levels. There were conflicts from the beginning about matters large and small, conflicts that were difficult to resolve during comprehensive planning processes and goal conformance reviews. The unfolding revolution was anything but quiet. Few states have adopted and sustained programs as far-reaching as Oregon's.

During the early years, activists and interested members of the public had been perpetually mobilized. The coastal commission and Project Foresight in the Willamette Valley reached out to, educated, and involved thousands of people. Publicity about the progress of SB 100 focused the attention of interested citizens during the 1973 legislative session, and hearings on the bill as it moved through the Senate were jammed. Thousands participated in developing the first set of statewide planning goals in 1974 and the Willamette River Greenway and coastal goals in 1975 and 1976. Ballot measure campaigns in 1970, 1976, 1978, and 1982 repeatedly placed arguments for and against the statewide land-use program in front of the electorate. All of those events and processes added to public participation in jurisdictions that had been actively engaged, however reluctantly and haltingly, in developing comprehensive plans since at least 1969. Public and private sector leaders—state and local elected officials, members of the business and professional communities, and environmental, women, and citizen-empowerment activists—were prominently involved throughout the period playing multiple and overlapping political and technical roles. Enacting and implementing SB 100 focused the attention of a great many Oregonians on land-use issues. Developing statewide land-use planning goals and making and implementing local comprehensive plans in Oregon became politically, economically, culturally, and legally significant—a situation that was unique in the United States at the time.

References

DLCD – Department of Land Conservation and Development, Salem
LCDC – Land Conservation and Development Commission
LGRD – Local Government Relations Division
OEC – Oregon Environmental Council
OHS – Oregon Historical Society Research Library, Portland
One Thousand Friends of Oregon – Portland
OSA – Oregon State Archives, Salem
PSU – Portland State University Library Special Collections, Portland
University of Oregon – Special Collections Library, Eugene

*Items marked with an asterisk are on deposit at Portland State University Library
    Special Collections

1967-69 Interim Committee on Agriculture. 1967a. Minutes. 7/24/67-1/23/68. 9/25
    Hearing. OSA.
1967-69 Interim Committee on Agriculture. 1967b. Minutes. 7/24/67-1/23/68.
    10/26 Hearing. OSA.
1967-69 Interim Committee on Agriculture. 1968a. Minutes. 7/24/67-1/23/68. 3/25
    Hearing. OSA.
1967-69 Interim Committee on Agriculture. 1968b. Minutes. 7/24/67-1/23/68. 3/26
    Hearing. OSA.
1967-69 Interim Committee on Agriculture, 1968c. Minutes. 7/24-67-1/23/68. 6/24
    Hearing. OSA.
1967-69 Interim Committee on Agriculture, 1968d. Minutes. 7/24/67-1/23/68. 7/22
    Hearing. OSA.
Aamodt, David. 1973. Oregon's Prime Agricultural Lands: An Area of Critical
    Statewide Concern. OSPIRG. Multnomah County Library.*
Aamodt, David. 1974a. Administrative Control Over the Conservation and
    Development of Prime Agricultural Land in Oregon. LCDC Commission
    Meeting Material, 4/26/74-7/26/74. OSA.
Abbott, Carl, Sy Adler, and Marge Abbott. 1997. *Planning a New West: The Columbia
    River Gorge National Scenic Area*, Corvallis: Oregon State University Press.
Abbott, Carl, Sy Adler, and Deborah Howe. 2003. "A Quiet Counterrevolution in
    Land Use Regulation: The Origins and Impacts of Oregon's Ballot Measure 7."
    Housing Policy Debate, Volume 14, Number 3: 383-425.
Allen, David. 1972. Letter to Robert Mendelsohn. October 16. McCall Records, Box
    28, Folder 3. OSA.*

Allen, Eric. 1974. Letter to Henry Richmond. September 30. 1977 Board Mailings
    Box, 1976 Board Records Folder. 1000 Friends of Oregon.*

Allen, Eric, 1975. Letter to Henry Richmond. December 23. 1977 Board Mailings
    Box, 1976 Board Records Folder. 1000 Friends of Oregon.*

Allison, Jim. 1974. Statement. December 13. Final Public Hearing. FH 1021. DLCD.*

American Law Institute. 1974. *A Model Land Development Code*. Philadelphia:
    American Law Institute.

Anderson, Dorothy. 1973a. Statement on SB100. February 12. Senate Environment
    and Land Use Committee, Box 59, Folder 59/5. OSA.*

Anderson, Dorothy. 1973b. Statement in Support of Revised SB 100. March 8.
    Senate Environment and Land Use Committee, Box 60, Folder 60/1. OSA.*

Anderson, Lloyd. 1973. Statement on the Revised SB 100. March 8. Senate
    Environment and Land Use Committee, Box 60, Folder 60/1. OSA.*

Angstrom, Richard. 1974. Statement on behalf of Associated Oregon Industries.
    February 2. Land Conservation and Development Commission Meeting
    Materials, Box 1, 10/73-10/74. OSA.*

Armstrong, Ward. 1974. Testimony. December 13. FH 1043. DLCD.*

Associated Oregon Industries. 1974. Statement. December 13. Final Public Hearing,
    FH 1013. DLCD.*

Attorney General. 1974. Letters of Advice. Opinion 2871.

Bacon, Larry. 1974a. "Estuary rules drafted." *Register-Guard* (Eugene). December 6.*

Bacon, Larry. 1974b. "Official to Fight for State Authority." *Register-Guard* (Eugene).
    December 26. 12B.*

Bacon, Robert. 1974. Statement on behalf of Oregon Shores Conservation Coalition.
    February 2. LCDC Meeting Materials, Box 1, 10/73-10/74. OSA.*

Banks, Maxine. 1969. Testimony. Senate Agriculture Committee. February 24. Box
    112, SB 10 Folder. OSA.

Bauer, Steve. 1974. Letter to Steve Schell. April 30. LCDC Meeting Materials, 4/26-
    7/26. OSA.*

Bauer, Webb. 1980. *A Case Analysis of Oregon's Willamette River Greenway Program.*
    Unpublished doctoral dissertation. Oregon State University.

Beers, Roger. 1976. Comments of the Natural Resources Defense Council, Inc. on
    the Draft Oregon Coastal Management Program. September 27. Office of
    Coastal Zone Management. *Written Statements from Parties Who Commented on
    the Oregon Coastal Zone Management Program and the Draft Environmental Impact
    Statement*. Washington, DC. A109-21.*

Beggs, Charles. 1973. "Land Control Issue Draws Heated Views." *The Oregon
    Statesman* (Salem). January 26.

Benner, Richard. 1973a. *The Oregon Coast and the Oregon Coastal Conservation and
    Development Commission: Why Not Classify Estuaries?* Portland: OSPIRG.

Benner, Richard. 1973b. Letter to Wilbur Ternyik. August 22. Author's copy.*

Benner, Richard. 1973c. Letter to Wilbur Ternyik. October 26. Author's copy.*

Benner, Richard. 1976a. Comments of Richard Benner for 1000 Friends of Oregon.
    March 18. Joint Land Use Committee, Box 15 Folder 3. OSA.*

Benner, Richard. 1976b. Comments of 1000 Friends of Oregon on Draft Oregon
    Coastal Zone Management Program. October 8. Office of Coastal Zone
    Management. *Written Statements from Parties Who Commented on the Oregon
    Coastal Zone Management Program and the Draft Environmental Impact Statement.*
    Washington, D.C. A122-145.*

Benner, Richard. 1976c. Letter to Janet McLennan. October 26. Straub Papers, Box 45, LCDC: 1000 Friends Folder. OSA.*

Benner, Richard. 1976d. Letter to Robert Knecht. November 26. Office of Coastal Zone Management. *Written Statements from Parties Who Commented on the Oregon Coastal Zone Management Program and the Draft Environmental Impact Statement.* Washington, D.C. A234-236.*

"Benner Asks Permit Denial." 1973. *OSPIRG IMPACT* 3(3): November.

Bennett, Chuck.1975. "Day asks, What have you done right?" *Capital Journal* (Salem). December 30.*

"Bill to shape future." 1975. *The Oregonian* (Portland). Editorial. April 1.*

Bosselman, Fred. 1973. Letter to Ed Sullivan. May 25. Ed Sullivan Papers. OHS.

Bosselman, Fred, and David Callies. 1972. *The Quiet Revolution in Land Use Control.* Washington, D.C.: U.S. Government Printing Office.

Branchfield, Edward. 1972. Letter to Ervin Hogan. May 4. McCall Records, Box 28, Folder 2. OSA.*

Brauner, Harold. 1977. Memorandum to City Mayors, Chairman of County Board of Commissions. May 16. LCDC Meeting Materials, Box 9, 5/20/77 Folder. OSA.*

Bryce, Dean. 1973. Associated Oregon Industry's Testimony Regarding Senate Bill 100. Senate Environment and Land Use Committee, Box 60, Folder 60/1. February 13. OSA.*

Buckhorn, Robert. 1972. *Nader: The People's Lawyer.* Englewood Cliffs, N.J: Prentice-Hall.

Buel, Ronald. 1976. "1000 Friends nudge planners." *Willamette Week* (Portland). Week Ending March 1.*

Bullier, Albert, Sr. 1982. Oral History Interview. SR 9056. OHS.

Burdick, Ginny. 1975a. "Cogan Resigns as Director of Land Development." *The Oregon Statesman* (Salem). January 7.*

Burdick, Ginny. 1975b. "Planning chief hits realtors' proposals." *Capital Journal* (Salem). April 9.*

Bureau of Governmental Research and Service. 1974. *Local Government Policies for Urban Development: A Review of the State of the Art.* Eugene: University of Oregon.*

Callies, David. 1984. *Regulating Paradise: Land Use Controls in Hawaii.* Honolulu: University of Hawaii Press.

Carter, Kathleen. 1975a. Memorandum to LOAC Members. June 13. LCDC, Box 2, 5/16-7/25. OSA.*

Carter, Kathleen. 1975b. "Activities of Statewide Significance (Draft)." September 23. LCDC, Box 3, 8/75-12/75. OSA.

CFM Research. 2005. Oregon Statewide Land Use Survey: A Report for Oregon Business Association and Institute of Portland Metropolitan Studies, Toulan School of Urban Studies and Planning, Portland State University. March.

Church, Jim. 1976. "Day: Enforcement should be tighter." *Capital Journal* (Salem). July 29.*

Citizens to Save Oregon's Land. 1976. "Preliminary Campaign Plan Against Measure #10." Straub Papers, Box 47, Land Use: SB 100 Folder. OSA.*

"The City of Medford . . . " 1975. *Earthwatch Oregon.* March. OEC.

Clark, Donald. 1974. Statement. December 13. Final Public Hearing. FH 1032. DLCD.*

Clark, Donald. 2002. Interview with Ernie Bonner. March 8. Ernie Bonner Papers. PSU.

Clay, John. 1974a. "Cogan Optimistic About Agency." *News-Review* (Roseburg). March 6.*

Clay, John. 1974b. "LCD to Develop Statewide Land-Use Goals." News-Review (Roseburg). March 6.*

Clucas, Richard. 2003. "The Political Legacy of Robert W. Straub." *Oregon Historical Quarterly*, 104:4.

Coenen, Neal. 1977. LCDC Policy Discussion. February 10. Minutes. February 10-November 1977. OSA.*

Cogan, Arnold. 1969a. Testimony. Senate Agriculture Committee. 2/24/69. OSA.

Cogan, Arnold. 1973a. Letter to Tom McCall. July 2. Author's copy.*

Cogan, Arnold, 1973b. Letter to L. B. Day. October 29. Author's copy.*

Cogan, Arnold. 1974a. Report to Members of LCDC, Re: Federal Grant Request by OCCDC. February 22. LCDC, Box 1, 10/73-10/74. OSA.

Cogan, Arnold. 1974b. Presentation to Subcommittee No. 2 of the Emergency Board. June 27. LCDC Meeting Materials, 4/26-7/26. OSA.*

Cogan, Arnold. 1974c. Memo to LCDC Division Directors and staff. August 16. Author's Copy.*

Cogan, Arnold. 1974d. Memorandum to LCD Division Directors. October 4. Minutes. 10/11/74 – 10/24/74. OSA.

Cogan, Arnold. 1974e. Memorandum to LCDC: Activities of Statewide Significance and Key Facilities. October 11. LCDC Meeting Materials. 10/11-10/74. OSA.*

Cogan, Arnold. 1974f. Memorandum to LCDC: Areas of Critical State Concern. October 11. Minutes. 10/11/74 – 10/24/74. OSA.

Cogan, Arnold. 1974g. Memorandum to LCDC: October 11. Minutes. 10/11/74 – 10/24/74. OSA.

Cogan, Arnold. 1974h. LCDC Status Report to Joint Legislative Committee on Land Use. October 16. Author's copy.*

Cogan, Arnold. 1974i. Memo to LCDC. October 23. 1000 Friends Papers, Box 98. University of Oregon.*

Cogan, Arnold. 1974j. Year-End Report. December 27. LCDC, Box 2, 11/74-7/75 Folder. OSA.*

Cogan, Arnold. 1974k. Memorandum to CIAC. February 19. Author's copy.*

Cogan, Arnold. 1974l. Memorandum to Advisory Resource People. September 24. Author's copy.*

Cogan, Arnold. 1999. Interview with Ernie Bonner. March 10. Ernie Bonner Papers. PSU Library.

Cohan, Richard. 1972a. Key Points, Hector Macpherson's Land Use Planning Bill. September 1. OEC Papers, Box 21, Folder 25. OHS.

Cohan, Richard. 1972b. Memo: Land Use Planning. August 10. OEC Papers, Box 21, Folder 25. OHS.

Cohan, Richard. 1973. Preface: Analysis of Environmental Issues for Oregon Legislature 1973. OEC Papers, Box 18. OHS.

Cohen, Joyce. 1973a. Testimony in favor of enactment of Senate Bill 100. January 25. Senate Environment and Land Use Committee, Box 59, Folder 59/5. OSA.*

Cohen, Joyce. 1973b. Letter to Senator Hallock. February 7. Senate Environment and Land Use Committee, Box 59, Folder 59/5. OSA.*

Cohen, Joyce. 1973c. Testimony in favor of enactment of Senate Bill 100, revised. March 8. Senate Environment and Land Use Committee, Box 60, Folder 60/1. OSA.*

Colby, Richard. 1975. "Straub takes legislators to river greenway area." *The Oregonian* (Portland). April 12.*

Collins, Maggie. 1974. "LCDC on the Road: Impressions of Nineteen Public Workshops." *Land Use Oregon* 1(2).

Collins, Maggie. 1975. "LCDC Budget." *Land Use Oregon.* 1:12.

Collins, Maggie. 1976. "LCDC Status Report." *Land Use Oregon.* 2:1.

Collins, Maggie. 2008. Interview with author. May 7.

Conkling, Gary. 1975. "Flegel to spearhead planning group." *The Daily Astorian*, January 9.*

Conover, Kelly. 1976. Statement to Joint Legislative Committee on Land Use. March 18. Joint Land Use Committee, Box 15 Folder 3. OSA.*

"Conservation budget stirs pros, cons." 1975. *The Oregonian* (Portland). April 4.*

"Corvallis spotlights some building woes," Special to the *Portland Daily Journal of Commerce*, n.d. 1000 Friends of Oregon Records, Box 91, University of Oregon.

Coughlin, Robert, John Keene, J. Dixon Esseks, William Toner, and Lisa Rosenberg. 1981. *The Protection of Farmland: A Reference Guidebook for State and Local Governments. A Report to the National Agricultural Lands Study*. Washington, D.C.: U.S. Government Printing Office.*

Cramton, Martin. 1974. Testimony. November 25. Public Hearings Volume II. DLCD.*

Cramton, Martin, Adrianne Brockman, George Crandall, and Frances Diemoz. 1975. Testimony to LCDC. August 15. LCDC, Box 3, 8/15-10/1. OSA.

Crandall, George, and Frances Diemoz. 1975. Letter to Henry Richmond. June 23. Joint Land Use Committee, Box 14, Folder 13. OSA.*

Davis, Martin. 1971a. Environmental Planning Items. June 25. OEC Papers, Box 1, Folder 4. OHS.

Davis, Martin. 1971b. Letter to Hector Macpherson. July 21. OEC Papers, Box 1, Folder 24. OHS.

Davis, Martin. 1972a. "Environmental Planning Committee Report." *OEC Newsletter.* May.

Davis, Martin. 1972b. Letter to Governor McCall. June 9. McCall Records. Box 28, Folder 2. OSA.*

Davis, Martin. 1972c. Proposals for Land Use Planning. *OEC Newsletter.* June-July.

Davis, Martin, 1973a. Testimony by the OEC. January 25. Senate Environment and Land Use Committee, Box 59, Folder 59/5. OSA.*

Davis, Martin. 1973b. Senate Bill 100: Proposed Amendment. March 6. Senate Environment and Land Use Committee, Box 60, Folder 60/1. OSA.

Davis, Martin. 1974. Statement on behalf of OEC. February 2. LCDC, Box 1, 10/73-10/74. OSA.*

Davis, Peter. 1974. "A Citizen's View of the Workshops." *Land Use Oregon.* Volume 1, Number 6: October.

Day, L. B. 1967. Testimony. House Bill 1176. House Agriculture Committee, Box 83, Folder 3. OSA.*

Day, L. B. 1974a. Letter to B.J. Rogers. June 27. LCDC Meeting Materials, 4/26-726. OSA.*

Day, L. B. 1974b. Letter to Glenn Jackson. July 17. McCall Records. Correspondence, 1967-74, Box 37, LCDC File #1. OSA.

Day, L. B. 1974c. Memorandum to The Commission. October 10. LCDC Meeting Materials, 10/11/74. OSA.*

Day, L. B. 1974d. Letter to Glenn Jackson. December 4. LCDC Written Public Testimony. DLCD.*

Day, L. B. 1975. Memorandum to Oregon Environmental Quality Commission. June 26. LCDC, Box 2, 5/16-87/25. OSA.*

Day, L. B. n.d. Letter to John Taylor. 1977 Board Mailings Box, Office Correspondence 1976 Folder. 1000 Friends of Oregon.*

"Day rips local governments." 1975. *Capital Journal* (Salem). December 12. Section 2:13.*

DeBonny, Paul. 1975. Written Statement to LCDC. August 15. LCDC, Box 3, 8/15-10/1. OSA.*

DeGrove, John. 1994. "Following in Oregon's Footsteps: The Impact of Oregon's Planning Program on Other States." In Carl Abbott, Deborah Howe, and Sy Adler, eds., *Planning the Oregon Way: A Twenty-Year Evaluation*, Corvallis: Oregon State University Press.

DeGrove, John, and Nancy Stroud. 1980. *Oregon's State Urban Strategy*. Washington, D.C.: U.S. Government Printing Office.*

DLCD. 1974. Workshop. February 2. DLCD.*

DLCD. 1974. Final Public Hearing. December. DLCD.*

DLCD. 1976. Press Release. September 10. LCDC, Box 6, 9/10 Meeting. OSA.*

"Description of a Supplemental Community Involvement Proposal to Be Funded by the Pacific Northwest Regional Commission to the LCDC." 1974. August 23. Author's copy.*

Dickie, Lance. 1976. "Farm rezoning east of Salem is 'in violation' of LCDC goals." *The Oregon Statesman* (Salem). May 15.*

Diel, George. 1973a. Your Opportunity for Pioneering in Land-Use Legislation. February 8. Senate Environment and Land Use Committee, Box 59, Folder 59/5. OSA.*

Diel, George. 1973b. Summing Up Some Pivotal Factors in Your Decision on SB 100. Senate Environment and Land Use Committee, Box 60, Folder 60/2. OSA.*

Diel, George. 1974. Testimony. December 13. Final Public Hearing Written Testimony. DLCD.*

"East Salem Zoning Is Appealed to LCDC." 1975. *The Oregon Statesman* (Salem). August 12.*

Eber, Ron. 1974. Statement on behalf of Sierra Club. February 2. LCDC, Box 1, 10/73-10/74. OSA.*

Ervin, David, James Fitch, R. Kenneth Godwin, W. Bruce Shepard, and Herbert Stoevener. 1977. *Land Use Control: Evaluating Economic and Political Effects*. Cambridge, MA: Ballinger Publishing Company.

Fadeley, Nancy. 1997. Oral History Interview 3959. Kami Teramura Masters Project Oral Histories. OHS.

Federman, Stan. 1975. "Jobless Count in Oregon Highest since 1950." *The Oregonian* (Portland). January 14.

Feedback. 1974. Newsletter. January 24. OEC Papers, Box 22, Folder 2. OHS.*

Fitzgerald, Ken, and Marguerite Watkins. 1992. 20th Anniversary Review of Oregon Shores Conservation Coalition. In 20th Anniversary Celebration of Oregon Shores Conservation Coalition, 1971-1991. Not published. Rockaway.

Fobes, Ken. 1974. Letter to Gary Sund. August 19. Author's copy.*

Forrester, J. W. 1974. Letter to Henry Richmond. September 16. 1977 Board
    Mailings Box, 1976 Board Records Folder. 1000 Friends of Oregon.*
Fradkin, Philip. 1973. "Oregon Makes Striking Gains in Protecting Environment;
    Despite Bold Steps, Glaring Defects Remain." *Los Angeles Times*. April 15.
Frazier, Larry. 1975. Joint Ways and Means Committee. Exhibits, SB 5537. April 11.
    LCDC, Box 2, 5/16-7/25. OSA.*
Fritts, Greg. 1974. "Editorial Comments on Oregon City." *Land Use Oregon* 1(2).
Fujii, Howard. 1974a. Statement on behalf of Oregon Farm Bureau Federation.
    February 2. LCDC, Box 1, 10/73-10/74. OSA.*
Fujii, Howard. 1974b. Statement to the LCDC. November 26. Public Hearings
    Volume II. DLCD.
Fujii, Howard. 1974c. Testimony. December 13. Final Public Hearing, FH-1051.
    DLCD.*
Fultz, Gordon. 1973. Statement. March 8. Senate Environment and Land Use
    Committee, Box 60, Folder 60/1. OSA.*
Fultz, Gordon. 1974a. Statement on behalf of Association of Oregon Counties.
    February 2. LCDC Meeting Materials, Box 1, 10/73-10/74. OSA.*
Fultz, Gordon. 1974b. Memorandum to County Judges and Commissioners.
    November 8. 1000 Friends Papers, Box 98. University of Oregon.*
Fultz, Gordon. 1974c. Testimony for the LCDC. November 26. Public Hearings
    Volume II. DLCD.*
Fultz, Gordon. 1974d. Memorandum to County Judges, et al. December 6. 1000
    Friends Papers, Box 98. University of Oregon.*
Fultz, Gordon. 1974e. Testimony. December 13. Final Public Hearing. FH 1033.
    DLCD.*
Gale, Maradel. 1971. Letter to Senator Jack Bain. June 17. OEC Papers, Box 1,
    Folder 23. OHS.
Gale, Maradel, 1976. Statement before Office of Coastal Zone Management Hearing
    on Oregon Coastal Zone Program. September 16. Office of Coastal Zone
    Management. *Written Statements from Parties Who Commented on the Oregon
    Coastal Zone Management Program and the Draft Environmental Impact Statement.*
    Washington, D.C. A211-215.*
Garrish, Christopher. 2002/03. "Unscrambling the Omelette: Understanding British
    Columbia's Agricultural Land Reserve." *BC Studies*, no. 136: 25-55.*
Gassaway, Carolyn. 1976. "LCDC Explains Plan Compliance, Awards Grants to
    Assist Local Planning." *1,000 Friends of Oregon Newsletter*. 1:7 (April).
Gervais, Dick. 1975. Memorandum to LCDC. October 22. LCDC, Box 3, 8/75-12/75.
    OSA.
"Give us time to think." 1976. "Editorial." *The Daily Astorian*. March 23.*
Godwin, R. Kenneth, and W. Bruce Shepard. 1974. November 14. LCDC Written
    Public Testimony. DLCD.*
Goldschmidt, Neil. 1974. Memorandum to LCDC. December 10. LCDC, Box 2,
    11/74-7/75. OSA.*
Gordon, Mel. 1973. Statement before the Senate Environmental and Land Use
    Committee. February 13. Senate Environment and Land Use Committee, Box
    60, Folder 60/1. OSA.*
Gray, John. 1970. Letter to Tom McCall. July 22. McCall Records. Box 98, LGRD
    1969 Correspondence Folder. OSA.*

Gray, John. 1973a. Remarks by John Gray before the National Association of Home Builders: Land Use: Profits AND Environmental Integrity. January 8. OEC Papers, Box 21, Folder 25. OHS.

Gray, John. 1973b. Statement in support of Senate Bill 100. February 12. Senate Environment and Land Use Committee, Box 59, Folder 59/5. OSA.*

Greenleaf, Craig. 1975a. Letter to LCDC. August 14. Joint Land Use Committee, Box 15, Folder 1. OSA.*

Greenleaf, Craig. 1975b. Letter to Representative Stan Bunn. November 28. Joint Legislative Committee on Land Use, Box 15, Folder 1. OSA.*

Gustafson, John. 1973a. "Organizing for the future: State fires up for all-out program to provide balanced job growth, keep Oregon livable and maintain its place as pioneer of ideas." *The Oregonian* (Portland). September 16 (The Sunday Forum).*

Gustafson, John. 1973b. Letter to Governor Tom McCall. December 12. Author's copy.*

Gustafson, John. 1974. Memorandum to File. August 15. Author's copy.*

Hagman, Donald. 1973. Letter to McCall. May 24. McCall Records, Box 27, 8/6/72-4/11/73. OSA.*

Hallock, Ted. 1973. Memorandum to Senators Betty Roberts, et al. June 21. Straub Papers, Box 78, Folder 730.1. OSA.*

Hallock, Ted. 1976. Letter to Governor Straub. September 10. Straub Papers, Box 78, Folder 730.1. OSA.*

Hallock, Ted. 2000. Oral History Interview with Ernie Bonner. September 19. Ernie Bonner Papers. PSU.

Handler, Joel, Betsy Ginsberg and Arthur Snow. 1978. "The Public Interest Law Industry." In Burton Weisbrod, ed., *Public Interest Law*. Berkeley: University of California Press.

Hansell, Stafford. 1983. Oral History Interview. SR 0088. OHS.

Harris, Richard, and Sidney Milkis. 1989. *The Politics of Regulatory Change*. New York: Oxford University Press.

Hawaii's Thousand Friends. 2011. "About Us." Accessed at: http://www.hawaiis1000friends.org/about.php*

Hawes, Steve. 1974a. Testimony to LCDC. November 26. Public Hearings Volume II. DLCD.*

Hawes, Steve. 1974b. Statement. December 13. Final Public Hearing. FH 1016. DLCD.*

Hawes, Steve. 1976. Letter to Steven Kafoury. March 12. Joint Land Use Committee, Box 15 Folder 3. OSA.*

Hayes, John. 1975. "Coast officials score at LCDC meeting." *Capital Journal* (Salem). December 22: 13.*

Hayes, John. 1976. "LCDC 'no haven,' says new boss." *The Oregon Statesman* (Salem). September 12: 1.*

Hemingway, Roy. 1975a. "Legislative Outlook." *Earthwatch Oregon: News Report of the OEC*. April.

Hemingway, Roy. 1975b. "Legislative Outlook." *Earthwatch Oregon: News Report of the OEC*. May.

Hemingway, Roy. 1975c. "The 1975 Legislature: An Environmental Evaluation." *Earthwatch Oregon*. June-July.

Herman, Peter. 1975. Memorandum to Harold Brauner. January 23. LCDC, Box 2, 11/74-7/75. OSA.*

Hermann, Dale, and Penelope Hull. 1981. "Yaquina Head and Status of Yaquina Head." Oregon Shores Conservation Coalition. *The Oregon Coast: Looking Back and Looking Ahead.*

Hider, Mitchell. 1971. "Saving Willamette Valley From Sprawl." *Capital Journal* (Salem). January 29.*

Hildreth, Richard, and Ralph Johnson. 1985. "CZM in California, Oregon, and Washington." *Natural Resources Journal* 25(1).

Hout, Eldon. 1973. Letter to L. B. Day. November 26. McCall Records, Box 27, 12/31/72-10/15/73. OSA.*

Howe, Deborah, Carl Abbott, and Sy Adler. 2004. "What's on the Horizon for Oregon Planners?" *Journal of the American Planning Association,* Volume 70, Number 4: 391-97.

"Intern Report Urges Classification of Estuaries." 1974. *OSPIRG IMPACT,* Volume 3, Number 5, January.

Jepson, Don. 1975. "New Chief Hunted by LCDC." *Oregon Journal* (Portland). January 8.*

Joint Committee on Ways and Means. 1975. Budget Report, SB 5537. May 13. Author's copy.*

Joint Legislative Committee on Land Use. 1976. *Final Report.* November. Author's copy.*

Jones, Don. 1973. Letter to Robert Davis. November 30. McCall Records, Box 27, 12/31/72-10/15/73. OSA.*

Jones, Don. 1974. Statement on behalf of League of Oregon Cities. February 2. LCDC, Box 1, 10/73-10/74. OSA.*

Judson, Archie. 1976. Planning Seminar. January 22. 1977 Board Mailings Box, 1976 Board Records Folder. 1000 Friends of Oregon.*

Kafoury, Stephen. 1975. Letter to John Lobdell. October 9. Joint Land Use Committee, Box 15, Folder 1. OSA.*

Kafoury, Stephen. 1976. Statement. March 18. Joint Land Use Committee, Box 15 Folder 3. OSA.*

Kartez, Jack. 1982. "Affordable Housing: A Policy Challenge for Farmland Preservation." *Journal of Soil and Water Conservation,* 37(3): 137-40.*

KATU. 1972. Editorial. November 15. Author's copy.*

King, Joe. 2005. Oral History Interview. Conducted by Rita Campbell. Accessed at http://www.secstate.wa.gov/legacyproject//pdf/OH811.pdf*

Knight, James. 1975. Memorandum to Herb, et al. July 2. Knight papers, Box 4. PSU.*

Knight, James. 1976a. Letter to James Keller. August 6. Straub Papers, Box 44, LCDC: File 3/5. OSA.*

Knight, James. 1976b. Memorandum to Hal Brauner. October 1. Straub Papers, Box 44, LCDC: File 3/5. OSA.*

Kvarsten, Wesley. 1974. Letter to L. B. Day. January 17. Author's copy.*

Lake, Brent. 1976. Memorandum from Sub-Committee on Activities of Statewide Significance to LCDC. August 27. LCDC, Box 6, 8/30. OSA.

LCDC. 1973a. Minutes. October 24. LCDC, Box 1, 10/73-3/15/74. OSA.

LCDC. 1973b. Minutes. November 1. LCDC, Box 1, 10/73-3/15/74. OSA.

LCDC. 1973c. Minutes. December 1. LCDC, Box 1, 10/73-3/15/74. OSA.

LCDC. 1974a. Minutes. February 8. Box 1, 10/73-3/15/74. OSA.

LCDC. 1974b. Minutes. October 11. LCDC, Box 1, 10/73-10/74. OSA.

LCDC. 1974c. "Public Hearings" on <u>Draft</u> Statewide Land Use Goals, Guidelines, and Critical Areas. October 24. Salem. Author's copy.*

LCDC. 1974d. Final Public Hearing on Revised Draft of Statewide Land Use Goals, Guidelines, and the Columbia River Gorge as a Critical Area. November 30. Salem. Author's copy.*

LCDC. 1974e. State-Wide Planning Goals and Guidelines Adopted by the LCDC. December 27. Salem. Author's copy.*

LCDC. 1974f. "A Report on 'People and the Land' Public Workshops. July. Author's copy.*

LCDC. 1975a. Program Budget, 1975-1977. January 3. Author's copy.*

LCDC. 1975b. Minutes. January 24.LCDC, Box 2, 1/24/75. OSA.*

LCDC. 1975c. Minutes. August 15. LCDC, Box 3, 8/15-10/1. OSA.*

LCDC. 1975d. September 12 Public Hearing Information: Willamette River Greenway. Joint Legislative Committee on Land Use, Box 15, Folder 1. OSA.*

LCDC. 1976a. "Draft Land Use Planning Goals and Guidelines for the Coastal Zone." March. Author's copy.*

LCDC. 1976b. Minutes. August 18. LCDC, Box 6, 6/76-9/76. OSA.*

LCDC. 1977. Minutes. May 6-7. LCDC Meeting Materials Box 8, Book 1. OSA.*

"LCDC 1973-75 Biennial Budget." 1973. McCall Records, Box 27, Local Government 8/6-4/11. OSA.

"Land Use Planners Hit." 1972. OSPIRG *Newsletter*. October.*

"Land use resolution designed to fortify LCDC coast role." 1975. *The World* (Coos Bay). January 3.*

Langford, Ned and Lyle Stewart. 1971. Memo to Willamette Valley Steering Committee. March 25. Author's copy.*

LaRoe, Edward. 1976. Memorandum to LCDC. December 6. Author's copy.*

"L. B. Day Leaves DEQ." 1972. *Earthwatch Oregon*. December: 12.*

Lehman, Tim. 1995. *Public Values, Private Lands*. Chapel Hill: University of North Carolina Press.

Leland, David. 1970. Letter to Martin Davis. October 15. OEC papers, Box 21, Folder 26. OHS.

Little, A. D. 1974. *A Regional Analysis: Economic and Fiscal Impacts of the Aluminum Industry in the Pacific Northwest*. Report to Western Aluminum Producers.

Little, Charles. 1974. *The New Oregon Trail: An Account of the Development and Passage of State Land-Use Legislation in Oregon*. Washington, D.C: The Conservation Foundation.

Local Government Relations Division. 1971a. Background Paper on: The Willamette Valley Development Program. January 20. Author's copy.*

Local Government Relations Division. 1971c. Preliminary Status of Land Use Planning and Zoning by Counties. February 22. McCall Records, Box 98, 1969 LGRD Correspondence. OSA.*

Local Government Relations Division. 1971b. Charbonneau: An Intergovernmental Environmental Planning Scenario. October 5. McCall Records, Box 98, 1969 LGRD Correspondence. OSA.*

Local Government Relations Division. 1972a. Project Foresight. February 24. Author's copy.*

Local Government Relations Division. 1972b. Status of Planning and Zoning. March 27. McCall Records, Box 28, Local Government Folder 4. OSA.*

Local Government Relations Division. 1973a. Willamette Valley Mall: A Challenge to Community Planning. January 17. OEC Papers, Box 22, Folder 12. OHS.

Local Government Relations Division. 1973b. Status of Counties – SB 10. June 29. McCall Records, Box 27, Local Government 8/6-4/11. OSA.*

Local Government Relations Division. 1974a. The Oregon Land Use Story. January 7. OEC Papers, Box 21, Folder 26. OHS.

Local Government Relations Division. 1974b. S.B. 10 Status of Comprehensive Plans and Zoning Ordinances as of January, 1974. January. Straub Papers, Box 46, Land Use: Comprehensive Plan. OSA.*

Logan, Robert. 1969. Memo to Westerdahl. November 11. McCall Records, Box 98, 1969 LGRD Correspondence. OSA.

Logan, Robert. 1971. Memo to Robert Davis. November 1. McCall Records, Box 98, 1969 LGRD Correspondence. OSA.*

Logan, Robert, 1973a. Letter to Senator Ted Hallock. January 31. Senate Environment and Land Use Committee, Box 59, Folder 59/5. OSA.*

Logan, Robert. 1973b. Letter to Donald Hagman. May 31. McCall Records, Box 27, Local Government 8/6-4/11. OSA.*

Logan, Robert. 1973c. Memo to Governor McCall. June 12. McCall Records, Box 27, 8/6/72-4/11/73. OSA.*

Logan, Robert. 1974. Memorandum to Governor Tom McCall. March 18. LCDC Meeting Materials, 4/26-7/26. OSA.*

Logan, Robert, 1997. Oral History Interview SR 3961. Kami Teramura Masters Project Oral Histories. OHS.

Luce, Charles. n.d. *My Years with the Bonneville Power Administration: 1944-1946 and 1961-1967.* Manuscript. OHS.

Lyday, Noreen. 1976. *The Law of the Land: Debating National Land Use Legislation, 1970-75.* Washington, D.C.: The Urban Institute.

Macpherson, Hector. 1971a. Letter to Maradel Gale. July 1. OEC Papers, Box 1, Folder 24. OHS.

Macpherson, Hector. 1971b. Letter to Action Group Members. December 31. Norma Paulus Papers, Legislative Files, 1973. Land Use Planning. Box 4 of 11, Folder 2. OSA.*

Macpherson, Hector. 1972. Letter to those interested in land use planning. July. McCall Papers, Box 28, Local Government Folder 2. OSA.*

Macpherson, Hector. 1974a. Letter to Henry Richmond. December 2. 1977 Board Mailings Box, 1976 Board Records Folder, Correspondence of Advisory Board 1976 File. 1000 Friends of Oregon.*

Macpherson, Hector. 1974b. Testimony. December 13. Final Public Hearing, FH-1004. DLCD.*

Macpherson, Hector. 1979. Testimony. October 23. 1979-80 Interim-Joint Box, Land Use Committee, Exhibits 2 Folder. OSA.*

Macpherson, Hector. 1997. Oral History Interview 3962. Kami Teramura Masters Project Oral Histories. OHS.

Macpherson, Hector, and Norma Paulus. 1974. "Senate Bill 100: The Oregon Land Conservation and Development Act." *Willamette Law Journal.* 10(3): 414-21.*

Mattis, James. 1973. "The Year of Fasano: What Thirty-Two Acres Hath Wrought." Ed Sullivan Papers, Fasano vs. Washington County Board of Commissioners Case Files. OHS.

McCall, Tom. 1969. Message to the Legislature. February 7. Author's copy.*

McCall, Tom. 1970a. Letter to John Gray. August 13. McCall Records, Box 98, 1969
    LGRD Correspondence. OSA.*

McCall, Tom. 1970b. Letter to Lee Miller. October 15. McCall Records, Box 98, 1969
    LGRD Correspondence. OSA.*

McCall, Tom. 1970c. Letter to The Honorable Gordon L. Macpherson. August 3.
    McCall Records, Box 98, 1969 LGRD Correspondence. OSA.*

McCall, Tom. 1971. Governor McCall Announces Result of Willamette Valley
    Livability Survey. March 22. Author's copy.*

McCall, Tom. 1972. Letter to Wilbur Ternyik. June 22. McCall Papers, Box 28, Local
    Government Folder 2. OSA.*

McCall, Tom. 1973a. Special Message to the 57th Legislative Assembly. January 18.
    Author's copy.*

McCall, Tom. 1973b. Testimony. Committee on Interior and Insular Affairs, United
    States Senate. Hearings on the Land Use Policy and Planning Assistance Act:
    February 7: 42, 46. U.S. Government Printing Office.

McCall, Tom. 1973c. Testimony to SELUC. March 6. Author's copy.*

McCall, Tom. 1974a. Letter to John Gustafson. February 6. Author's copy.*

McCall, Tom. 1974b. Remarks by Governor Tom McCall. September 18. Author's
    copy.*

McCall, Tom. 1974c. Testimony. December 13. Final Public Hearing. FH 1001.
    DLCD.*

McCallum, Walt. 1974. Memorandum to John Gustafson. September 3. Author's
    copy.*

McCarthy, Steve. 1974. Letter to Governor McCall. March 29. McCall Records, Box
    30, Correspondence, 1967-1974, OSPIRG. OSA.

McFarland, Andrew. 1976. *Public Interest Lobbies*. Washington, D.C.: American
    Enterprise Institute.

McHarg, Ian. 1969. Design with Nature. Garden City, N.Y.: Natural History Press.

McLennan, Janet. 1976a. Memorandum to Governor. March 9. Straub Papers, Box
    44, LCDC: General File 3/5. OSA.*

McLennan, Janet. 1976b. Memorandum to John Mosser. June 17. Straub Papers,
    Box 44, LCDC: General File 3/5. OSA.*

McLennan, Janet. 1976c. Memorandum to Governor. June 23. Straub Papers, Box
    44, LCDC: General File 3/5. OSA.*

McLennan, Janet. 1976d. Memorandum to Governor. June 29. Straub Papers, Box
    44, LCDC: General File 3/5. OSA.

McLennan, Janet. 2008. Oral History Interview. Straub Archive. Western Oregon
    University.

McLennan, Janet. 2009. Interview with author. February 5.

Miller, Lee. 1970. Letter to Governor McCall. October 6. McCall Records, Box 98,
    1969 LGRD Correspondence. OSA.*

"The Missing Tooth in Environmental Smile." 1975. Editorial. *The Oregon Statesman*
    (Salem). January 16.*

Moore, James. 1973a. Statement on SB 100. February 12. Senate Environment and
    Land Use Committee, Box 59 Folder 59/5. OSA.*

Moore, James. 1973b. Statement on Revised SB 100. March 8. Senate Environment
    and Land Use Committee, Box 60, Folder 60/1. OSA.*

Moshofsky, William, 1973. Testimony. February 13. Senate Environment and Land
    Use Committee, Box 60, Folder 60/1. OSA.*

Moshofsky, William. 1976. Letter to Robert Straub. August 11. Straub Papers, Box 46, Land Use: SB 570, Folder 2. OSA.*

Mosser, John. 1990. Oral History Interview. SR 1122. OHS.

Multnomah County, 1973. Testimony. March 8. Senate Environment and Land Use Committee, Box 60, Folder 60/1. OSA.*

Myers, Clay. 1997. Oral History Interview SR 3956. Kami Teramura Masters Project Oral Histories. OHS.

Myers, Phyllis. 1976. *Zoning Hawaii: An Analysis of the Passage and Implementation of Hawaii's Land Classification Law*. Washington, D.C.: The Conservation Foundation.

Newbegin, Wade. 1991. *R.M. Wade and Company and Family: Four Generations*. Portland, Oregon: R.M. Wade and Company.

Newbegin, Wade, Jr. 1976. Letter to Governor Straub. October 22. Straub Papers, Box 47, Land Use: SB00, Folder 1. OSA.*

Niven, Betty. 1974. Memorandum to Land Conservation and Development Commission. December 13.*

Northwest Environmental Defense Center. 1973. Minutes. August 2. OEC Papers, Box 20, Northwest Environmental Defense Center. OHS.

"OCCDA will elect officers soon; economic study eyed." 1975. *The World* (Coos Bay). April 28.*

"OCCDC okays request for funds." 1974. *The Daily Astorian*. August 27.*

Olson, Louis, and Richard Carruthers. 1976. Memorandum to LCDC. February 3. Straub Papers, Box 65, 113.6: LCDC Folder 2. OSA.*

1000 Friends of Oregon. 1975a. Minutes. April 21. 1977 Board Mailings Box, 1976 Board Records Folder. 1000 Friends of Oregon.*

1000 Friends of Oregon. 1975b. "1000 Friends Asks DEQ to Apply LCDC Goals to Septic Tanks." *Progress Report*. Fall.

1000 Friends of Oregon. 1976. Minutes. April 7. 1977 Board Mailings Box, 1976 Board Records Folder.*

Oregon. 1947. *Oregon Laws*. Chapter 537: 951.

Oregon. 1963. *Oregon Laws*. Chapter 577: 1141.

Oregon Department of Transportation, 1974. Comments on Draft Statewide Land Use Goals. November 26. LCDC Written Public Testimony. DLCD.*

Oregon Environmental Council. 1973. Further Information on Senate Bill 100 – 3/8/73. OEC Papers, Box 1, Folder 44. OHS.

Oregon Environmental Council, et al. 1974. Revisions and Comments. November 25. LCDC Written Public Testimony. DLCD.*

"Oregon Industries Unit Supports Land-Use Plan." 1976. *Oregon Journal* (Portland). August 10: 4.*

Oregon Supreme Court. 1973. *Fasano v. Washington County*. 264 Or 574. March 2: 588.

Oregon Wildlife Commission and Fish Commission of Oregon. 1974. Joint Statement. November 25. LCDC Written Public Testimony. DLCD.*

OSPIRG. 1973. "OSPIRG Calls on OCCDC to Classify Estuaries." September 8. Press Release. Author's copy.*

O'Toole, Randal. 1974. Testimony. Final Public Hearing. FH-1055. DLCD.*

Ouderkirk, Jeff. 1992. "Yaquina Head and Penelope Hall." Oregon Shores Conservation Coalition. *20th Anniversary Celebration of Oregon Shores Conservation Coalition 1971-1991*.

Paulus, Norma. 1997. Oral History Interview 3957. Kami Teramura Masters Project Oral Histories. OHS.

Peterson, George, and Harvey Yampolsky. 1975. *Urban Development and the Protection of Metropolitan Farmland.* Washington, D.C.: The Urban Institute.

Pickard, Robert. 1979. "Oregon's 'Friends' Give Environmentalism a New Image." *Star-Bulletin* (Honolulu, Hawaii). December 3.*

Pierce, John. 1981. "The B.C. Agricultural Land Commission: A Review and Evaluation." *Plan Canada* 21:2, June.*

Pierce, J., and O. Furuseth. 1982. "Farmland Protection Planning in British Columbia." *GeoJournal* 6.6, 555-60.*

Pintarich, Paul. 1974. "Oregon land use planners seek 50,000 public helpers." *The Oregonian* (Portland). March 10.*

Plotkin, Sidney. 1987. *Keep Out: The Struggle for Land Use Control.* Berkeley and Los Angeles: University of California Press.

Ponzi, Richard, and William Blosser. 1973. Letter to Governor McCall. April 3. McCall Records, Box 27, Local Government 4/30-4/4. OSA.*

Pope, Daniel. 1993. "Demand Forecasts and Electrical Energy Politics: The Pacific Northwest." *Business and Economic History.* 22(1): 234-43.

Popper, Frank. 1981. *The Politics of Land Use Reform.* Madison: University of Wisconsin Press.

Popper, Frank. 1988. "Understanding American Land Use Regulation Since 1970: A Revisionist Interpretation." *Journal of the American Planning Association* 54(3): 291-301.

Porter, John. 1974a. Memorandum to LCDC. November 26. Author's copy.*

Porter, John. 1974b. Testimony. December 13. Final Public Hearing. FH 1039. DLCD.*

"Proposed Budget to Accomplish Financing of SB 100 as Recommended by the Senate Environment and Land Use Committee." 1973. Senate Environment and Land Use Committee, Box 60. OSA.*

Proposed Land Use Organization. 1974. Minutes. September 19. 1977 Board Mailings Box, 1976 Office Correspondence Folder. 1000 Friends of Oregon.*

Read, Herschel, Louis Olson, and Gordon Galbraith. 1972. Letter to Governor Tom McCall. December 8. McCall Papers, Box 28, Local Government Folder 2. OSA.*

Richen, C. W. 1974. Statement. December 13. FH 1007. DLCD.*

Richmond, Henry. 1973a. "Land Use Bill 'Thrown to Wolves.'" *OSPIRG IMPACT.* Volume 2, Number 8. April.*

Richmond, Henry. 1973b. *The Oregon Coast and the Oregon Coastal Conservation and Development Commission: The Fox Guarding the Chickens?* Portland, OR: OSPIRG.*

Richmond, Henry. 1974a. Memorandum to L. B. Day. February 21. LCDC, Box 1, 10/73-10/74, 2/22 Meeting. OSA.

Richmond, Henry. 1974b. Letter to L. B. Day. March 20. 1000 Friends Papers. Box 91. University of Oregon.*

Richmond, Henry. 1974c. Memo, Finance Committee (HRR) to NEDC Executive Committee, n.d. OEC Papers, Box 20, Folder 9. OHS.

Richmond, Henry. 1974d. Letter to Arnold Cogan. June 28. LCDC Meeting Material, 4/26/74-7/26/74. OSA.

Richmond, Henry. 1974e. Letter to L. B. Day. July 25. LCDC Meeting Material, 4/26/74-7/26/74. OSA.*

Richmond, Henry. 1974f. Letter to William Hutchison. July 29. Author's copy.*

Richmond, Henry. 1974g. Letter to Governor Tom McCall. August 1. 1000 Friends
    of Oregon Records, Box 91. University of Oregon.*
Richmond, Henry. 1974h. Letter to Steve Schell. August 30. LCDC Meeting
    Materials, 7/29-10/6. OSA.*
Richmond, Henry. 1974j. Letter to Glenn Jackson. September 12. 1977 Board
    Mailings Box, 1976 Board Records Folder, Correspondence of Advisory Board
    1976 File. 1000 Friends of Oregon.*
Richmond, Henry. 1974k. Letter to J. W. Forrester. September 24. 1977 Board
    Mailings Box, 1976 Board Records Folder, Correspondence of Advisory Board
    1976 File. 1000 Friends of Oregon.*
Richmond, Henry. 1974l. Letter to L. B. Day. September 24. 1977 Board Mailings,
    Etc., Box, Office Correspondence 1976 Folder, Board Meeting, 9/19/74. 1000
    Friends of Oregon.*
Richmond, Henry. 1974m. Memorandum to Senator Ted Hallock. September 27.
    1000 Friends of Oregon Papers, Box 91. University of Oregon.*
Richmond, Henry. 1974n. Memorandum to L. B. Day. October 21. Author's copy.*
Richmond, Henry. 1974o. Statement. November 25. Public Testimony (Written).
    DLCD Office, Salem.*
Richmond, Henry. 1974p. Statement. December 13. Final Public Hearing. FH 1052.
    DLCD.*
Richmond, Henry. 1975a. Letter to Friends. January 6. 1000 Friends Papers. Box 91.
    University of Oregon.
Richmond, Henry. 1975b. Letter to Wade Newbegin, Jr. April 4. 1977 Board
    Mailings, Etc., Box, 1976 Board Records Folder, Correspondence with Board
    of Directors Members 1976 File. 1000 Friends of Oregon.*
Richmond, Henry. 1975c. Memo to Board of Directors, Advisory Board. April 21.
    1000 Friends of Oregon Records, Box 91. University of Oregon.
Richmond, Henry. 1975d. Memorandum to L. B. Day. June 24. 1977 Board Mailings
    Box, 1976 Board Records Folder. 1000 Friends of Oregon.*
Richmond, Henry. 1975e. Memorandum to L. B. Day. June 27. Joint Land Use
    Committee, Box 14, Folder 13. OSA.*
Richmond, Henry. 1975f. Letter to Governor Straub. August 11. Straub Papers, Box
    44, LCDC: Appeals Process. OSA.*
Richmond, Henry. 1975g. Letter to Governor Straub. August 22. Straub Papers, Box
    45, LCDC: 1000 Friends. OSA.*
Richmond, Henry. 1975h. "Land Use and Economics." *1,000 Friends of Oregon
    Newsletter*. Volume 1, Number 1. October.
Richmond, Henry. 1975i. Letter to Governor Tom McCall, October 28. 1000 Friends
    of Oregon Records, Box 91. University of Oregon Library.*
Richmond, Henry. 1975j. Memorandum to Board of Directors, Advisory Board.
    December 8. 1977 Board Mailings Box, 1976 Board Records Folder. 1000
    Friends of Oregon.*
Richmond, Henry. 1975l. Letter to J. W. Forrester, Jr. December 15. HRR-
    General Correspondence, January, 1976. 1977 Board Mailings Box, Office
    Correspondence 1976 Folder. 1000 Friends of Oregon.*
Richmond, Henry. 1976a. Letter to L. B. Day. July 2. 1977 Board Mailings Box,
    1976 Office Correspondence Folder. 1000 Friends of Oregon.*
Richmond, Henry. 1976b. Letter to John Gray. October 27. 1977 Board Mailings,
    Etc. Box, Office Correspondence 1976 Folder, HRR Correspondence. 1000
    Friends of Oregon.*

Richmond, Henry. 1977a. Letter to Honorable Robert Straub. January 19. Straub Papers, Box 47, Folder 1. OSA.*

Richmond, Henry. 1977b. "Proposal to Ford Foundation." 1000 Friends Papers. University of Oregon.*

Richmond, Henry, and Richard Benner. 1976. Memorandum to LCDC. December 9. Straub Papers, Box 65, Folder 730.1. OSA.*

Richmond, Henry, and OSPIRG. 1991. OSPIRG celebrates two decades of working to make Oregon a better place to live: 20th Anniversary. Portland: OSPIRG.

Richmond, Henry, Ken Bonnem, and Greg Fritts. 1974. "Potpourri." *Land Use Oregon* (1)1: April 4.

Rindy, Bob. 2004. Memorandum to Lane Shetterly. May 11. Author's copy.*

Roberts, Carlisle. 1967. "The Taxation of Farm Land in Oregon." *Willamette Law Journal*, 4(4): 431-61.

Robinson, Sue. 1976. "Day predicts win for land use law." *Capital Journal* (Salem). July 12.*

Roby, Larry. 1975a. "Greenway film is halted, but not because McCall is 'star.'" *Capital Journal* (Salem). January 23.*

Roby, Larry. 1975b. "Straub has his own ideas about Greenway law." *Capital Journal* (Salem). January 23.*

Roby, Larry. 1976. "Ex-LCDC member opposes land use duties shift to land board." *Capital Journal* (Salem). September 11: 12A.*

Rockefeller, Laurance. 1975. "Letter to Governor Tom McCall." March 17. 1000 Friends of Oregon Papers, Box 91. University of Oregon.*

Rogers, B. J. 1973. Testimony. February 12. Senate Environment and Land Use Committee, Box 60, Folder 60/1. OSA.

Rogers, B. J. 1974a. Speech to Portland Board of Realtors. February 6. OEC Papers, Box 21. OHS.*

Rogers, B. J. 1974b. Letter to L. B. Day. June 21. LCDC Meeting Materials, 4/26-7/26. OSA.*

Rohse, Mitch. 1985. "Farmland Protection in Oregon: Evaluating the Most Extensive Program in the Country." Salem: DLCD.*

Rome, Adam. 2001. *The Bulldozer in the Countryside: Suburban Sprawl and the Rise of American Environmentalism.* New York: Cambridge University Press.

Rosenbaum, Nelson. 1977. *Private Property and the Public Interest: Citizen Involvement in State Land Use Control.* Washington, D.C: Urban Institute. Land Use Center Working Paper 1226-08. June.*

Ross, James. 1974. Memorandum of Understanding to Arnold Cogan. May 24. LCDC Meeting Materials, 4/26-7/26. OSA.*

Ross, James. 1976. Memorandum to LCDC. December 28. LCDC, Box 7, 1/7/77. OSA.*

Ross, James, and Donna Hepp. 1974. "Estuarine Sanctuaries – The Oregon Experience." *Coastal Zone Management Journal,* 1(4): 433-46.*

Roy, Richard. 1973. Memo to Don Waggoner, et al. January 3. OEC Records, Box 20, Folder 9. OHS.

Rudel, Thomas. 1989. *Situations and Strategies in American Land-Use Planning.* Cambridge, England: Cambridge University Press.

Runka, G. Gary. 2006. "BC's Agricultural Land Reserve – Its Historical Roots." Paper presented at Post World Planners Congress Seminar, June 21.*

Scharf, Andrea. 1976. "Revolt Against Land Use Planning." *Oregon Times Magazine.* August: 26.*

Schell, Steven. 1971. Letters to Wilbur Ternyik. August 3 and 26. McCall Records, Box 98, 1969 LGRD Correspondence. OSA.*

Schell, Steven. 1973a. Statement of Oregon Shores Conservation Coalition. February 12. Senate Environment and Land Use Committee, Box 59, Folder 59/5. OSA.*

Schell, Steven. 1973b. Letter to Senator John Burns. February 14. Senate Environment and Land Use Committee, Box 60, Folder 60/2. OSA.*

Schell, Steve. 1974a. Letter to Arnold Cogan. June 21. LCDC Meeting Materials, 4/26-7/26. OSA.*

Schell, Steve. 1974b. Memo to LCDC. August 30. Author's copy.*

Schell, Steve. 1974c. Statement. December 27. LCDC, Box 2, 11/74-7/75. OSA.*

Schell, Steve. 1974d. Letter to Technical Committee Member. November 1. Author's copy.*

Schell, Steve. 1975. Memorandum to Interested Legislators. June 3. Straub Papers, Box 46, Land Use: Comprehensive Plan. OSA.*

Schell, Steve. 2001. Interview with Ernie Bonner. December 3. Ernie Bonner Papers. PSU.

Schell, Steve. 2008. Interview with author.

Schroeder, J. E. 1974. Letter to Arnold Cogan. November 27. LCDC Written Public Testimony. DLCD.*

Sidor, Ted. 1970. Status of County Land Use Planning and Zoning in the State of Oregon. July 14. McCall Records, Box 98, 1969 LGRD Correspondence. OSA.*

Smith, Dean. 1974. "Land Use Goals Sought." *Oregon Journal* (Portland). October 14.*

Smith, M. Gregg. 1974. Letter to Arnold Cogan. November 18. Public Hearings, Volume II. DLCD.*

"The South Slough Estuarine Reserve." 1992. Oregon Shores Conservation Coalition. *20th Anniversary Celebration of Oregon Shores Conservation Coalition 1971-1991.*

Springer, Vera. 1976. *Power and the Pacific Northwest: A History of the Bonneville Power Administration.* Portland: Bonneville Power Administration.

Squier, Anne. n.d. Letter to Richard Benner. Author's copy.*

Stacey, Bob. 1974a. "LCDC Budget Slashed." *Land Use Oregon* 1(4).

Stacey, Bob. 1974b. "LCDC Progress Report." *Land Use Oregon* 1(5).

Stacey, Bob. 1974c. "LCDC Progress Report." *Land Use Oregon* 1(6).

Stacey, Bob. 1974d. "LCDC Status Report." *Land Use Oregon* 1(7).

Stacey, Bob. 1974e. LCDC Goals. N.d. LCDC Written Public Testimony. DLCD.

Stacey, Bob. 1974f. "LCDC Status Report." *Land Use Oregon* 1(8).

Stacey, Bob. 1975a. "LCDC Report: Statewide Goals and Guidelines." *Land Use Oregon* (1)9.

Stacey, Bob. 1975b. "LCDC Status Report." *Land Use Oregon* 1(10).

Stacey, Robert E., Jr. 1975c. *State Involvement in Land Use Planning in Oregon: An Inauspicious Beginning.* Washington, D.C.: Population Institute.*

Stacey, Robert E., Jr. 1976a. "LCDC Keeps Tight Rein on Planning Extensions, Stresses Growth Boundaries and Farm Land Protection." *1,000 Friends of Oregon Newsletter.* 1:4 (January).

Stacey, Robert E., Jr. 1976b. "LCDC Reduces Emphasis on Agricultural Goal in Review of Lane County Plan." *1,000 Friends of Oregon Newsletter.* 1:8 (May).

Stacey, Robert E., Jr. 1976c. Memorandum to Members. June 23. Joint Legislative Committee on Land Use. Box 15, Folder 3. OSA.*

State Housing Council. 1974. Proposal for a Statewide Housing Goal. November 26. Public Hearings, Volume II. DLCD.*

"State's dilemma in planning." 1974. Editorial. *Register-Guard* (Eugene). November 14.*

Stimmel, Tom. 1975. "1000 Friends: A Concern For Land." *Oregon Journal* (Portland). July 28.*

Stoel, Thomas, Jr. 1975. "Environmental Litigation from the Viewpoint of the Environmentalist," *Environmental Law Review – 1975.*

Straub, Robert. 1974. Testimony. December 13. Final Public Hearing, FH-1002. DLCD.*

Straub, Bob. 1975. "Our Willamette Greenway: A Plan for the Future." *1,000 Friends of Oregon Newsletter.* 1(3). December.

Straub, Bob. 1976a. "By Bob Straub, Governor of Oregon." Straub Papers, Box 47, Land Use: SB 100 Folder 1. OSA.*

Straub, Robert. 1976b. Press Briefing. July 8. Straub Papers, Box 44, LCDC: General File 3/5. OSA.*

Straub, Robert. 1976c. Letter to Ted Hallock. September 29. Straub Papers, Box 78, Folder 730.1. OSA.*

Sullivan, Edward. 1972a. Letter to John Porter. January 10. Ed Sullivan Papers. OHS.

Sullivan, Edward. 1972b. "Brief." *Fasano vs. Washington County* Board of Commissioners Case Files. Ed Sullivan Papers. OHS.

Sullivan, Edward. 1973a. Letter from Ed Sullivan. March 12. *Fasano vs. Washington* County Board of Commissioners Case Files. Ed Sullivan Papers. OHS.

Sullivan, Edward. 1973b. "The Greening of the Taxpayer: The Relationship of Farm Zone Taxation in Oregon to Land Use." *Willamette Law Journal* 9(1): 1-25.*

Sullivan, Ed. 1975. Memorandum to Senator Atiyeh. Joint Trade and Economic Development Committee, Container 117, Exhibits: SB 122. May 28. OSA.*

Sullivan, Edward, and Laurence Kressel. 1975. "Twenty Years After – Renewed Significance of the Comprehensive Plan Requirement." *Urban Law Annual.* 9:3. 33-67.

Sullivan, Rachel. 1974. "Who Killed 2607? Fact and Fiction in the Land Consumer Protection Act." *Oregon Times.* March: 20-23.*

Ternyik, Wilbur. 1973. Letter to Richard Benner. September 10. Author's copy.*

Thompson, John. 1975. "Coast Policies to be Aired." *The Daily Astorian* (Astoria, OR). April 29.*

Thompson, Wayne. 1974. "Bob has a lot in common with Tom, but it's a new deal." *The Oregonian* (Portland). December 15. D1.*

"Tillamook County Planning Commission Makes Waves." 1971. OEC *Newsletter.* September-October.

Tollefson, Gene. 1987. *BPA and the Struggle for Power at Cost.* Portland: Bonneville Power Administration.

Uhrhammer, Jerry. 1973. "Tight initial funding seen for land-use bill." *Register-Guard* (Eugene). May 16.*

Uhrhammer, Jerry. 1976. "A new guy sits on Oregon hot seat." *Register-Guard* (Eugene). July 13.*

VanNatta, Fred. 1974a. Statement on behalf of Oregon Homebuilders' Association. February 2. LCDC Meeting Materials, Box 1, 10/73-10/74. OSA.*

VanNatta, Fred. 1974b. Statement on behalf of Oregon Homebuilders' Association. November 26. Public Hearings, Volume II. DLCD.*

VanNatta, Fred. 1974c. Presentation. December 13. Final Public Hearing. FH 1030. DLCD.*

VanNatta, Fred. 1975. Testimony of Fred Van Natta on behalf of the Oregon State Home Builders Association. May 29. OSA.*

VanNatta, Fred. 1976. Comments on the Draft Coastal Goals Resolution. March 18. Joint Land Use Committee, Box 15 Folder 3. OSA.*

VanNatta, Fred. 2008. Interview with author. May 1.

Vogel, David. 1980-81. "The Public-Interest Movement and the American Reform Tradition." *Political Science Quarterly* 95(4): Winter.*

Walth, Brent. 1994. *Fire at Eden's Gate*. Portland: Oregon Historical Society Press.

Weir, Margaret. 2000. "Planning, Environmentalism, and Urban Poverty: The Political Failure of National Land-Use Planning Legislation, 1970-1975. In Robert Fishman, ed., *The American Planning Tradition: Culture and Policy*. Washington, D.C.: The Woodrow Wilson Center Press.

Williams, Larry. 1971. Letter to Wade Newbegin, Jr. February 3. OEC Papers, Box 1, Folder 19. OHS.

Williams, Larry. 1972a. Letter to Council for the Preservation of Rural England. April 25. OEC Papers, Box 1, Folder 33. OHS.

Williams, Larry. 1972b. Letter to John Gray. September 15. OEC Papers, Box 1, Folder 38. OHS.

Williams, Larry. 1973a. Letter to L. B. Day. January 12. OEC Papers, Box 1, Folder 42. OHS.

Williams, Larry, 1973b. Letter to Governor McCall. May 9. OEC Papers, Box 1, Folder 46. OHS.*

Williams, Larry. 1973c. Letter to Steve Schell. August 6. OEC Papers, Box 1, Folder 49. OHS.

Williams, Larry. 2007. *Memories of an Oregon Conservationist*. OEC 40th Anniversary. Author's copy.*

Williams, Norman. 1975. [1985 Revision] *American Land Planning Law: Land Use and the Police Power*. Wilmette, Ill: Callaghan and Co. Volume 5: 607.

Wingard, George. 1993. Oral History Interview SR 1144. OHS.

Wright, Albert. 1974. Letter to Cogan. December 3. LCDC Written Public Testimony. DLCD.*

Zachary, Kathleen. 1978. *Politics of Land Use: The Lengthy Saga of Senate Bill 100*. MA Thesis, PSU.

Zedwick. Andrew. 1977. Letter to Robert White. January 10. Office of Coastal Zone Management. *Written Statements from Parties Who Commented on the Oregon Coastal Zone Management Program and the Draft Environmental Impact Statement*. Washington, D.C. A156-159.*

Index